SOFTWARE QUALITY
PRODUCING PRACTICAL, CONSISTENT SOFTWARE

Slaying the Software Dragon Series

This series provides software developers and managers with practical guides to developing quality software, covering each major aspect of this process. A key theme is the importance of implementing effective maintenance strategies at every stage of development. The series covers both technical and management perspectives in order to aid both software engineers and business managers involved in software development. Future book topics include software planning and maintenance, software testing and test planning, and software inspections and reviews.

Other titles by Mordechai Ben-Menachem

The PATRIARCH Series in Software Quality Assurance:

> *The PATRIARCH SQA Handbook*
> *The PATRIARCH Manager's SQA Guidebook*
> *The PATRIARCH Developer's SQA Guidebook*
> *The PATRIARCH Implementer's SQA Guidebook*
> *The PATRIARCH Document Quality Assurance and Verification and Validation Handbook*
> *The PATRIARCH SQA Planning & Auditing Manual*

Software development procedures manuals:

> *Software Technical Procedures Manual*
> *Software Management Procedures Manual*

Books specially prepared for use with United States Department of Defense Standards:

> *US Department of Defense Std-2167/2168 Companion – An Aid and Training Guide for use of the Military Standard for Mission Critical Software Development*
> *DoD Standards 2167/2167A/2168 Auditor's Manual (in a five-volume set) for Data Item Descriptions and Procedures*

SOFTWARE QUALITY
PRODUCING PRACTICAL, CONSISTENT SOFTWARE

Mordechai Ben-Menachem

and

Garry S. Marliss

INTERNATIONAL THOMSON COMPUTER PRESS
I ⓣ P® An International Thomson Publishing Company

Boston • London • Bonn • Johannesburg • Madrid • Melbourne • Mexico City • New York • Paris
Singapore • Tokyo • Toronto • Albany, NY • Belmont, CA • Cincinnati, OH • Detroit, MI

Copyright © 1997 Mordechai Ben-Menachem

International Thomson Computer Press is
a division of International Thomson Publishing Inc.
The ITP logo is a trademark under licence.

For more information, contact:

International Thomson Computer Press
20 Park Plaza, 13th Floor
Boston, MA 02116 USA

International Thomson Computer Press
Berkshire House
168-173 High Holborn
London WC1V 7AA England

Nelson International Thomson Publishing Australia
102 Dodds Street
South Melbourne, NSW
Victoria 3205 Australia

Nelson Canada
1120 Birchmount Road
Scarborough, Ontario
Canada M1K SG4

International Thomson Publishing Southern Africa
Building 18, Constantia Park
240 Old Pretoria Road
P.O. Box 2459
Halfway House 1685 South Africa

International Thomson Publishing GmbH
Königswinterer Straße 418
53227 Bonn, Germany

International Thomson Publishing Asia
60 Albert Street # 15-01
Albert Complex
Singapore 189969

International Thomson Publishing Japan
Hirakawa-cho Kyowa Building, 3F
2-2-1 Hirakawa-cho
Chiyoda-ku, Tokyo 102 Japan

International Thomson Editores
Seneca 53
Colonia Polanco
11560 Mexico D. F. Mexico

International Thomson Publishing France
Tour Maine-Montparnasse
33 avenue du Maine
75755 Paris Cedex 15
France

Library of Congress Cataloging-in-Publication Data
Ben-Menachem, Mordechai.
    Software quality: producing practical, consistent software/
Mordechai Ben-Menachem and Garry S. Marliss.
       p.   cm.
    Includes bibliographical references and index.
    ISBN 1-85032-326-7
    1. Computer software—Quality control.   I. Marliss, Garry S.
II. Title.
QA76.76.Q35B46   1997
005.1′068′4—dc21

97-15926
CIP

Commissioning Editor: Liz Israel Oppedijk, ITCP/Boston
Publisher/Vice President: Jim DeWolf, ITCP/Boston
Marketing Manager: Christine Nagle, ITCP/Boston

Projects Director: Vivienne Toye, ITCP/Boston
Manufacturing Manager: Sandra Sabathy, ITCP/Boston

Production: Gray Publishing, Tunbridge Wells, UK

Cover design: Codesign, Jamaica Plain, MA, USA

This book is dedicated with love and warmth to my ever lovely and much-esteemed wife – Malki. Simple words can never be sufficient to express what needs to be said.

And also, to ECI Telecom, the present managing director (Mr David Rubner) and the director of development (Mr Danny Etz-Hadar): one of the best and most pleasant companies with whom this author has had the pleasure to work and two of the finest professionals.

CONTENTS

PREFACE

This is a guidebook for the software practitioner.

The professionals addressed are those who have recognized a need for the application of software process management in projects. This book will be of no interest to the "unprofessional" practitioner, for the aficionado who dabbles in software because it is fun (and it certainly is), but does not really develop serious projects. The book is, however, relevant for university courses, albeit certainly not for those of a low level. As a management reference this book is applicable to all types of software development.

We now possess the knowledge and experience needed for the successful development of software and its maintenance. However, there is probably no endeavor where the gap between the knowledge and performance of the leaders and that of the average professional practitioner is wider or less well understood. This book is a bridge across the gap of what is accomplished by the leaders and the learners – between what is done and what ought to be done. As a guidebook, the prime goal is to help you get the job done: better, less expensively, and with greater fulfillment and satisfaction.

This book is written from a background of many years of experience both in following the developments published in the professional literature and, more importantly, working with software organizations – of small projects in small and large companies as well as very large projects (thousands of staff-years) within large companies, and projects jointly developed by several companies at once. The aim is to guide you, the professional, to examine your own work and performance. Self-diagnosis of one's weaknesses is never easy, and frequently unpleasant, but it is always necessary to improve effectiveness and to understand the results of the activities for which one is responsible.

For those readers who intend to make management their career path, we hope to provide the vision and guidance, knowledge and discipline that are needed to qualify you for your next position.

Users of computer systems will also find this book of great value, especially those who are responsible for acquiring systems. Such users need to know software management and the limitations of the resources and techniques in use, perhaps as much as the producers. This knowledge will enable you to understand what can reasonably be expected from those who are developing and maintaining the systems on which we all are dependent. Ignorance of management, its work, standards, responsibilities, functions and capabilities (i.e., limitations) is one of the most serious weaknesses of our society. This weakness is universal (it is not limited to software, but we will limit ourselves to that field).

Why this Book Needed to be Written

At the beginning of modern computing, say in the 1950s, the *software revolution* had not yet been recognized. It was not until the end of the 1970s that we realized the degree to which computers and computing were going to affect our lives. To many, this was very frightening. In the light of experience, perhaps this was justifiable. Over time, there grew to be an increasing awareness that software (computing) is very different from hardware – but still possesses many similarities. Interestingly, this new awareness grew in parallel, both within the developer and in the "user" communities. The two things that were most noticeable were first that as computers entered into and controlled more aspects of our lives the criticality (risk) of this "resource" became more difficult to control, second it was also realized that many of the perceived similarities between hardware and software could be utilized to decrease some of the risk (degrees of uncertainty) that were inherent in the processes of creating, maintaining, acquiring, and operating software. These risks were particularly apparent in large software-rich projects which went out of control.

We will discuss the concept of projects and the implications of *size*. Although these are extremely important, many people have lost sight of the reasons behind things. The major advantage to introducing computer/software technology into an existing process is to **accommodate change**. As you progress through the book you will see that while the **facilitator** of change is the software configuration management function the **arbiter** (the "umpire") for change in software technology is the software quality function. From management's standpoint, an out-of-control project/resource is disastrous, independently of whether you are managing it for acquisition, for sale or for in-house use. We know that an increasing amount of money is devoted to software (as opposed to hardware – it is claimed that some 60% of all large corporation data processing budgets are devoted to the correction of erroneous or questionable lines of COBOL code) and that the problems with systems are usually more directly related to the software than the hardware. Specifically, as the percentage of software in a product increased, the percentage of the failures from software increased – and at a faster rate; that is the *percentage* increased at a higher rate. This is rather shocking and conceptually difficult. This trend has caused a great deal of fear. Rightfully so. Processes, analyses, experiments and research were initiated all over the (technological) world to discover what could be done about this problem. One of the results of this activity was an enhanced awareness that software, and software professionals, **can be managed**. This was actually quite a revelation. It took the professional community an embarrassingly long time to understand this. As it turns out, the greatest boon to developing good software and releasing it on time and within budget is what has always worked best in every human endeavor – courageous men and women doing their job in the best way they know how and managing their endeavors conscientiously. Sounds simple? It is far from it! The other result, and this was a lot more painful, was that programmers could not both play the role of "high priests of the future" and continue to not have to be responsible for budgets, quality, reliability, and timeliness.

Interestingly, at the same time that the software community was undergoing this revelation, the rest of the industrial world was also going through a similar evolutionary process. In their case, this was precipitated by an increasing fear and awareness that industries in the so-called newly industrialized countries were overtaking them in their home markets. One of the perceived solutions to this problem was that quality of the products and services must improve. For this reason, the International Standards Organization (ISO) initiated the specification of the series of standards now called ISO 9000 (actually, it all began with the British Standards Institution but was taken over by the ISO). This set of standards is unique in that it does not discuss how to go about doing or building something, but rather how to go about organizing to achieve quality and make improvements visible. For these reasons, the standards have achieved a great deal of international success. It is important that the reader understands that quality has become, and will remain, a critical management criterion. The organization's ability, in terms of producing a quality solution, is probably the single most important competitive resource the organization can have. Clearly, this is something which must be both controlled and developed. Let's illustrate this with an example. For several years, the first author has conducted informal quality perception surveys. Participants were asked: "Who has a stereo system at home?" Generally, everyone raised their hand. Afterwards, the question asked was: "Who has a stereo which is not Japanese?" Very few could attest that their stereo system was not at least partially Japanese. Among those surveyed were some senior managers of prominent international corporations which manufacture stereo systems. We have never discovered any technical person whose stereo system was not at least partially made by a Japanese company. This is the perception of quality. These manufacturers are certainly skilled, the difference is more one of perception than actual.

So then, why did this book need to be written? Simply because, while there are many books that describe software quality techniques, there are none that bridge the gap between the practitioner and management. The book is divided into chapters which reflect the design of a standard software quality assurance plan. The reasons for this organization are to both help you to create such a plan and also to show you the methods to apply in order to actually perform the planning.

INTRODUCTION TO SOFTWARE QUALITY

1

WORLDWIDE, SOFTWARE DEVELOPMENT ORGANIZATIONS are becoming much more concerned with the process of developing quality software. Many software organizations have already established specialized groups to assess and define formal processes for development. Not all authorities agree that formal development processes are of overriding importance. Certainly, quality systems certification is becoming more important. CMM, ISO 9000 (its European equivalent, EN29000 and the various national versions) are turning into strategic instruments for many organizations. As public procurement authorities are basing their purchasing decisions on such certification, it has even become a matter of corporate survival. The growth of certification importance is due to the software project world becoming more competitive and precarious. Customers and suppliers are both seeking to shift the burden of risk-taking onto others. On the other hand, risk-taking is potentially very profitable. In order to limit the risks, project management must adopt new proactive professional approaches.

This book presents a methodology that controls risk using quality management integrated with advanced software project management. The methodology is practical and implementable so that you can use it *now*. Furthermore, adopting quality management procedures will prove valuable no matter whether your intention is simply to improve your software production or to achieve certification in some standard such as ISO 9000 or CMM or IEEE1074. Note that considerable attention is placed upon continuing to improve development and product practices. For those who are aiming at certification, remember, once ISO 9000 (or CMM, or whatever) certification is won, the job is not over. Certification must be maintained and renewed, usually on a yearly basis.

The emphasis of the 1990s is global competition. This has caused a tremendous increase in the awareness of quality as a prime strategic weapon. The unprecedented speed at which the ISO 9000 series of standards have become the *status quo ante* of quality systems is the best possible proof of this statement. Even if this standard is "replaced" by something improved, this does not change the result, only strengthens it. Quality systems certification is a ripening concept in the industrial world. Anyone not doing it is going to be left behind.

Your next question is probably: " ... but this book is about software ... ?" That is part of the point. Do you really believe that if purchasers (customers, those pests that just happen to pay the bills) who are increasingly accustomed to demanding and receiving quality are going to continue to make an exception for software? Do you really think that we can continue to say silly things, as we all do in our "warranty" statements, that we do not accept any responsibility for our systems? How long do you think the courts of the world are going to continue to accept that?

Many countries have now established ISO 9000, CMM level 2 or 3, or an equivalent, as a prerequisite for purchases by government authorities. Since governments always buy a lot, this is going to help these countries to compete against you. This is not something that is going to happen five years from now. This is happening *now*, in the software that you are competing against.

> The ISO 9000 series has quickly been adopted by many nations and regional bodies and is rapidly supplanting prior national and industry standards. It has been adopted by the European Committee for Standardization (CEN). One of CEN's purposes is to harmonize quality standards and eliminate trade restrictions within the EEC.
>
> (*Quality Progress, May 1991*)

The objectives of this book are to guide the planning and organizing for quality in the software produced by organizations. Among the procedures to be implemented are the processes of organizing various methodologies for quality metric analysis. In particular, instructions on how and when to deploy them.

Total quality management (TQM) means the use of control techniques for making and achieving goals. These goals are usually taken to mean all of the company's goals. Somehow, software has usually managed to remain the exception. Even in very well-managed organizations, software frequently runs out of control. Why? Mostly because we simply do not really fully understand how to control the creative processes. Software TQM must include the use of plans, analysis and control of software and the goals that cause (or allow) quality software "to happen." TQM for software includes extensive and detailed explanations of software quality assurance plans and the processes of planning. The standard for plans to be used is based on a mixture of the IEEE standard for software quality assurance plans as well as several other US and international standards.

Quality, as a Management Information System

The purpose of a management information system (MIS) is to supply *management* with *information* required to reach policy decisions, make plans, set objectives and exercise control over operations and to ensure that those objectives are achieved. However, an information system is unlikely to prove successful unless combined with sound *strategic planning* – short-term goals must be based on long-term plans. Without strategic planning, management becomes opportunism with limited chances for success. It is important that such a management information system be as simple as possible to use, and produce only useful information. In common with all such systems, it is very dependent upon the quality of its *input data*. For the past 150 years, systems analysts have labored to improve management, manufacturing and sales/distribution processes. While in many cases, the best information systems may very well be manual, for the past 35 years, this has increasingly been performed by computer (or rather, with the aid of one). It has long been axiomatic that complex activities can only be managed via *accurate* information systems.

It is known that sound *budget* and *costing systems* are vital as sources for planning and pricing decisions. A basic control procedure consists of a comparison of actual costs with expected costs and of actual volumes with standard volumes. When variances begin to infer an increase in risk, the information system must provide for communication to management so that remedial action may begin. Other commonly expected reports to management may be weekly production or backlog reports. Information should include rudimentary production control with links to *inventory* and *scheduling*.

This type of reporting takes place for almost all endeavors today – except that of creating and maintaining software. It is our belief that this has been the case primarily because the process has been basically little understood, or perhaps even misunderstood. Very recently, great progress has been made in the understanding of the software process. This includes coalescing and maintaining definitions of processes. Among the functions supported partially or fully by software engineering methodologies, are the following (see Figure 1.1).

- Definition of software development processes and life-cycle models.
- Tailoring of organizational standard processes to a defined project-specific development process.
- Production of plans, including tasks, resources and technologies.
- Guided enactment of process tasks.
- Tracking of project progress and measurement of work products and process performance (including modifications, as needed).
- Reviews and audits of defined project artifacts for conformance with internal and external standards.
- Selection and use of pre-defined generic and standard software engineering artifacts, if desired, based on a variety of de-facto and official international standards.

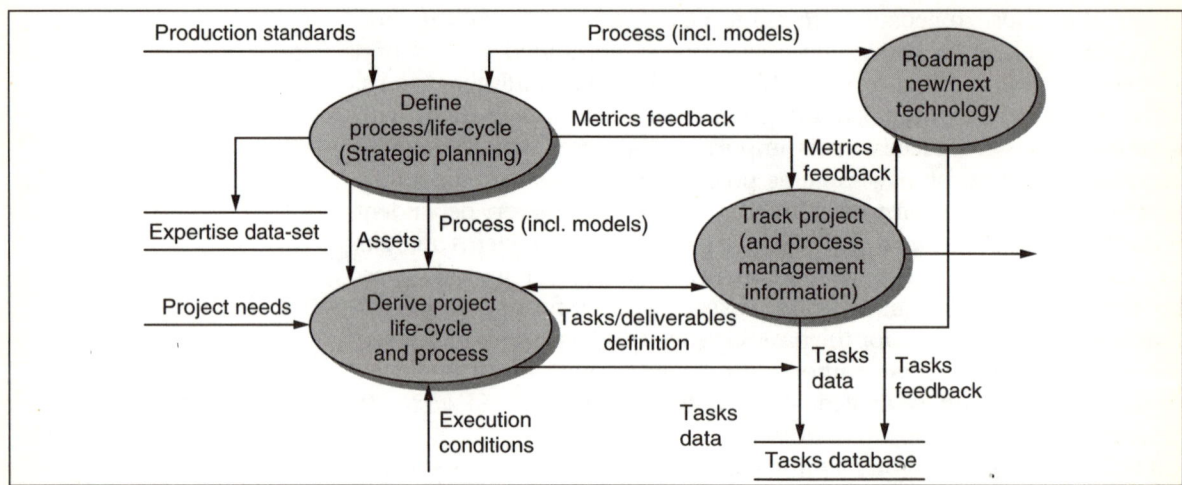

Figure 1.1   Software development processes, as a system.

The underlying philosophy of the system/methodology is the following:

- We believe that the process of creating and maintaining software is now sufficiently understood that an **information system** for the *management of information systems*, can be implemented. This is discussed in detail in the section on records collection and quality metrics.
- We believe that a system which takes into account only processes or only deliverables, is basically insufficient. At the very minimum, both *must* be accounted for. Preferably, more than that. The checklists accompanying this book show, extensively, how this is done.

- We believe that a primary difficulty facing any systems analysis is to ascertain the existence of a continuous source of accurate and dependable data. The task of gathering this data must be performed without becoming a burden.
- We believe that software quality assurance (coupled with software engineering) is systems analysis of the software development process.

At some philosophical level, it could be said that this book is about: **systems analysis, of systems analysis**. Or more properly, a systems analysis view of how software development and maintenance needs to be better managed.

Software Modeling and Commonly Used Models

There are many models in use today to describe what software professionals do and how software is, or may be, produced. Some of these models are very good, some acceptable and others rather less than adequate. Some of these are very generic and some are very parochial. In developing the approach for this book, there were a number of choices as to which models to use and which would be largely ignored. In the end what governed the choice primarily was: (a) that the model addresses efficiently the subject chosen, i.e., software quality management and (b) those models which are most important in the marketplace. If you will, those that have the best "salesmen" – though this does a certain disservice.

For example, there are the so-called "waterfall model" and "spiral model" of approaching software development management. These are excellent, for what they cover. However, they only cover very little.

Another example, is a model called "Trillium"[1] developed by Bell Canada, Northern Telecom and Bell-Northern Research. This is an excellent model and deserves more attention than the industry has awarded it. Unfortunately, it is not very well known, possibly because it was developed to be specific for a particular environment. As its name implies, it is designed for the Telecom market and hence is too narrow in scope to be widely adopted, or for this book.

There is also the IEEE Std 1074 model for software life-cycle management.[2] This is both reasonably good and includes thorough coverage (though it is overly complex). Perhaps this is the reason that it does not seem to be used very much – only by a few organizations inside the USA and almost not at all outside. Most of this book is devoted to the view of software quality management as defined by the model in IEEE Std 730.

In the end the choice was to base the book upon the IEEE model for software quality planning, and to compare it with the ISO 9000 model for quality management, even though this is very far from software, and the Software Engineering Institute's (SEI) Capability Maturity Model (CMM). The reasons for the ISO 9000 model is first in the communality in the titles and second (admittedly) its importance in the marketplace (popularity). It is very important for this book to be useful and applicable. Much more important then for it to be "academically correct" whatever that means. The reason for choosing the second is slightly more complex. Certainly, it should be chosen for its technical merits. But it covers all of the software life-cycle, which is rather more than needed for this book – software quality management is a "nonphase oriented" task. The details of the software life-cycle are not directly of interest. However, the CMM model is too important to be ignored in this book. In the end, the decision there was mostly a question of what would be most relevant to readers.

One final word about models. Throughout the book a lot will be written about all three models (ISO 9000, CMM and IEEE Std 730). It is important for the reader to understand that this book is attempting to discuss the best possible ways for assuring the quality of software that is being developed or maintained. The standard models have different objectives. ISO 9000 discusses organizing a **quality management** function for a company. CMM discusses how to assess the **processes** being used for developing software functionality. These are different. However, the *model at the head* of this effort is IEEE Std 730. Its objectives are precisely the same as those of this book (other than the question of criticality of the software, which is avoided). We may make critical remarks about ISO 9000. However, these critiques are only in terms of the goal that this book is discussing. Please, do not misunderstand our intentions. We think that ISO 9000 is an excellent standard, but its goals are not the book's goals. We may make critical remarks about CMM. Once again, these critiques are only in the terms of our goals. CMM is an excellent tool if process assessment is your goal. It is not the goal of this book. That is why they are both secondary while IEEE Std 730 is the primary model. One can compare models that have affinity, without claiming that they are the same and without forcing the issues.

One of the most basic, and important tasks of quality assurance is evaluation; that is to know the value of what you are doing and the value of any possible improvements, whether this is self-evaluation, self-assessment or an external assessment. This is one of the basic goals of this book. To help you to understand how to go about doing this for yourself and your company, and to do this quickly and inexpensively. As external assessments cost in the order of tens of thousands of dollars, this alone may be all you need the book for.

Webster's dictionary[3] defines **evaluate** as:
'To determine value of; appraise; express numerically.'
While the same book defines **assessment** as:
'Act of appraising and fixing proportionate levy; the amount at which a property is valued for taxation.'

While the people performing *assessments* of companies are not referring to taxes, the concepts of appraisal and proportionment are appropriate.

The Structure of the Model

This book intends to serve the software developing organization as a tool for designing and implementing **software quality assurance and software quality management** functions. In this sense, the book is eminently suitable for use with ISO 9000 or the SEI's CMM. (More on both of these later. If you do not recognize these acronyms, do not worry about it, you will. Otherwise you would not be reading this book.) While this is not a "cookbook," it is intended to allow fast and convenient implementation of quality management of the software process. As such, the book includes specific subsections to help the practitioner expedite task implementation.

Part of any quality implementation process must include tools which can be used to readily evaluate the quality level of a task or process being performed. For this purpose, we provide various checklists. Some of them are for management of the software process, as performed by the installation (or project). In this case, they will be similar to the kinds of things you will see when you are externally audited for ISO 9000 certification or for CMM "level *n*" certification. But at least as important, you will also use them for both self-evaluation and for evaluating any subcontractors. (If you try to use them to evaluate an employee you will be hung up to dry over a burning briar patch! This is not what they are intended for.) In any case, the major problem addressed is a swift and accurate collection of data that reflects how processes are being performed. In most cases, there *is* a process of some kind for management of the software process. What we are adding, is the ability to evaluate *quickly* and *consistently* both of which are very important. In addition to the checklists, there are also worksheets and forms which have proven very useful and applicable.

Guidebook Design Concepts

This book is designed to benefit all those organizations which are too large to be managed trivially – that means more than, say, five people. There is a basic need to simply get started! This is, by no means, an easy thing to do. Many projects, staffed by first-rate professionals, simply have no idea how to begin the subject of quality management. This puts them off the subject and so they do nothing. At very least, this makes their competition very happy. The project team may think that they are working "lean and mean." Usually they are just working much harder than is necessary. For some reason, quality management of software is still not taught, certainly not as part of the computer science curriculum. Viewing the development of the computer milieu, it is obvious that an increased emphasis upon optimization of management techniques could potentially benefit the majority of projects.

In utilizing the tools of quality management, we can more easily know what we are supposed to build, what we are building and what we have built. Not only that, but we can measure progress. That does not mean we cannot use quality management incorrectly. (Remember the old rule of the system's analyst: "computerizing a sloppy factory, makes for computerized slop!") With almost no effort, anything can be made to go wrong. However, the tools of quality management, when implemented intelligently and with proper forethought, can serve as the focal point for a real discipline, at a very low cost to the project. This means that not only can we know what has happened, we can support the product effectively. We can repeat the good things we have done and learn from them.

The general structure of the book is intended to imitate, as much as possible, the structure of IEEE 730. This is an excellent model for the design of the quality assurance function – the function and the plan of operations for the function will then appear similar. Unfortunately, there are still some weaknesses in the standard. These are discussed later on in the book. Where the standard is lacking, we have taken the liberty to expand upon the subject. Occasionally, the reason for expansion is not really a weakness in the standard or a lack of some function, but a decision by the various committees upon a specific delegation of tasks to different documents. The best example of this is the ideas of reviews and audits. The standard defines them in a very minimal manner because they are relegated to a different standard (IEEE 1061, Verification and Validation). This is, of course, perfectly legitimate and proper. Delegation of authority is a necessity of any management. So it is, and was for the committees that wrote the standards. However, this book needs to address all relevant issues so that you, the practitioner, can have the needed tools to accomplish your job, quickly and efficiently.

The Three CPIs

The concept of TQM is beginning to spread throughout the world and is now starting to make an impact on software development organizations. This is more then just a "new fad." The implementation of TQM in an organization *forces* management to push the primary focus of all activities in a direction of continuous process improvement (CPI). Continuously improving all of the organization's processes is, in any case, very difficult. In the "western world" (Europe and North America) productivity enhancements over the past 100 years have averaged about 4.5% per annum for industrial processes and about 0.9% per annum for services. Clearly, the competitive imperative forces us to at least understand this, but even more so, to improve upon it. The concept of TQM for software is an overall technique for organizing and using methods of quality planning and metric analysis, such that results obtained are usable and *repeatable*.

The concept of *software total quality management* is intended to guide the quality assurance practitioner in planning and organizing for quality of software produced by the organization from which his or her living is coming. Quality planning is a primary tool – you cannot know where you are going if you do not know where you intended to go. Clearly, a first real step must be building the quality assurance (QA) plan and managing the quality goals defined by the plan. The quality task is particularly difficult when attempting to plan the quality of software, which is only little understood. This is true even for engineers who have had quality assurance training (whether hardware engineers or software engineers). Such training itself is rare enough. For those engineers (even first-rate professionals) who have not had such (QA) training, very little understanding exists of the issues involved *vis-à-vis* software.

Experience has repeatedly demonstrated that attempting to understand software quality and the assurance of software's quality, as simply an extension of software engineering techniques, is doomed to fail. **Software engineering is an iterative system for knowledge acquisition**. The major problems in systems today are error fixing and the problems caused by this (collectively called maintenance). These problems are most poignantly described by error propagation, which is the logical equivalent of wear-down in hardware. "Total quality management for software" acts firstly as an aid to the process of organizing the various methods for quality planning and metric analysis. But also, to instruct the user in proper methods of employing these methods, such that results obtained are usable and repeatable. Too often, the literature is rife with "statistics" which cannot be independently verified.

Quality metric analysis is used as a tool for understanding effects of various variables upon the way systems are developed and maintained. This must have both an immediate and a long-term effect upon systems acquisition. The knowledge thus gained is incorporated into the QA plan (of the system, and/or the software). It then becomes a primary management aid for enhanced understanding and improved management of the systems: in operation, in production and in acquisition by the organization. This feedback is then used by management for bettering the quality goals defined via the QA plan. No feedback mechanism can be of value if these input values cannot be verified.

While planning for quality, as in any other management discipline, a good understanding of "where you are going" – what your quality *goals* are – is a prerequisite for effectiveness of the planning process. Knowing "where you are going" means to be able to plan what the quality attributes are to be, and what the proposed "relative value" (quantitative) of each attribute *needs* to be. Not only that, but all this usually needs to be done before the system itself is particularly clear. The software QA practitioner needs to have a set of tools for both professional purposes, and for allowing project management/client management to quantify **their** quality goals for the project/product in development. (To eliminate overuse of the "/" double terms, for the remainder of this book, the words "project" and "product," and the terms "client management" and "project management" will be used interchangeably.)

Most organizations selling consulting for TQM claim, at least in their marketing literature, that the type of organization is not relevant to their techniques. This is quite simply not correct. When one of the authors discussed the questions with some of them (and actually discussed it personally with executive officers of Crosby Associates International Inc., Conway Quality Inc., Organizational Dynamics Inc., and representatives of the Juran organization) they all acknowledged that they had no real understanding of software and had never analyzed when software was similar to other kinds of problems and when it was not. In instances of implementing their techniques there have been very pointed differences, where a software-oriented organization has been concerned. Particularly, when I mentioned to them that in software there is no manufacturing process, but only design, they were universally unhappy. This forced them to re-evaluate the comment that organization type is irrelevant. The result is that they may need some sort of a "mental fix" – actually, we all do. What is more important for us, is that this now causes us to change the mode of thought based upon the software producers being accustomed to being always "feared" by the organization. Nonetheless, they still think that way, and it is still always the case that we cannot afford the luxury.

TQM uses control techniques for making and achieving goals. This is usually taken to mean all corporate goals. Somehow, software has usually managed to remain the exception. Even in very well-managed organizations, the software frequently runs out of control. Why? Mostly because we simply do not really understand how to fully control the creative processes. Software TQM must include the use of plans, analysis and control of software and goals which allow for quality software to happen. Quality planning is a primary tool. Clearly, a first real step must be establishing an agreed baseline, followed by building a quality plan and managing defined goals. A basis of control must be an understanding of how software quality may be measured. It is imperative that we base analysis upon these measurements. This analysis must have both an immediate and a long-term effect upon systems acquisition. This ensures deeper understanding and allows better management of the system: in operation, production and in acquisition by the organization.

Total Quality Management Practice

As stated above, the usually accepted concepts of TQM, as promulgated by the various "management gurus," are based upon the same concepts being discussed here. The only difference is that your normal, everyday management guru does not know software. They seem to think that products just happen. Clearly, this is not the case in a software company. Nor is it the case in an engineering company that develops and markets products which happen to be software rich. Many products today may have as much as a 90% software content (measured in terms of total investment in their development). In discussions that one of the authors has had with several of these highly skilled professionals (and, do not misunderstand us, we have a great deal of respect for these people and both admire and learn from their work), they have always emphasized that they really did not understand software, but they thought it was essentially the same as anything else! This is not quite accurate. Figure 1.2 on the next page, shows a *typical* enterprise structure. Notice that software is simply not there. Why? Is this simply an oversight on their part? Hardly! These people are much too professional and experienced for that. We must be aware that certain kinds of systems are too complex for trivial analysis (e.g., traffic, weather, biological, economic). Major information systems of all kinds, whether oriented towards information processing or real-time may be as complex as biological systems. In any case, the discussion centers around the idea that one must *plan* to do better and that all these ideas are a challenge to traditional management philosophy.

The difference then, is that software is all development (design). Remember, industrial processes are intrinsically stable – they are algorithmic processes. Information sciences are intrinsically unstable. The usual models just do not work.

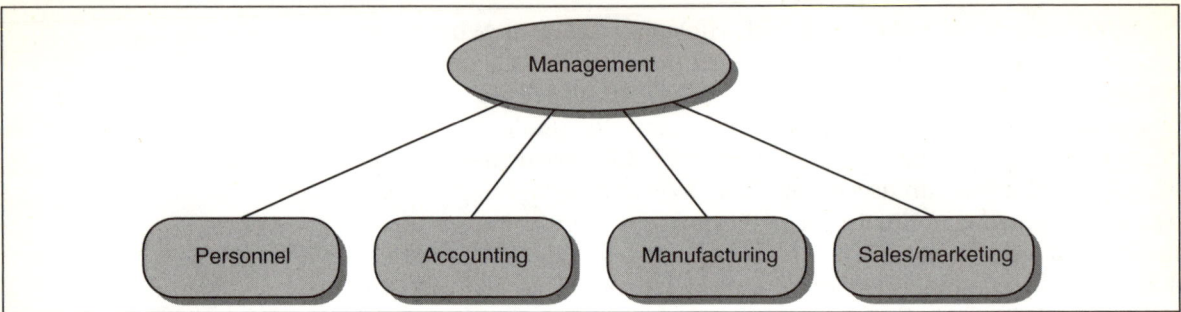

Figure 1.2 GURUware.

Well, if the usual models do not work, what, if anything, can be learned from them?
The answer is: the three CPIs!

- Continuous process improvement.
- Continuous product improvement.
- Continuous productivity improvement.

Interesting, is it not? We said three different things with the same acronym. The great big secret is, in software they are all the same. The stupid expression: "If it ain't broke, don't fix it!" Is simply that, *stupid!* That is the surest way to not stay in business for any length of time. Even monopolies understand that today.

We are asking you, on a continuous basis, to think about what you are doing, about how you are doing it and about how much it is (and should be) costing you. We are asking you, on a continuous basis:

- to improve your *products*
- to improve your *processes* and
- to improve your *productivity*.

As TJ Watson said, we are asking you to *think*. Nasty, isn't it?

The First Steps to Planning for Quality

An organization engaged in the development, acquisition or maintenance of software – whether for profit or as an internal service to the company – must have a view of quality and its meaning to them in relation to the proposed product. Our wish at this point is to suggest what that view might be to achieve the sort of results we think you desire. Look at Figure 1.3. It displays the relationship with which management needs to be

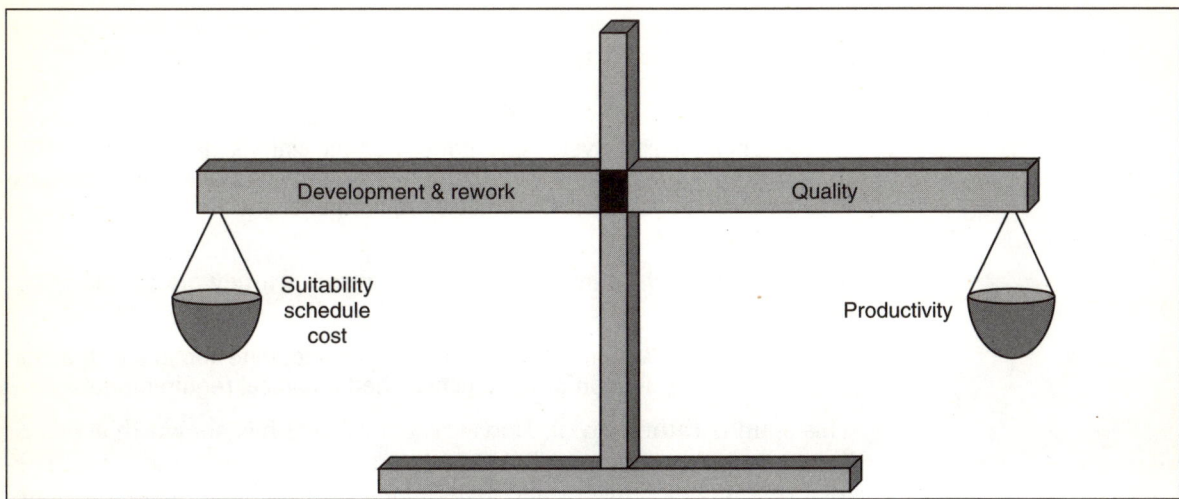

Figure 1.3   Management relations for quality.[6]

concerned for software. Let us use this drawing to establish a few basic principles and put them in their place. Let's look at the right-hand side of the drawing. Notice that quality is the *arm*, from which *productivity swings*. **In software, quality and productivity just do not separate!** They are part of the same thing. This is axiomatic to any understanding of quality, as it relates to software. Crosby's famous book said "Quality is free." This is not quite true (close, but not quite). What is absolutely true (certainly for software) is that what really is costly, is a lack of quality. Generating, then hunting and fixing bugs is a very expensive, wasteful and unproductive way of life.

There is a major difference between software and hardware. **In software the defects are built in. In hardware they are a function of time**. Understanding this is a prerequisite to a plan for quality.

Now let's look at the left-hand side. Development *and* rework are the balance arm of quality. What swings from them are the three keys to any project's success: *suitability* of the produced system to the clients' expectations, *delivery* on the agreed date and *price* that is considered appropriate. Now isn't that a nasty lot of things to say? If you do not like it, you deserve it.

To be kept in perspective, quality concepts must be understood in terms of accepted definitions. "Accepted" means definitions as used by commonly used industry standards. The standards "ANSI/IEEE STD 730" and "ANSI/IEEE STD 610.12"; the American National Standard Institute/Institute of Electrical and Electronic Engineers Standards for Software Quality Assurance Plans and for Software Engineering Terminology. From those sources, one can see that the definition, is actually composed of two parts. The definition of what quality means:

> The totality of features and characteristics of a product or service that bear on its ability to satisfy given needs (ANSI/ASQC A3-1978).

And, the definition of what quality assurance means:

> A planned and systematic pattern of all actions necessary to provide adequate confidence that material, data, supplies, and services conform to established technical requirements and achieve satisfactory performance.

The software QA plan provides the necessary framework for planning of:

> ... systematic actions necessary to provide adequate confidence that the item or product conforms to established technical requirements.

This sounds rather trivial. However, experience has shown that this is quite a complicated and delicate – not to mention, diplomatic – task. The total quantity of activities and tasks which need to be addressed is quite large. In a general term, we call it software auditing.

The software audit process improves the *availability and reliability* of software and the products supported by software. The process is designed to be analogous to the quality control function in manufacturing of "regular" products. This concept of quality auditing, like any quality audit concept, must be soundly based. Standards are one of the necessary parts of the baseline against which things can be measured. For our application, we are in need of more than this. We need an overall concept of planning. The resulting plan must include both the procedures and planned analysis of productivity and quality.[5]

The procedure

There are certain fundamental requirements for any quality improvement process to be successful. These requirements can be stated as a list of points as shown in Table 1.1.

Now, how is this to be accomplished? A set of four activities must be implemented by the organization.

- **First,** establish a *baseline* for measurement. Whether this process is called software practices assessment or software maturity index (as the SEI calls it) or software process model is not important. This process measures the state-of-the-practice used by the organization in its development activities.
- **Second**, develop a comprehensive quality plan, which includes productivity and goals, along with the technology goals to be used by the organization. Software engineering is immature on principles. That is why pure SE activities have not really had a major impact on the productivity of our systems (by the by, the most profound impact has come from reusable packages such as trans-

Table 1.1

Accept the quality process

Management commits to the improvement process as corporate culture

There is always room to improve what is being done

Preventing problems is smarter than reacting to them

Management focus, leadership and participation

A performance standard of zero defects

Participation by all employees, as individuals and as groups

Focus improvement on processes, not people

action monitors and databases). This plan is wholly dependent upon the total *commitment* of management. TQM, particularly for software, begins with the most senior management of the concern (e.g., the CEO).

- **Third**, implement your *plan*. The implementation must include all three types of goals (productivity, quality and technology).
- Finally, the **fourth** aspect. Everything must include measurement, measurement and *measurement*! Of course, as stated in several other places in this book, this measurement is not a religious rite. It is used, after rigorous analysis, as feedback for the software organization.

The most difficult comprehension problem is establishing your corporate baseline. Even all the corporate awareness discussed previously is not sufficient if there is not a reliable picture of where the organization stands in comparison to the industry, and what the plan for improvement needs to be. Also, of course, we cannot prove improvement unless we have means for measuring it. This implies that we need to start measuring our current state before starting to improve it.

Only after this measurement can the quality attributes be determined, along with their constituent parts. Once these parts exist and are allocated to attributes of suitability, maintainability or both, the last and final aspect may be determined, that of the quality attribute relationships. This closes the circle. Once this framework exists, determining the software quality through the product life-cycle (concept, requirements, design, implementation, testing, installation and checkout, operations and maintenance[6] and finally retirement[7]).

An excellent example of how things should be accomplished can be taken from the quest for quality at the Philips Corporation. They call this quest, "company-wide quality improvement principles." This particular example is taken from their Singapore subsidiary, and was reported in a newsletter of the American Society for Quality Control (ASQC).

- **Customer satisfaction**. A perfect interface must be achieved between company performance and customer needs in all aspects that customers consider to be important.
- **Leadership.** Quality improvement is primarily a task and responsibility of management as a whole.
- **Total involvement.** There must be total involvement of all employees at all levels and in all functions. Equally important is the complete involvement of all suppliers of goods and services.
- **Integrated approach.** Integration must be achieved between functions and between levels. Traditional organizational barriers must be removed.
- **Systematic approach**. A systematic approach must start with a clearly defined business strategy, which is then translated into an improvement policy with objectives and priorities. These must be followed by detailed planning, implementation and monitoring of progress.
- **Defect prevention**. Defects must be prevented from occurring. Performance must be the result of built-in capabilities.
- **Continuous improvement**. The approach should not have the character of a campaign or a project. Excellence can only be achieved by continuously investing in improvement, step-by-step, year after year.
- **Maximum quality.** Long-term objectives must be set which reflect the will to strive for excellence. The path towards excellence must be marked by challenging but achievable and acceptable targets.
- **Education** and **training**. Widespread attention will be given to education and training. A new work culture can only be realized if people are more than ever prepared to make their contribution.

The point referring to continuous improvement is particularly interesting. It "just happens" to be a fact of business life that nearly every major successful corporation in the world places continuous quality improvement as a primary corporate policy. A sadder example was reported by *Business Week* on July 4, 1988; under the title; "Missed deadlines at Lotus Development Corporation" (see Table 1.2, below). Lotus was clearly one of the brightest and most interesting of companies in the software marketplace. They enjoyed some amazing successes. They also had some very interesting failures (we can, of course, say the same for any other major software company) which have been publicly reported. An intelligent manager learns from the mistakes of others. Lotus learned their lessons, and they should be applauded for that – but it was too late, they are no longer an independent company and their upper management has been replaced. That is what the *Business Week* article was about and, in a very real sense, that is what "total quality management for software" is all about.

Problems of products being delayed, or even canceled, have multidimensional costs. These costs include both *lost product sales* and

Table 1.2   An example of what is happening in industry

Product	Announced	Promised for	Status
Modern Jazz	March, 1987	1Q 1988	Canceled June 16, 1988
1-2-3 rel. 3	April, 1987[3]	1Q 1988	4Q 1988
1-2-3G	April, 1987	4Q 1988	1Q 1989
1-2-3M	April, 1987	1Q 1988	1Q 1989
DBMS	April, 1987	4Q 1988	2Q 1989
1-2-3 MAC	October, 1987	3Q 1988	1Q 1989
AGENDA	November, 1987	2Q 1988	3Q 1988

decreased customer confidence. Both of these are intangibles which are difficult to measure directly, but this difficulty must not be allowed as an excuse to ignore them. We all remember that Lotus started at about the same time as Microsoft and in the beginning they were in competition as to who would be the leader. Lotus has now been purchased by the largest fish. They are not going to be leading anything now.

A Case Study

John Cullyer from the Royal Signals and Radar Establishment (RSRE), UK Ministry of Defence (MOD). VIPER microprocessor, a 32-bit RISC chip designed for safety-critical applications.

RSRE performed a study of NATO software in the 1980s, using a static analysis technique in which a program is represented as a directed graph, various expressions are associated with the arcs and conclusions regarding correctness are derived from them. Of the modules (not necessarily whole programs) which RSRE sampled from the NATO inventory, one in ten were found to contain errors, and of those, one in 20 (or one in 200 overall) had errors serious enough to result in loss of the vehicle or plant! About the same findings were made whether the code came from Britain, the USA, or West Germany.

VIPER is an attempt to address this problem. The project was felt to be so urgent that it was funded within 48 hours of submission. There is no stack ("We don't like stacks – they overflow"). There are no interrupts; all device handling must be done by polling. Cullyer said that it is not possible to verify programs that permit interrupts. "I don't think we have all persuaded our bosses that there is a problem. If we do not implement these methods, there will be a lot of accidents and a lot of people will die. If we do implement them there will still be accidents, but we will limit the casualties." He also mentioned that new MOD software procurement standards require formal development techniques for critical software. MOD regulations explicitly prohibit any cost saving that might increase hazard to life – you are not allowed to trade lives off against money.

The shuttle is a totally "fly-by-wire" craft. The onboard flight control software is built from about 500,000 lines of HAL/S source code; the total error rate for the software was 0.11 errors/thousand source lines (or about 55 errors). IBM got the error rate down to 2.2 errors per 1000 lines in 1982 and to 0.11 per 1000 lines at the end of 1985. The figures referred to errors discovered by the customer and undiscovered errors remain. For instance, how they could be sure the abort sequence software was error free, since it had never actually been used? The answer is that they exercised it in a software simulator.

How can one determine how many consecutive failure-free tests would be needed to establish with 99% confidence that the probability of failure is less than one in a billion? Commonsense suggests that it must be at least a billion, perhaps more. Miller derived that you actually need around 4.61 billion, and presented the rule of thumb that to obtain confidence that the probability of failure is less than 10^{-N}, you need about $10^{+(N+0.5)}$ trials. He pointed out that in most cases it is only practical to test up to around 10^5 trials, which can only reveal bugs that appear with frequency $10^{-4.5}$ or greater.

People sometimes say that good engineering practices ensure that the probability of failure is much less than $10^{-4.5}$. This is rather illogical if testing reveals any errors at all. If the tests reveal frequent bugs, why should you believe that your good engineering practices have prevented the subtle ones? Performing binary patches to weapons software in the field is a common practice in the US services; the UK standards prohibit this. Cullyer mentioned that the UK has only 11 scientists and engineers who review the entire avionics; he estimated that there were only about 50 people in whole western world looking after civil avionics safety.[8]

Notes

1 The copy I am referring to is: "Trillium: Model for Telecom Product Development and Support Process Capability," Bell Canada, Release 3.0, December 1994. The word "Trillium" is not listed as trade marked by this document.
2 Currently undergoing a process of revision.
3 Webster's *New Illustrated Dictionary*, Editors-in-chief Allan S. Kullen and Frederick Reinstein, Books, Inc., 1970.
4 In software, quality and productivity just do not separate!
5 In 1985, software costs for the United States Department of Defense were roughly $11 billion. In the USA, as a whole, the total outlay for software was about $70 billion; worldwide the costs for software reached about $140 billion – that was 11 years ago. The present rate of growth in the worldwide software market is about 12%. (As reported by Barry W. Boehm, TRW, September, 1987, *IEEE Computer*.)
6 Operations and maintenance is called here, one stage. This is where the majority of resources are consumed. While it is true that, conceptually, every maintenance

project is a development project in the small, it is also very important to remember the additional onus that is placed upon these activities.

7 The actual fact of retirement seldom needs to be examined. By this point it is usually too late to do anything significant or to learn a great deal about it. Most software systems live for 15–20 years. At that point, no one cares anymore, they simply wish to get the old stuff out of the way and get on with the new system.

8 Taken from "Testing for the individual programmer," JC Cherniavsky and WR Adrion, NTIS, US Department of Commerce, PB 166960.

ESTABLISHMENT OF A SOFTWARE QUALITY PROGRAM

2

THE EFFECTIVE ESTABLISHMENT OF A QUALITY ASSURANCE function in an organization is a complex process. Probably the most important aspect for success is that the organization actually believes that this is necessary for its own health and on-going survival. Hopefully, most organizations recognize the need and initiate their software quality program in time like the people in the following case study.

In 1986 the first author was approached by the assistant general manager of a small company to discuss a problem. The executive asserted that there was a project in the organization which had the potential to **make** or **break** them. He further claimed that if the project succeeded the organization would double in size every two years. If it failed, the company would close for lack of working capital. The company was at the level of about $25 million in revenue, with a small loss for the past fiscal year. Most of their revenue came from defense electronics. The management was already aware that they needed to diversify. (I have seldom seen such far-seeing management! Brilliant!)

The project had a client willing to try the system and even more important, willing to pay for the system, if it worked (British Telecom, clearly a nontrivial client). In addition, several other clients were very likely to buy if the first did. Even clients whose governments would be unhappy if they did (for example, the German Bundespost – the German government wanted them to buy from Siemens, whose system could not be demonstrable in the same time-frame as this client's). In telephony, time is always critical, even for monopolies. Sometimes much more so than money.

We sat in a Chinese restaurant for lunch and discussed the project. It turned out that the project's software was the critical success factor. The software was based upon an existing product which they had marketed with mild success. It was a line-doubling system for telephones (voice).[1] However, this was their first really serious try at the nondefense market. The new technology which they were attempting to develop would multiply lines by a factor of five. The advice given was that they should make every effort to ensure (and assure) the success of the software. To that point in time (for them) software was defined as a nuisance, not a resource. They had seven software developers for all of their products (including maintenance).

Ensuring that the software was a success was not a trivial factor. While software quality assurance was an existing concept (this first author had helped create it when an article was published called *Software Quality Management*, in 1980) very few people in the world really knew what *to ensure* might really mean in real life. There were, however, a few things which the software community had learned and which could be applied to this situation. Luckily, the head of development was (and is) one of the best managers of the kind this author has had the pleasure to deal with. ***This is important because in an endeavor of this type, people are everything.***

The first suggestion was to appoint a skilled professional to look at what was going on and create a **feedback loop** within the organization. Today, this kind of a loop is called *software quality assurance*. When I used this term with the development manager, the reaction was that software is written and then makes problems. **One cannot assure it!** Nevertheless, the simple terminology remained. This decision was also helpful.

The feedback loops were important for another reason. The primary client wanted to be able to follow the progress of the project which, of course, had a "hopeless" time scale. This process would have the secondary objective of creating the information to be provided to the client for perusal whenever deemed by them to be necessary (this was to be "periodically," the periods had not yet been defined). Even the method of perusal was not defined, since parts of the documentation were written in a language which the client could not read, and no one was willing to pay to have them translated. (A good thing too, at the time, they were awful!)

The first author was to supply the company with the professional advice needed and to make certain that all required training was provided. In addition, there was to be an overseeing of the general work dealing with methods of documentation, development, testing and reporting which was to be the personal area of the first author. (As well as being responsible to company management and for reporting to the client's representatives, when they came.) In short, what was established was indeed a *software quality assurance* (SQA) function. Afterwards, the company developed these skills in-house and took full responsibility after the end of this project and two follow-on projects.

The project was a success. The company did double in size every two years, it is now approaching some $500 million and is the technology and market leader in its field. (Some of their competitors may disagree with that statement. If so, I apologize for the inconvenience, but these are the facts as the first author understands them.) This chapter is intended to provide the people who are to develop the software quality function with the list of items needed by them for the establishment or the evaluation of the software quality program, if one already exists. The program, as it is envisioned here, may be applied for a single project. Nevertheless, it is strongly recommended that it would be better if it were implemented throughout a whole installation. Ideally, the program should be for the entire organization, but this is frequently more than can be accomplished at one time.

The first task is a swift and accurate collection of data – as much data as possible. This collected data must reflect how the software development process is being performed, and how it is being audited (assured). In most installations there is, of course, some process in place to perform the task of checking, storing and releasing software. Frequently, this process has developed over time and has never been formally audited. The process is perhaps not the most sophisticated and may never have been computerized, and this may not have any importance.

The second task is to develop a *plan for quality*. The major problems in assuring the level of systems today are **error propagation** and **error fixing**. While planning for quality, as in any other management discipline, a good understanding of "where you are going" – what your quality goals are – is a prerequisite for effectiveness of the planning process. Knowing "where you are going" means to be able to plan both what the quality attributes are to be, and also what the proposed "relative value" (quantitative) of each attribute needs to be. Not only that, but all this usually needs to be done before the system itself is particularly clear. The software quality assurance practitioner needs to have a set of tools both for professional purposes, and for allowing project management/client management to quantify their quality goals for the project/product in development.

Scope of the Software Quality Program

Requirements for the establishment and implementation of the project software quality program must be defined and made public knowledge. These requirements include:

- Planning for and conducting assessments of the quality of the software.
- Planning for and conducting assessments of the quality of the documentation.
- Planning for and conducting assessments of the quality of workmanship of all contractors (and subcontractors) for the software.
- Planning for and conducting assessments of the quality of all work which will need to be performed for the on-going maintenance of the software.
- All deliverable and nondeliverable items which are to be developed as part of the project need to be clearly identified and labeled.
- All deliverable and nondeliverable items which are to be purchased as part of the project need to be clearly identified and labeled.
- The project may include client-supplied items which will need to be verified or which will need to be included within another object (item) which will, in tern, need to be validated and/or verified.
- System boundaries, as regards items to be stored and released need to be clearly defined.

Professional Ethics

Software quality assurance practitioners have access to confidential corporate data (such as trade secrets) and confidential personal data. The successful establishment of quality assurance is wholly dependent upon the cooperation of the developers and management. Personal and corporate confidences must be respected and handled with the utmost care. Please do not think that because this section is very short, it is of small importance. I have personally seen failures which directly resulted from actions which caused a lack of person confidence in the SQA practitioner. Bad ethics is not just bad practice. It is always stupid.

Such general statements are not only unhelpful, but most people find them obnoxious. Certainly managers worried about the next quarter and next year – and tired of hearing about the next year's panacea – do not find these particularly useful.

Achievement of top management comprehension of how quality leads naturally to productivity is dependent upon supplying them with a coherent concept of what it means. Once this has been accomplished, a realistic definition of quality management can be agreed upon. What quality and productivity mean for corporate management are low costs and expenses, and enhanced product capability. But this is only the "bottom line" issue, the final result of doing things right the first time. This must be backed-up up by a "technical" definition. The technical definition proposed has three parts; requirements, client confidence and constant improvement.

First, requirements

The organization must develop, manufacture and distribute consistently low-cost products and services. More importantly, the products must be what customers believe they want.

Second, confidence

The products must be supplied at the level of reliability which matches the client's needs, and remain there. Even if those needs have not been clearly defined.

Third, constant improvement

For the client to continue to perceive a supplier as a quality producer, constant improvement of all products and all processes must be made an integral part of the corporate culture.

The process of constant improvement must be in all areas of corporate operations, including suppliers and distributors. All participants in the product cycle must be forced to eliminate waste. All kinds of waste. There are three kinds of waste which must be dealt with: scrapped material and work (re-work or over-specification); poorly utilized assets (capital-inventory, receivables, plant or equipment); or, the most difficult (and common) of them all, time of people – all people of all levels.

The managers of many important corporations now understand, and are implementing, the use of statistical process control to achieve and maintain consistent quality in engineering, manufacturing and maintenance. Some corporations have also begun using statistics from customer satisfaction surveys. Unfortunately, most managers have not had any significant education concerning the new management systems. Systems whose central concern must be attacking the aforementioned areas of waste in material, capital and time of people. Management is now beginning to learn that quality management includes elimination of waste of time. That waste includes idle time, "busy" work, errors, complexities, poor methods, and so on.

There are three tools which accompany the five parts of software quality assurance. These three tools are: statistical surveys and tools, "imagineering", and industrial engineering. The five parts are: quality planning, quality analysis, reviews and inspections, configuration management and testing. These are not "panacea" concepts. This is the real thing! The practical and tried method for really accomplishing the job. After all, that is what "total quality" is really supposed to be all about. The strong use of industrial engineering techniques is absolutely essential.What are the people doing, and when? How long is needed for each step? The effective use of the tools in a coordinated system leads directly to a major reduction of costs and expenses. When management is brought to understand that, they will lead the way. Leaving people out of the quality definition gives everyone (managers and employees) incorrect signals. The prime task of quality management is elimination of waste of time.

Top management must be made aware of the systems, policies, and procedures that really control the effectiveness of their organization. Standards of workmanship and operational procedure, must be agreed upon and used to measure improvements in productivity and quality. Managers need to determine the optimal complement of personnel for their areas of responsibility. This must be audited via some sort of work sampling technique (relating to work quantity and pace). Work processes need to be regularly analyzed for possibilities of simplification. A system of awards, based upon monetary incentives (pay, promotion, bonus, stock options) should be determined for people who adhere to the new management philosophy. Nonmonetary awards may also be applied. People should be rewarded for preventing problems, rather than fixing them. Perhaps more than any other single aspect, fear must not be a part of the corporate culture. This is firstly accomplished via clear channels of upward communication.

Management must be made aware that there are many systems of policies and procedures that need constant re-examination. Some of the techniques for this re-examination are quite simple, for instance, employee surveys and work-flow charts. When the analysis shows a necessity, improved systems may be installed, or new systems established. These systems must be designed, from the very beginning, for major improvements in quality and productivity. Major changes in quality and productivity just do not occur unless top management understands these systems and leads the changes required.

Without direct top management involvement, the organization will not believe that there exists a genuine need or desire for improvements. All these required changes move at a slow pace. If productivity improvements of 2–5% can be achieved annually and constantly, vast changes can be expected. While history has not yet shown many who have attained that goal, most industry experts believe it realistic.

A prime imperative of any quality management program must be based upon the notion that management must see what is both necessary and possible. Most corporate management wants and needs real help, and has, over the past decade, become aware of it. No management wants destructive criticism. The education of top level managers to a more realistic, up-to-date definition of quality management (the newer system of management controlled by management) leads to much greater top management understanding, leadership and commitment. That, in turn, determines how the organization works and leads to the necessary improvements in quality and productivity.

Note

1   This means that the system effectively converts one physical line into multiple "logical" lines. Very clever electronics, coupled with extremely clever software.

THE TRILLION DOLLAR DILEMMA – THE YEAR 2000

3

IN A SHORT WHILE, THE YEAR'S DATE WILL BE 2000. WHY IS this important? Economists know that the "western" economy functions by 250 year cycles. Two hundred years of relative stability followed by 50 years of rapid change. We seem to be at the end of one of these cycles. We are all aware of the imminence of the so-called "information age" which is now to follow the industrial age. Perhaps, if you read the news media, you may be aware of a problem which is being called by many: the "year 2000 problem" (Y2K). This is one of many names. It is also called the "millennium problem," the "century problem" and also the "1000 Year glitch."[1] Notice that all of the "names" define the year 2000,[2] as a problem. Why?

In the origins of computing (in the 1960s) the cost of storage was the major issue. This was dealt with by preserving space, in every way possible. One of the commonest, and cheapest, ways was to store only two digits for the year (for example, 1996 is stored as "96"). This seems very little, but "time/date stamps" are one of the most common data items in all of computing. One major company we know of counted the number of fields *defined* as dates in their databases. The total is 6202 (it is the "and two" that really got me!). Clearly, this is not a trivial number, for it does not include fields used for dates not described as date fields nor working storage fields nor REDEFINEs, and so on. These things are so prevalent that they are used for many other things, which are seemingly unrelated to a "date." For instance, many games use a time/date stamp as "seed" value for a pseudo-random number generator. These games will not work when that value is zero ("00"). No computer can divide by zero – one automobile rental company's computer goes down several times a day because of licenses which expire in the year 2000. Many elevator companies use the year "00" as a test pattern, causing them to stop at the nearest floor. Many radar systems use the date to compute where stars are to be expected, and hence to calibrate themselves. They will not "see" correctly. Federal Aviation Administration computer systems are 30 years old.[3] Most major systems, defense included, will not function unless some very basic changes are implemented.

Why It Is a Problem

The idea that the coming new decade, the move from 31 December 1999 to 1 January 2000, has the potential to cause significant problems to computer-dependent systems, is becoming increasingly accepted. But why is it a problem? Even the nontechnical person understands that simply changing the size of a "date field" from two characters wide to four characters, in a program, is not significant enough to be classed as a real problem. Certainly not the world-shattering difficulty that Y2K is considered. Let us try to understand what the problem really comprises. It appears to be composed of four parts: size, prevalence, complexity and testability.

Size

The problem is not just a question of changing a few fields. The quantity of fields that are themselves dates, or that are (or may be) derived from dates, is astounding. Dates are an extraordinarily common data representation. They are used for computing the positions of stars (for navigation), calculating interest, setting the periods when an elevator (lift) must be maintained, predicting inventories to random number generators, and so on ad nauseam. In addition to this, many systems may have tens or hundreds of the pesky things. With the best technologies and the most sophisticated tools, there is simply a lot of work to do to find them and correct them.

Prevalence

As stated, the quantity is vast and they appear in every kind of system. But it is still more than that. There is almost no application type which is immune. Most operating systems are in danger of failure. During an interview with an prospective employee one of the authors expressed the opinion that the F16 aircraft may be in trouble. The interviewee had formerly been responsible for a F16 flight training simulator. When this was mentioned, she thought for a moment and agreed, the F16 will not fly. Problems will occur with telephones, and not just billing; electricity supply (the actual flow); and this is just the beginning. Those dates are everywhere and used in strange and mysterious ways.

Complexity

Many companies may have been aware of the problem and thought that they had it under control. They forgot human nature. This author knows of a bank that bought their software, stipulating that all dates be in the millennium format. However, the programmers, over the years, had "masked out" the first two characters, assuming that they were not relevant. All software now needs to be corrected.

Testability

The most basic premise when testing anything, regardless of how complex or simple it may be, is that the systems used to test it are trustworthy with a predictable level of confidence. This is not the case with Y2K problems. No systems can be assumed to be completely reliable, not even the mainframe.

A Y2K Life-cycle Model

What should a Y2K (Year 2000) oriented maintenance life-cycle model be like? What are the determining factors and the critical enabling technologies for a successful Y2K project? It must be made clear that the size and complexity of these projects, coupled with the very narrow bandwidth of programming resources within organizations, are going to be the primary controlling factors. You can put all of the tools in the world in a corner and ignore them if you do not have the people to do the job. And you can take all of the people that you can possibly hire, and stand them in the corner if you do not have access to the technology to perform the work in the available time. (That is, if there are any people to hire.)

Table 3.1 Y2K life-cycle

Work task	Percent of total
Inventory and analyze systems	25%
Plan tasks and remediation	5%
Change/remediate (execute plan)	20–30%
Verify and test	40–50%

Verification and Testing

Verification of the systems, after remediation, is critical. How may this be done?

A well-known testing technique is boundary values. The list of possible boundary values for Y2K is interesting:

- 31 December 1999 and 1 January 2000 are the obvious ones.
- 2 January 2000 *can* be obvious, on reflection.
- 28, 29 February and 1 March 2000 – Y2K is a leap year, which is not a well-known fact.
- 29 February 2004.
- 1 January 2000 minus the system's range – plus one day, minus one day … (there may be a large number of these).

This list is by no means complete.

New Equipment/New Systems

Has the purchase of new systems made this a nonissue? Most installed PC systems store a two-digit year as their system date. Certainly, all systems prior to the Pentium, and most of **them**, including many sold today. Try it. Set your system date to 31 December 1999, one minute to midnight. Wait for the clock to turn over, then power down the system. Reboot and check what the date reads. Remember that if you are connected to a network, your system will take its date from there. Be aware of what you are testing, as well as how you test it. So much for the hardware (actually, it is the firmware, the BIOS). What about the software applications. Surely, new applications should be okay? Old habits die hard.

- A small mortgage bank has a software system developed by their computer vendor, some ten years ago. Management was far-sighted enough to demand all dates be four digits. So, no problem right? Wrong! **Old habits die hard**. Remember what we said above, about programmers using two digits, via a "mask." Luckily, this is a very small bank and the problem was caught early by their head of systems.
- The head of *Software Methodology & Tools* for one of the world's largest corporations purchased a small, relatively trivial, commercial program in a noted chain of computer shops. This application was completely new and was prominently labelled: "**Year 2000 Certified**." It was produced by one of the largest software manufacturers. He installed the software, set his clock forward and tried it. The application did not work. He then called the Help Desk and some clever consultant, realizing with whom

they were speaking, put him through to the head of software technology. They agreed that the buyer would look at the source code. **He found *824* errors**. This highly skilled professional then asked (us): "If one of the largest software houses produced a brand new application, called it 'Year 2000 Certified' and had 824 errors, what am I to do with two billion lines of undocumented code?"

Notice two things about this story.

- There was no notification by whom the application was certified.
- That number: 2,000,000,000 lines of code! This is an amazing quantity.

Two billion lines of undocumented source code!

Lessons

- Certification should mean that it was certified by a qualified professional, who has been trained for this kind of certification activity. **The certification process must be *verifiable* and *repeatable*.**
- The basic action of changing dates in code is simple. However, the quantities involved, and the convoluted ways in which dates have been used are causing a problem of horrendous proportions.

Realities

Most analysts estimate costs of one to two dollars per line of source code, to fully correct all *basic* date fields and *resulting* fields including verification and testing. Regardless of budget, there is a question concerning the quantity of lines of code (LOC) that can be corrected in one year using normal, industry accepted tools and techniques (usually between four and five million LOC). Remember that corrections are performed while maintaining service levels and continuing with normal maintenance tasks. It is frequently very difficult to do this with existing staff (no "bandwidth"). This means that what has been corrected must continue to accept input coming from uncorrected systems (there is an implied assumption that this input can be corrected, on-the-fly). Additionally, all this must be **corrected, tested and verified** on a functionally equivalent operational system, but which allows its system date to be changed – otherwise, you **cannot** know that the correction works correctly.

> **Note**: Not all date fields need correction. We can allow many things to continue as they are. For example, screen displays or fields not used computationally may very well be left to some later time, for normal maintenance to take care of them.

The first author has asked **tens** of very highly placed MIS executives throughout corporate America what they plan to do. Most of them have answered with one word, **retire**! One life insurance corporation with some 27 million lines of source code, performed three significant pilot projects. Their conclusion: *"With seven years' more work, we would need 50 years to finish. There just aren't enough people or the right tools."* The company has been sold.

The Programmer's Paradigm

Anyone can write (well almost) but *you* are a *programmer*. You write odd looking lines of text that most of your relations do not understand and your spouse does not even want to! You make a point of stretching your imagination to make a piece of hardware or software do things that no one has done before. Your work is creative, sometimes screamingly so! Like any creative person, as your tools improve, your work flows better, as do your results. Sometimes, you are asked to write a program "from scratch" but not often. Most of the time (statistics say 80% of the time) you improve your existing code, in an evolutionary manner. The evolution of a good program into a better one can be challenging. Making a "not so good" program (particularly someone else's) into a good one is horrendous. You make a good (better than average) salary and the word "on the street" is that this is likely to move up very steeply in the near future.

Moore's law states that computing power increases by 48% per year. This has been true since about the time of Charles Babbage (the 1850s). What is less well known, is that expressiveness of computer languages is increasing at a rate of 11% while actual programmer productivity is increasing at about 4.8%[4] **There is an order of magnitude difference between Moore's law** (the rate at which computing power increases) **and programmer's productivity**. This does not sound too good.

Information technology[5] activity has contributed about 5% to business efficiency, despite the enormous quantity of existing source code – some have reported about 50 billion lines of Cobol source code on the island of Manhattan (good thing they do not weigh anything, or take up any space, or even that rock might be in trouble), others have reported some 600 billion lines of Cobol source, throughout the world. Software is that part of a system which ought to be capable of most quickly adapting to changes, of all kinds. Changes may be to the environment, the mission or operational elements, changes in the quantities of data or the complexity of data needs or the milieu in which the system functions. It may include several or all of these at the same time. Today we react to these changes, we do not anticipate them. We make changes to our software but always at considerable risk. The cost of change is disproportionate to its apparent size. Maintaining software is an expensive and demoralizing task. We almost never know in advance the effort and resources needed. We frequently estimate, but the degree of inaccuracy is astounding. Expenditures on software maintenance approached US$100 billion in the USA alone at the beginning of this decade and are approaching about US$400 billion now, at the end of 1996. We make changes from an imperfect understanding of the current system. In no other engineering discipline would major structural changes be made to a functioning system with the impunity and lack of understanding that is applied to our software systems. When a user requests a change, it should be our obvious duty to inform them of the expected impact (and costs). We do not do this, nor do we usually know how.

The Basic Assumptions Behind Development

- A single application is being developed.
- There are, or can be (if we do not know them) fixed requirements.
- Resources are the major limiting factor.
- We perceive a finite life time for the system that we are developing.

While these assumptions are true for software development, they are almost **never** true for maintenance. That is one of the reasons the makers of **CASE** products always try to sell a rewrite. It is not only the tool vendors that are at fault. Neither ISO 9000 nor SEI's CMM address software maintenance. Software engineering methods take little account for on-going, evolutionary development. University professors mostly still deny that it exists or that it is a major issue. They all offer strategic concepts yet 80% of system changes result from simple, evolutionary changes, such as altering a screen or a report. **Change *is inevitable***, both over the life-time of the system and during initial development. Most systems are **enterprise systems** with interfaces to many others, which coexist and co-operate. System life-times are very long. No technological artefact exists as long as does the average software system. Resources at our disposal constantly develop, though this is seldom the limiting factor we assumed it to be. We need to maintain a delicate balance between our need for a quality product and our demands to enhance what we already have. So what **is** the "reality" in which we work?

- Too much to do.
- Too little time in which to do it.
- Too few good people.
- Too many options.

A Paradigm Shift

What is proposed is a basic shift in the way we think about software. The idea of: first specify everything; then build it all; then maintain it forever **is bankrupt**! **What exists is continuous evolution.** Our problem is predictability, orderliness and clearly comprehensible management. **We CAN do this.**

"... 60% of all business expenditures on computing are for maintenance of software written in Cobol."[6]

• Mike Hammer said:	• We say:
Old rule: Plans get revised periodically. **New rule**: Plans get revised instantaneously.	Old rules can stay as they were. The **only rule** is that everything (including plans) is a baseline for change. The timing for change cannot be predicted, nor should it. **Right thinking** is to plan for continuous change.

We know that 80% of software professionals' time is spent on maintenance, while only 20% is devoted to development of new systems. If we can save even a trivial amount from the 80%, we make a major change to overall software productivity. By-the-bye, these are important numbers, they are discussed later! Where do problems in software actually appear? We divide problems into three categories: redesign problems, 50%; logic problems, 30%; and coding problems, 20%. Redesign means the requirements were insufficiently understood. Logic means that design needs were not understood or were incorrectly translated from the requirements.

Many logic problems are created during maintenance by an overly limited view of the systems' requirements or design. Making a change in software is multidimensional, with many areas of possible error. A

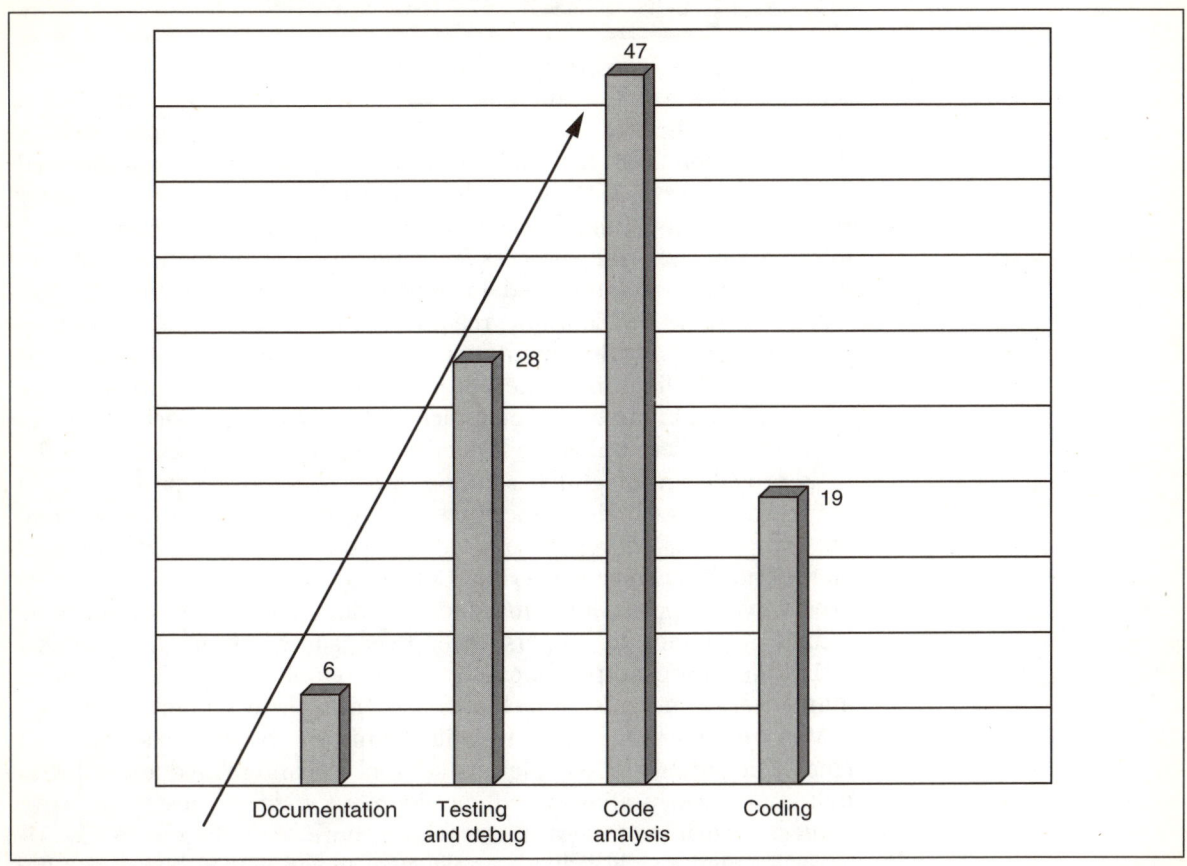

Figure 3.1 Proportions spent in maintenance activities. As shown in the graph, code analysis is where the big payoff lies. If this can be more efficient we have a tremendous productivity gain. This is very interesting as we seem to have discovered a dichotomy. We know that the major cause of disruption, of software wear-down, is an insufficient understanding of the process logic. Now we see that this is where the programmers are spending the greatest part of their time. What is wrong here?

change always causes a rippling effect. This is before we have even fully analyzed the ramifications of our proposed change. For this reason, it is axiomatic that when maintaining software, one must always document all of the changes. This is a great idea, but in practical terms it **never** happens. One of the prevalent phenomena is that **errors cluster**. That explains why we need to maintain statistics (read: metrics) in order to learn from our mistakes. But fixing a problem is always urgent, and it always has to be done in a short period of time. Couple all this with the fact that no one wants to be a "maintenance programmer," with the enormous increase of Cobol programmers' costs and that today's users are more demanding, and you begin to have an understanding of the problem.

Locating and Reusing Hidden Assets

Legacy systems store much of the information needed to operate a business. However, the quantities involved have hidden this information from view. The quality of existing systems, their *normal* lack of documentation and the tools that are available have not allowed individual *programs* to be easily understood, not to mention major software systems. Manual system rewrites often attempt to reuse existing information, but the process is laborious. Maintenance and re-development tasks enhanced by reverse engineering technology can make this more efficient and reliable. "Maintenance tools" analyzers, restructuring tools, documentation aids and measurement tools have been available for some time but most of them still work in isolation. They have not inhibited maintenance and costs growth. Each addresses a specific problem but is too limited to resolve broad tasks. Nor do the tools provide an integrated solution. Most focus at the program level but the key to true maintenance productivity is to treat the *entire system*, not components. Piecemeal upgrades to your applications are not only inefficient; they can be dangerous. Current tools do not encompass broad productivity aspects. Some tools address data, some process, but none resolve all issues developers face. Even some seemingly advanced techniques (for example function points) are only very partly integrated into our environments for lack of consistent tools to support them.

Many maintenance tools are still mainframe based. This approach ignores advantages of complementary tool sets and related technologies that make workstation-based development today's most productive strategy. Providing programmers with a more rewarding work experience also significantly reduces employee turnover. Rather than constantly reworking existing applications they can have the time to develop entirely new applications or apply themselves to the **Year 2000**.

System-wide standardization of naming conventions is one of the greatest single factors in enhancing maintenance productivity. Through productive redevelopment, the organization transforms old code into the corporate asset it should be. Imagine being able to clearly see processing paths of a whole system, even including the worst kinds of old *spaghetti-code* programs, and which areas will be affected if you make a change to one data field or copy. **(Try that on your "end-of-century" problem!)** Fan-In/Fan-Out models provide clear views of program flow, even if it is unstructured. A field/program cross reference allows system-wide resolution and reconciliation of data field names, regardless of how they are used. This facility allows you to recognize, test, rename in short, to regain control of these synonyms. **This also goes a very long way to solving the** "year 2000 problem." **An automated tool set may save 50% of the costs.** The complete "inventory" of a system and its associated relationships (interfaces) must be captured and stored in a rapidly accessible form. All invocation information and all interface information **can** be learned from the existing code. This allows implementation of portable software because it is supportable and documented. Not object-oriented "bubbles," but real existing, functionality made reusable.

Analysis and Design For Maintenance

The **analysis process** is essentially what you expect it to be. **Essentially**, but not identical. For **maintenance**, it is an iterative process composed of:

- Feasibility analysis
- Risk analysis
- Detailed requirements analysis

This stage always demands detailed perusal of systems' documentation and source code, to determine feasibility and to establish real technical requirements. Remember, we are trying to understand what was not understood previously. Perhaps because it was badly presented or overly complex. We are now trying to understand it through the stink of previous misunderstandings.

There are very strong differences between design in a maintenance vs a development environment. For **maintenance**, the process is composed of:

- Identify affected software modules
- Modify documentation (schematics, program design language, and so on); this is essentially the design of the new functionality
- Create test cases for the new code
- Identify relevant regression tests or create new ones
- Identify user documentation update requirements

There are also differences between kinds of maintenance developments: preventive, corrective and so on. This always demands very detailed perusal of major parts of the systems' documentation and source code to interweave newly designed parts into existing structures and to establish testing needs.

Implementing and Testing a Maintenance Change

The source code of the existing system is the major driving force, and major limiting factor. For **maintenance**, this stage always demands very extensive perusal of the existing system. If reliable documentation exists, it must be used together with the source code, but their *parallel update* is very difficult to achieve. Particularly in corrective maintenance, we need to heed the ***error clustering***. This means that we need to learn both to **recognize** clusters and to **measure** their effects. Remember, errors cluster in all parts of the system, not just in the code, but in the code the phenomenon is most common. This means that for every section of code, the more errors we find, the more that there still are. This complicates our task of finding and correcting the errors, enormously!

Regression testing is the process of establishing, beyond reasonable doubt, that existing system functionality has not been damaged by the new, modified functionality. A set of tests, which have previously proven to be effective in establishing system performance metrics (measuring performance) is used to show that everything still works correctly. This stage always demands very detailed knowledge of the system and its construction and includes both documentation and source code. This is necessary in order to determine exactly which set of tests need to be used and in what manner. It is very rare that we have the budget luxury of being able to run tests that are not really needed, just to *play safe*.

Systems Testing

Notice the plural? Testing the system**s**. This stage needs to determine that the new system (the old system plus the new functionality) works to expectations. That is almost never sufficient. It must also work with the other systems that interface with it. This demands knowledge of the entire system and all other systems which interact with it. As always, this includes both documentation (technical and user) and source code. **Deployed systems are depended upon!**

What is needed is an analysis and documentation tool. The system must be equally usable by all "types" of software engineers. That is to say, whether you are active in an "information systems" environment (and therefore likely to be using Cobol or a similar/derived language) or in an "engineering" environment (and therefore likely to be using C or C++, or a similar/derived language). A "legacy systems workbench" must examine software source code, extract data and analyze it for information content. The information created from this data analysis should be both low level and high level. Additionally the system must:

- Process existing applications with extremely fast turn-around time
- Not be dependent on other tools (for example CASE) but rather open to communication
- Be very user friendly and straightforward to use
- Operate on many languages, and any language it operates on must be processed in such a way that it is not dialect dependent

The scanning and analysis facilities recover design details (everything except computational algorithms). In many cases, understanding may depend on detailed knowledge of history and raison d'etre of the application. A facility is provided for adding this into the *created* documentation. The system uses Hypertext as its documentation database. This makes software quality assurance tasks much simpler and more accurate. Metrics are implemented at two levels: per-program metrics and system-wide metrics. Per-program metrics include objects counts in the program and value analyses. System metrics include comparisons of program sizes, program readability and maintainability, and more. The emphasis of system metrics is to aid management to decide on maintenance schedules and preventive maintenance of the software.

The key to maintenance productivity lies in understanding entire systems. Preventive maintenance should be an obvious concept. In software this is difficult to implement, if for no other reason than the constant work overload. A tool like this will fundamentally change this so that time can be allotted for problem prevention and continuous process improvement. Other tools do not encompass *all aspects* of a system: process, data, external and internal interfaces and the user interface.

Notes

1 *Newsweek International*, 1 July 1996.
2 By the way, 2000 is not the millennium, 2001 is.
3 I do not intend to be outside of my home from the end of December 1999 through January of 2000, nor do most of those whose profession is IT. If you do, good luck.
4 Lewis, Ted; The next $10,000_2$ years: Part 1 and Part 2; *IEEE Computer,* April 1996.
5 Information technology does not mean accounting, it is equally applicable to telephony or Inter-netting or controlled flight, as well. In fact, the term has come to mean almost anything in which a computer is intimately involved.
6 *CACM*, November 1993.

SOFTWARE QUALITY ASSURANCE PLANNING – AN OVERVIEW

THIS SECTION DESCRIBES THE PURPOSE, OUTLINE AND content of a software quality program, and the methods to be used to prepare software quality assurance plans (SQAP). The plan itself is based on the widely accepted standard: ANSI/IEEE Standard 730.1-1989; IEEE Standard for Software Quality Assurance Plans.

The methodologies are applicable to both data processing and real-time software and may be applied both to critical and noncritical systems. For those who are interested in gaining certification, they are compatible with all demands of ISO 9000-3 and ISO 9001.[1] When an organization or corporation engages in development, acquisition and/or maintenance of software, whether for profit (sale or resale) or as an internal service to the company, management must have a view of quality, and what it **needs to mean to them** in relation to the proposed software. That is what this is all about!

History of the Standard

The standard for software quality assurance plans was developed by the IEEE (Institute of Electrical and Electronic Engineers) Software Engineering Standards Subcommittee[2] (IEEE SESS). Initially it was designated as IEEE Std-730-1981 and was derived as a result of the usual process for standards formulation. A working group was formed with international representation. This working group composed the text of the standard while providing timely opportunities for members of the group and interested parties to make comments. The text was finalized from the sum-total of all comments. Finally, the text was voted on by a broadly based international balloting group. The standard's date of first approval by the IEEE SESS, and subsequently by the IEEE Standards Board was September, 1981. After approval of the standards board, the document was submitted to the American National Standards Institute (ANSI) for acceptance, this approval was finalized in June, 1982. The approval of the standard was contingent on it being corrected for use with critical software relating to nuclear reactors. This project was begun with the ANSI approval. The subsequently updated, document was given IEEE Standards Board approval in June, 1984.

> This version of the document (730-1990) is a total of 12 pages, approximately six pages of actual text, the remainder is "overhead."

Contents and Structure of the Standard

To be kept in the correct perspective, the quality assurance/quality planning concept must be understood in lieu of the accepted definition of quality assurance (QA). By "accepted" we mean the definition employed by the most commonly used industry standards. Those standards are "ANSI/IEEE STD 730" and "ANSI/IEEE STD 729"; the American National Standard Institute/Institute of Electrical and Electronic Engineers Standards for Software Quality Assurance Plans and for Software Engineering Terminology. From those sources, one can see that the definition is actually composed of two parts. The definition of quality is:

> The totality of features and characteristics of a product or service that bear on its ability to satisfy given needs. (ANSI/ASQC A3-1978)

And the definition of what quality assurance means:

> A planned and systematic pattern of all actions necessary to provide adequate confidence that material, data, supplies, and services conform to established technical requirements and achieve satisfactory performance.

The software quality assurance plan provides the necessary framework to plan the "... systematic actions necessary to provide adequate confidence that the item or product conforms to established technical requirements..." This sounds rather trivial. However, experience has shown that this is quite a complicated and delicate, not to mention diplomatic, task. The number of activities and tasks which need to be addressed is quite large. As a general term, we call it software auditing.

The software audit process improves the availability and reliability of software and the products supported by software. The process is designed to relate to the quality control function in manufacturing of "regular" products. This concept of quality auditing, like any quality audit, must be based on use of standards. Standards provide the "baseline" against which things can be measured. The minimal set of standards for the software development and maintenance process must consist of:

- Planning and procedures.
- Analysis of productivity and quality data.
- Reviews, audits and inspections.
- Configuration management.
- Software testing.
- Specifications and documentation (of all kinds and levels).

No quality assurance program for software can call itself properly constructed unless all of these elements have been taken into account. In very small or very unsophisticated organizations, you may think that it is possible to get by with less. Unfortunately, the piper will always collect his pay. The nasty part is that when you delay **this** payment, there is a very high penalty fine.

Getting back to the standard, as is the case with most documents of this kind, the standard can be generally divided into two major parts. The first part, which is quite short, is general information for the user of the standard. This consists of the scope and purpose (of 730), the definitions and the acronyms used by the standard. Afterwards, (section three of the document) is the standard for the plan itself. This standard is supported by an additional document, the "ANSI/IEEE-Std 983-1986 Guide for Software Quality Assurance Planning."[3] This "commentary" on the standard can be quite useful. Since this book is not meant to replace the standard, the explanations provided by the standard are not repeated. However, where experience has shown that additional information is needed, annotations are provided. Remember, the IEEE Std 730 is designed for critical software! Of course, not all software is critical in the sense of the standard and even if it is, the definition of criticality can be quite fluid. Our annotations are designed to enable the user to apply the 730 concepts to real-life projects, many of which may be quite small.

For example, most organizations have projects of various size. Nearly all have quantities of small projects (under three staff-years) with a great deal in common. These shall be called "mini-projects." Despite their relatively small size, they still cause quite a few of the problems that need to be addressed. The technique is to try to write one software quality assurance plan (SQAP) which will be usable for all the mini-projects (or as many of them as possible), then apply it to them. Merely applying a standardization activity across a set of mini-projects will increase quality by a quantum leap, at a very small cost! Of course, a basic assumption is that mini-project SQAPs are also based on the IEEE 730 Standard. This is very easy to do once the basics are understood.

Possible Problems with Use of 730

IEEE 730 is a very good standard. However, the user should be aware of its limitations. The following list of items attempts to relate what quality assurance planning needs are not covered by the standard but must be addressed by the quality assurance plan.

Metrics

More needs to be said about integration of the SQAP with metrics. The state of the practice has advanced enough so that a standard can legitimately demand intelligent use of measuring devices. Simple metrics (essentially metrics for measuring program code) just do not suffice anymore. We must not forget that code – particularly for critical (read **big**) projects is only 10% of the whole development and only 20% of the problems we fix in maintenance! Life-cycle metrics are really needed! Good life-cycle metrics need to provide the practitioner with a clear path towards the kinds of information to be gathered and stored on a quality/productivity database. Metrics are referenced in section 13 of 730 (which, unfortunately, is rather weak).

Management

Not enough is said by the standard about the role of management with respect to quality assurance. This is most unfortunate. Not only will QA not exist (in any real sense) without requisite management involvement and support, but management will itself be a major loser since QA is a primary tool for effective management.

QA role

Nothing is stated about the role of QA in the product/project, nor does the standard provide guidelines for resource allocation to the quality organization. There is a bland statement that it is meant for critical software but can be used by other people. The standard needs to provide guidelines for this.

Establishing Quality Goals

The Purpose of Quality Goals

This section discusses establishment of quality goals for a software project or system. That probably makes this chapter one of the most important chapters of the book. What a seemingly silly thing to say! Why should the establishment of quality goals be of such overriding importance? We have already hinted earlier that the set of quality goals is the basis for the entire activity for achieving quality

Meaningful quality goals are difficult to achieve agreement on, and then to establish, particularly in our area. The reason for this is that many of the people who have to be involved really have no understanding of the interplay required. Even fewer understand the interface complexity that this task entails. This section provides a series of tables to help plan and balance these interactions and assist discussing the various goals with management and developers. One of the jobs of software quality assurance in the organization is to *translate* this technical display of information into media that **your** people will understand, and appreciate.

To repeat, the quality goals that are established are the baseline for a large number of activities. These include: guidance and control of system development, delivery and conversion of the system, assessment of whether the system meets the quality requirements as specified and finally, control of long-term maintenance of the system. Intermediate quality goals and metrics are used as the mechanism for management control to achieve these targets. What we mean by "intermediate" is that goals change, evolve and migrate throughout the life-cycle of a system. In identifying applicable quality goals, many different (and occasionally, conflicting) criteria and concerns may be relevant. There are always acquisition concerns which must be identified, such as cost, warranties and schedules. Laws, regulations, organizational structure and objectives and system characteristics also affect relevance of specific quality goals. Clearly, some quality goals are mutually exclusive, while others are mutually supportive. The proper "mix" must be chosen with care to ensure a reasonable set of attainable goals. Not only that, but there may frequently be a need to balance the weights applied to the different goals and attributes. Just to get a very basic feel for this, look at Figure 4.1 overleaf and you will see where the money is spent today.

To attain the system goals, intermediate goals must be considered within the software system life-cycle (including development and maintenance). These goals contain early indicators of final system characteristics. A useful example to illustrate this point is to consider design errors discovered by auditing techniques during development. These provide an effective prediction basis for final system error rates

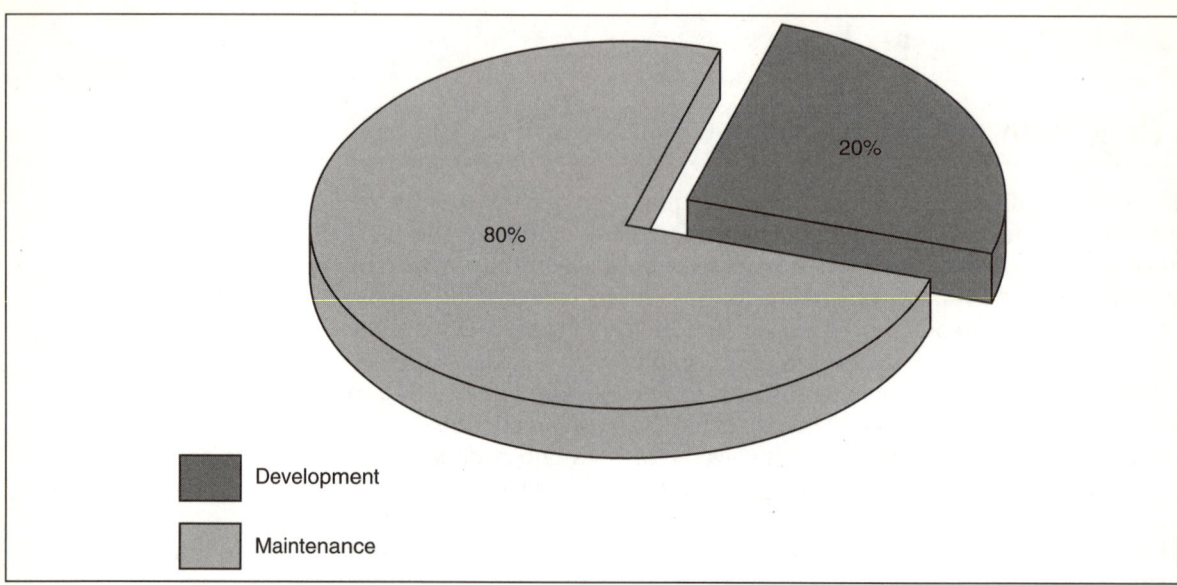

Figure 4.1 Life-cycle costs.

and failure modes. This can also provide a tool for a preview (almost a prediction) of FMEA (failure mode and effects analysis).

Establishment of software quality goals is not a "one-time" activity, performed at a specific time during the system life-cycle. It is an on-going activity, regularly performed throughout the *life of the product*. While the initial software quality assurance plan must contain the quality goals being strived for, these goals *must* be updated as the system matures. Once initially established, the quality goals are used to guide and control the **acquisition** (from within the organization or from a contractor) and the **verification** and operation of the system. They will also be used during the on-going **maintenance** to ensure the system remains "on track."

The Quality Goal Methodology

Remember, the quality goals established during planning will become the quality attributes later on. The first step of the methodology for quality goals planning is to identify all the possible (applicable) quality goals for the system. How is this done? Begin by referring to worksheets # 4.1 and # 4.2 to understand what the quality attributes of the system can be. Note that the first worksheet concerns **suitability** of the product to user intentions, and the second concerns the ability to retain this suitability at later times – **maintainability**. This step is very important. The user should be encouraged to make changes to the worksheet as experience (corporate and personal) warrant. However, the present versions of these tables have been developed over a great deal of time and contain an enormous amount of embedded experience. That means that these changes must be made with caution and only with the agreement of a large majority of the user community! [Remember what we said above about using this information to communicate to management and users, the conflicts and trade-offs that need to be taken into account.]

Inconsistencies should not be excluded at this point. Exclusion of a goal because of a perceived inconsistency, without a thorough understanding of the meaning of this inconsistency, is intuitive and may not be productive. A goal itself cannot be inconsistent. It is "in conflict" with one or more others. Which of them should be included and which excluded? Perhaps none need be excluded, but they must have various "weights" attached to them – de-emphasize or strengthen them. Goals which may affect organizational self-interest are among the more important quality goals. Once the initial list of quality goals has been established, the goals listed will then be rated by significance (weight) to the project/product. The quality planner must try to reach as general an agreement as is possible. Ideally, all parties concerned with the product will be in agreement.

Thus we have created a simple process of three steps:

- Compile the quality goals from each interested party. Ensuring that all viewpoints are considered and represented will increase satisfaction when the time comes for the system to be used. Clearly, some desires will be in conflict. For example, marketing may push for the product to be delivered before engineering is satisfied with performance. Cost or schedule constraints may conflict with optimal design considerations.
- A quality/reliability engineering analysis must be performed to ascertain the effects of the various quality attributes. This analysis must consider goals which reinforce one another as well as those which "compete" with one another. Obviously, there will be some users who are unhappy with the results of the analysis. Nonetheless, a consensus must be reached. This is not a question of desire. This is an absolute necessity for goal attainment, and even more so, for quality perception. The results must be supportable and must be "sold" to everyone involved. (By-the-bye, a great deal of software quality assurance is internal sales.)
- The end result of this process will be the creation of a **prioritized list** of the *desired* and agreed on **quality goals**.

When the quality goals for the software have been agreed on by all interested parties, one can proceed to identification of the software measures which will relate to those goals. A software measure is a software metric. The terms can be intermixed if that improves under-

**Software Quality Planning Worksheet # 4-1
Mapping of software systems quality characteristics –
Suitability attributes**

Project: _____   Planner: _____

Date: _____   SQAP: _____

#	Attribute	Components	Concept[4]	Require.	Design	Coding	Test	I & C	Operations
1	Useability	Operability	x	x	x	x			
		Training	x	x	x	x	x		
2	Efficiency	Conciseness			x	x	x		
		Execution			x	x	x		
		Operability		x	x	x	x	x	x
		Size			x	x			
3	Reliability	Completeness	x	x	x	x	x		
		Accuracy		x	x	x	x	x	x
		Consistency	x	x	x	x	x	x	
		Error tolerance			x	x	x	x	x
		Size			x	x	x	x	
		Fail-softness		x	x	x	x	x	x
4	Integrity	Auditability	x	x	x	x	x	x	x
		Security			x	x	x	x	
		Size			x	x	x	x	
		Penetrability[5]			x	x		x	
5	Appropriateness	Requirements	x	x					
		Auditability							
		Requirements	x	x	x				
		Understandability							
		Readability	x	x	x	x			
		Design auditability			x	x	x		
6	Correctness	Product auditability	x	x	x	x			
		Design			x	x	x		
		Understandability							
		Design auditability	x	x	x	x			

Software Quality Planning Worksheet # 4-2
Mapping of software systems quality characteristics – Maintainability attributes

Project: _____   Planner: _____

Date: _____   SQAP: _____

#	Attribute	Components	Concept	Require.	Design	Coding	Test	I & C	Operations
1	Portability and reusability	Generality	x	x	x	x	x		
		Modularity			x	x	x		
		H/W-S/W independence	x	x	x	x	x	x	x
		Self documentation			x	x		x	
		Fault rate		x	x	x	x		
		Fault density			x	x	x		
		Size		x	x	x	x	x	x
2	Testability	Auditability		x	x	x	x	x	
		Complexity[6]							
		High level design	x	x	x	x			
		Computational		x	x	x			
		Control			x	x			
		Interface		x	x	x	x		
		Coupling			x	x	x		
		Fault rate		x	x	x	x		
		Self documentation				x		x	
		Modularity			x	x	x	x	x
		Simplicity		x	x	x		x	
		Test coverage	x	x	x		x		
3	Modifiability	Modularity			x	x		x	
		Documentation				x	x	x	
		Readability	x	x	x	x	x	x	x
		Change rate		x	x	x	x	x	
4	Understandability	Readability	x	x	x	x	x	x	x
		Documentation	x	x	x	x	x	x	x
		Modularity			x	x		x	
		Size		x	x	x	x		x
		Change rate		x	x	x		x	
5	Interoperability	Change rate		x	x	x	x	x	
		Change count	x	x	x	x	x	x	
		Complexity		x	x	x			
		Modularity			x	x		x	
		Self-documentation			x	x			

standing. (In most of this book, the preferred term is software metric, as that is more commonly used.) These metrics need to measure, to include, the **development process**, the **product** and the **operations and maintenance** stages.

> **A quality axiom:**
>
> A nonmeasurable process is a nonmanageable process.

Quality Goals

Considerations for quality goals establishment

While establishing quality goals, the quality planning function must weigh several considerations. This section discusses the five most basic of these considerations.

System characteristics

The system characteristics must include at least the following:

- functionality
- performance
- constraints
- technological innovativeness (for the organization doing the developing) and
- technological and managerial risk (see Table 4.1)

Table 4.1   Sample system characteristics vs. goals comparison

System characteristic	Goal
1. National security	System integrity
2. Interactive	Responsiveness Useability Soft fail
3. Long system life	Portability Testability
4. Human lives depend on it	Reliability Testability
5. Corporate stability depends on it	(Write your own list here)

The quality goals for a system depend on system characteristics. Some goals and the characteristics which interact with them may be illustrated by the examples in the table.

Obviously, this list is neither exhaustive in characteristics nor in goals, there was no intention that it should be. Many more goals and many more system characteristics may be considered for every system, even the seemingly trivial. The table is provided to form a basis for each organization to create their own. One should use the lists of quality goals, referring to Table 4.1, to help identify those goals pertinent to each system characteristic. The table should then be recreated as a "personalized" table. Once the "personalized" characteristics/goals table has been agreed on, the management priorities can then be set.

Trade-offs

The next consideration will then be to consider the detailed trade-offs. Conflicts and/or support of various quality goals (see Worksheet # 4.3) and the cost/benefit trade-offs concerning their implementation. Worksheet # 4.4 has proven to be an effective aid to understanding quality attributes which support one another and those which conflict with one another. Clearly, the implementation of conflicting goals is an expensive, difficult and frustrating process. While using information from this table/worksheet, the priorities previously set will be the most helpful guide for reconciliation. Cost/benefit is also part of this equation, as this is another form of conflict.

This section of the guidebook consists of the eleven basic quality attributes and many of their detailed breakdowns (obviously, others are still possible). The first problem for understanding the effect an attribute may have on the system, must be to identify what the quality attributes of the system are going to be (are going to need to be). In addition, these needed attributes cannot be defined without a realistic viewpoint of what they mean to the developers – who always are in a state of fright that something or someone will slow them down. What they neglect of course, is that the activity that slows them down the most is error correction and the resultant error propagation. To elicit the real support of developers, an effective bi-directional conversation must exist. This means that the developers must be made to understand what each of the quality attributes of the system means to them.

Caveats

The relationships displayed above are quite general. Clearly there can be many instances when the particular relationship between any two quality attributes may be different from the one shown here. What this table supplies is the general case. An example is in order: efficiency will generally be supportive of reliability and conflict with our ability to port the software to a different platform. However, there will be cases when

Software Quality Planning Worksheet # 4-3
The interactions of the quality attributes
Conflicts and supports

Project: _____   Planner: _____

Date: _____   SQAP: _____

	1	2	3	4	5	6	7	8	9	10	11
1.	\										
2.	+ −	\									
3.	+	+	\								
4.	−	−	+	\							
5.	+	+	+		\						
6.	+	+	+			\					
7.	+	−	+	−	+	+	\				
8.		−	+	−	+	+	+	\			
9.		−	+	−	+	+	+	+	\		
10.		−		−	+	+	+	+	+	\	
11.	+	−	−	−	+	+	+	+	+		\

Note. The numbers in the heading and the left column are the quality attributes listed in Worksheet # 4.4. The positive attributes ("+") are mutually supportive, the negative attributes ("−") are in conflict.

this relationship can be reversed. The important point to bear in mind is that while this table is very informative and useful in the metric planning process, it is only a model. It is only your reality, after you adopt and adapt it. For each application environment the model must be carefully checked. The **specific** applicability of the table must be evaluated and ascertained. It should then be used. We strongly suggest that the accuracy check be performed by at least three professionals.

Quality perceptions

The third consideration is the quality perceptions of all staff and users involved with the system. This refers also to the consensus discussed above. One of the most important considerations, while building the software quality assurance plan and the quality goals which will direct it (building, administering and using it) is an agreed concept of the system's goals. Of course, the future quality of the proposed system is part of the system's goals. To understand this, all of the personnel

Software Quality Planning Worksheet # 4-4

Quality attribute interactions

Attributes

	Attributes	Suitability	Maintainability
1.	Useability	5	1
2.	Efficiency	5	3
3.	Reliability	5	3
4.	Integrity	5	2
5.	Appropriateness	5	1
6.	Correctness	5	4
7.	Portability/reusability	3	5
8.	Testability	4	5
9.	Modifiability	2	5
10.	Understandability	2	5
11.	Interoperability	2	4

Note. A scale of 1–5 has been chosen. One means that there is no real effect, five means a great effect.

involved with the system must be involved with directing the quality goal activity. These perceptions may be attained via a survey. Clearly, all surveyed personnel must be briefed to understand the various trade-offs discussed here. The result is an independent set of subjective opinions regarding levels of importance of the various quality goals.

Quality functions

The next consideration is to select which of the various quality functions (see Worksheet # 4.5) can be applied to the particular project, taking into account the needs of the project along with the capabilities and restrictions of: the personnel; the corporate/organization and the technology.

Training

The final consideration is that management, the quality assurance personnel and the developers have been trained in the various quality assurance techniques they will need to implement the quality plan (see Worksheets # 4.6 and # 4.7).

Software Quality Planning Worksheet # 4-5
Mapping quality functions to the system life-cycle

Project: _____   Planner: _____

Date: _____   SQAP: _____

#	Activity	Components	Concept	Require.	Design	Coding	Testing	I & C[7]	Operations
1	Auditing	Documents	x	x	x	x	x	x	x
		Code				x	x	x	x
		Tests		x	x	x	x	x	x
		Configuration management	x	x	x	x	x	x	x
		Change process		x	x	x	x	x	x
2	Methodology	Standards		x	x	x	x	x	
		Procedures	x	x	x	x	x	x	x
		Tools	x	x	x	x	x	x	x
		Techniques	x	x	x	x	x	x	x
		Training	x	x	x	x	x	x	x
3	Analyzing	Activity measurements		x	x	x	x	x	x
		Product measurements		x	x	x	x	x	x
		Error data		x	x	x	x	x	x
		Failure data				x	x	x	x
		Event data				x	x	x	x
		Historical data		x	x	x	x	x	x
4	Reporting	Status			x	x	x	x	x
		Deviations		x	x	x	x		
		Problems		x	x	x	x	x	
		Productivity		x	x	x	x	x	
		Test results		x	x	x	x	x	x

Software Quality Planning Worksheet # 4-6
Mapping of quality assurance techniques
Technical

Project: _____

Planner: _____

Date: _____

SQAP: _____

#	Technique	Components	Concept	Require.	Design	Coding	Testing	I & C	Operations
1	Testing	Path					x	x	x
		Logical			x	x	x	x	
		White box/ black box			x	x			
		Stress				x	x		
		Regression							x
2	Verification & Validation	Reviews	x	x	x	x	x	x	x
		Inspections		x	x	x	x		
		Testing		x	x	x	x		
		Change control board	x	x	x			x	
		Audit	x	x	x	x	x	x	x
3	Tooling	Development tools	x	x	x	x	x	x	x
		QA tools		x	x	x	x	x	x

Software Quality Planning Worksheet # 4-7
Mapping of quality assurance techniques
Managerial

Project: _____ Planner: _____

Date: _____ SQAP: _____

#	Activity	Components	Concept	Require.	Design	Coding	Testing	I & C	Operations
1	Auditing	Product review	x	x	x	x	x	x	x
		Config. management		x	x	x		x	
		Post Mortem reviews		x	x	x		x	
		Change audit	x	x	x		x		
2	Analyzing	Data acquisition		x	x	x	x	x	x
		Data logging		x	x	x	x	x	x
		Reporting		x	x	x	x	x	x
		Metrics use				x	x	x	x
3	QM Planning	Risk assessment	x	x	x				
		Risk management	x	x	x				
		Status review			x	x	x	x	
		Quality goal planning	x						
		Attribute assessment	x	x			x		

SQA Planning Software
Productivity and Documentation – A Case Study

XXX Software productivity

This part of the chapter is a case study which provides an example of exemplary planning as performed by one systems development organization. This is a simulacrum of an actual document presented to the client company.

Theoretical model

The XXX-240 software is approximately 300 K Bytes of compiled code. An industry accepted, normalized productivity model for embedded, multi-processor systems, when developed by a highly experienced team, familiar with the technology and application to be produced, is 0.5 staff-hours per byte [@ 152 staff-hours per month, 1820 hours per year]:

```
    300 * 1024 * 0.5 = 153600 staff-hours
153,600/152 = 1010 staff-months, theoretical
```

Actual model

Through intensive application of sophisticated techniques of project management and software quality assurance, and software engineering tools, attainable software development productivity has been increased by a factor of one third. The theoretically required 1010 staff-months could be reduced to 670 staff-months needed for the project as a whole.

Actual productivity

In the final result, this could also be improved, as a result of reuse of existing, field proven software. The resulting actual investment in software for the XXX-240 system, including differing country versions and conversion to the UNIVERSAL software, cost only approximately one-third of the improved productivity model. Actual software investment (to date) 240 staff-months.

Documentation types for XXX-240

The following table exhibits the types of documentation existing for the various parts of the XXX-240 system. The documentation language may be either English or Hebrew. The list is as previously reported to the client quality representatives.

CPU ⇒	OPS	CCPU	VCPU	ACPU	MCPU
Requirements specification	+	+	+		
Design specification			+	+	+
Changes specification				+	+
S/W test specification					+
System test specification	+	+	+	+	+
Open problems list	+	+	+	+	+
Software change follow-up					+
Software test examples	+	+	+	+	+
Language	Pascal	C/asm.	C/asm.	C/asm.	C/asm.
Size :: K Bytes	NA	15	15/30	60	150

Planned documentation types for XXX-240

The following table contains the projected documentation of the XXX-240 system. The target date for this documentation update is the end of second quarter. To accomplish this, very sophisticated documentation and analysis techniques and tools will have to be used.

CPU ⇒	OPS	CCPU	VCPU	ACPU	MCPU
Requirements specification	+	+	+	+	+
Design specification	+	+	+	+	+
Changes specification					
Software test specification	+	+	+	+	+
System test specification	+	+	+	+	+
Open problems list	+	+	+	+	+
Software change follow-up	+	+	+	+	+
Software test examples	+	+	+	+	+
Language	Pascal	C/asm.	C/asm.	C/asm.	C/asm.

Notes

1 Throughout this book, whenever I refer to ISO 9001, I am referring to the second edition, which is dated 1994-07-01. As this is a rather significant update, there may be differences if you are looking at the older version.

2 In July of 1990 the name of this organization was changed to the IEEE Software Engineering Technical Council (IEEE SETC). The text contains the former name in order to be historically correct.

3 This document is in the process of being redesignated as 730.2 and reissued. This process will complete when the balloting is finished and it is approved. At the present it is classified as "obsolete". In any case, the document is interesting as it stands, and will be much more so when it has been fully updated.

4 All of the following tables are based on the same list of life-cycle processes:
  (a) conceptualize the problem
  (b) requirements analysis and specification
  (c) software architectural (high-level) design and detailed design
  (d) implementation and coding
  (e) test – including (at least) unit, integration and system
  (f) installation and checkout (including porting of data and work culture)
  (g) operations and maintenance – operations and maintenance use up the greatest quantity of resources.

5 Penetrability is the opposite of integrity.

6 "Complexity," as a specialized quality attribute, is subdivided into component parts.

7 Installation and checkout.

SOFTWARE QUALITY ASSURANCE PLAN – PURPOSE AND SCOPE

This chapter defines the purposes and scope of the software quality assurance plan.

All system level software items covered by the plan are listed along with all portions of the software life-cycle to be covered.

THE SOFTWARE QUALITY ASSURANCE PLAN (SQAP) NEEDS TO be a formal document which describes the activities to be carried out by the software quality assurance team along with a detailed list of the subjects of the activities. The SQA team writing the plan begins in Chapter 1 of the plan to describe details of the software quality assurance plan and starts to provide a look at the process (or processes) used by quality assurance to guarantee that the desired level of quality of the software product (or software portion of the whole product) will be achieved. As in any technical document, and particularly those used to plan work performed by (sometimes very large) groups of people, the SQAP must state the specific purpose and scope of what is planned. This means that the names of all software products covered by the plan must be listed, and this list must be absolutely clear to the reader of the document from the very beginning. As a matter of common courtesy, and also to ensure readability of the document, all documents referenced in the text of the plan should be listed clearly.

A professional level SQAP describes managerial and technical procedures applied by the project developing agency in the development, deployment and on-going maintenance and modification of all software that is written or adapted for the system. The SQAP applies to both development and maintenance of software. While the IEEE 730 standard claims that it is intended for critical software, there may be many different definitions for what constitutes criticality. At one extreme, the software under consideration may be *critical* to the developing organization's fiscal health, while at the other, a failure of a system may cause loss of life, impact public safety or cause large financial or social losses. These are all examples of criticality and such occurrences are all too common today.

Note. Within the context of this book, any uses of the terms, "QA" or "Quality Assurance" refer to "SQA" and "Software Quality Assurance," respectively unless they are obviously independent (for example the QA department). In the case of this software effort being a part of a larger effort, the book does not reference to the general quality assurance of the project, as that is usually covered by a separate plan, to which the SQA plan should be a subordinate part.

Chapter 1 of the plan will be divided into paragraphs for purpose, scope and document organization. The second part (chapter 2) contains a listing of all of the documents that are directly referenced by the plan. This is usually entitled referenced documents but sometimes may be called applicable documents – the two names are equivalent.

Document Organization

We strongly recommend that the intended format of a software quality assurance plan be based on the American National Standard, developed by the Institute of Electrical and Electronic Engineers, called ANSI/IEEE Standard 730 "ANSI/IEEE Standard for Software Quality Assurance Plans". The version of the standard used for this book is the revised edition as approved by the American National Standards Institute on 10 October 1989. However, care has been taken to ensure the book's applicability to the International Standards Organization ISO 9000 standard series, the American military standards and the Software Engineering Institute's (SEI) Capability Maturity Model (CMM). For example, if the following questions can be answered "yes," then the basic requirements of ISO and CMM will be satisfied.

Does the SQAP apply to development and maintenance of critical software?

For example, can failure impact safety or cause large financial or social losses?

Must the SQAP state the specific purpose and scope of what is planned?

Must names of all software products covered by the plan be listed?

Are all documents referenced in the text of the plan listed clearly?

Software Quality Assurance Plan – Management

This chapter defines roles and responsibilities of every individual person and organization who react with the plan for assuring the quality of the software. In particular, this section describes how all quality assurance tasks are to be managed. The structure of chapter 3 of the software quality assurance plan is defined below.

CONTINUING THE SQAP, CHAPTER 3 DESCRIBES THE STRUCTURE of the organization with respect to quality. This includes the structure of the quality assurance function, of course. In addition, every organizational body that has a role to play in achieving and maintaining quality must be defined and their roles reviewed. Senior management, and even the board of directors, should have quality responsibilities, though this level need not necessarily be a part of the project plan. For those interested in certification, this is the section which is most critical for ISO 9000 compliance. In this particular case, reference to senior management responsibilities will probably be needed for ISO 9000 compatibility.

At very least, the plan should point the reader to the highest level in the organization that has direct responsibility for the quality of the specific development, and should also indicate, if only by reference to another document, the ultimate quality responsibility. This must be a member of senior management. ISO 9000 demands this, and they are absolutely correct. If your plan is for a bespoke system, a purchaser's representative should be appointed, as soon as possible, as liaison with the developer. This role must include all technical and contractual requirements. For very large developments, this function may be a team of people, one or more persons per area of activity.

To avoid any misunderstandings, the senior person ultimately responsible for quality is board-level responsible for any and all deficiencies and problems with the quality system. That does not mean that the salary or bonuses will be determined by a counting of the numbers of bugs discovered in the delivered product (though this might be a good idea as a long-term goal). He or she is responsible for deficiencies in the **quality system**, not for the quality of the system, i.e. the delivered product. It is the quality system which must take responsibility for the level of workmanship attained. Clearly, if there is a major failure, then this person is the one responsible for post-mortem activities to ascertain reasons for failures and to establish means to ensure that the error cannot be repeated. The quality system should be the example to the rest of the company for what good practice means. If this is not the case, then this person is found deficient, indeed.

Remember please, that the objectives of this book are not only to show you what needs to be written into your plan, but also how to get there. Usually, the order in which things are presented will be helpful to you, if you pay attention to the way things are written here.

Organization

Earlier we described the organization responsible for fulfillment of and for ensuring compliance with the software quality program requirements, including the authority and responsibilities of each organization and its relationships to other organizational entities (e.g. the organization(s) responsible for performing configuration management). A chart should be used (see Figure 6.1) to illustrate the structure of the organization(s) performing software quality activities and their position within the project management system.

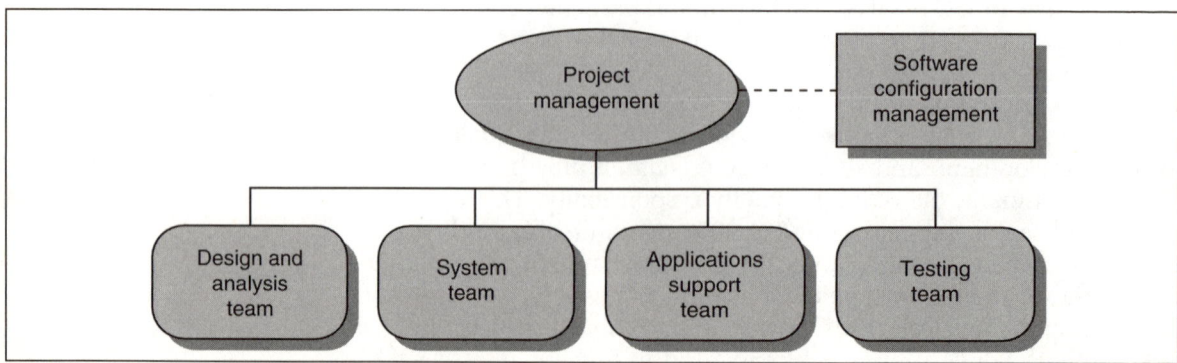

Figure 6.1 A sample organization structure chart as relates to . . . SQA.

Software Quality Planning Worksheet # 6-1
Documents and tasks, prior to coding

Project: _____   Planner: _____

Date: _____   SQAP: _____

Item #	Development product	Document delivery date	Quantity expected	QA activity (A, R, W, I)	Performed on (%)	Performed by
1	SSS		1	W	100	T, D
2	SSDD		1	W	100	T, D
3	SRS		5	A	80	Q
				A	100	M
4	Test plan		1	R	100	M, T, C, Q
				A	60	Q
5	Test design		5	R	100	T, C, Q
				A	60	Q
6	TLD/DD		5	W	100	D, T
				W	100	D, T
7	IRS		1	A	100	Q
				R	100	D, Q
				W	100	D, T
8	IDD		1	A	100	Q
				R	100	D, Q, T
9	SQAP		1	A	100	M
10	Source code		5	A	20	Q
				W	100	D
11	SPS		5			D, M, C
12	Test results		18			Q
13	User's manual		1			D, M, Q

Software Quality Planning Worksheet # 6-2

Key abbreviations for Worksheet 6-1[1]

Software product	Full name
SSS	System subsystem specification
SSDD	System/subsystem design document
SRS	Software requirements specification
TLD/DD	Top level design/detailed design
IRS	Interface requirements specification
IDD	Interface design description
SPS	Software product specification
Letter	**Meaning**
A	Audit
R	Peer review
W	Walkthrough
I	Inspection
D	Developers
T	Testers
C	Configuration management
M	Management
Q	Quality assurance
–	Entire work group

Quality Tasks

This paragraph of your plan defines the roles of each individual (do not be embarrassed to name names here, this emphasizes real responsibility). Merely naming the role is insufficient. The specific tasks assigned to each role for assuring the quality of the software products or items to be produced (as covered by this SQAP) are just as important. There must be a *whole* description here.

Once the resources needed to implement a software quality program have been ascertained, the next step is to establish a schedule for implementation and resource usage. **The quality schedule *must* be established in consonance with the development schedule.** Indeed, it is probably a good idea to have development management audit and sign-off on the SQA schedule, for increased feedback between the two groups.

For each activity and task, indicate activity initiation, dependencies on other events (such as availability of draft documents) and expected activity completion times. Include key development milestones such as formal reviews, audits, and key meetings. In a similar manner, a schedule should be established for the acquisition of QA support tools.

All of these schedules should be laid out in a manner that is both readable and auditable. Remember that *you cannot be an effective auditor if you are not effectively audited*. All tasks associated with portions of the software life-cycle covered by the plan need to be described. These task descriptions should provide special emphasis on SQA activities. Finally, the task sequence should be clearly, and carefully, defined.

Responsibilities

This section of the plan must define all those individuals for whom the final quality of the product, or any intermediate deliverables, falls within their areas of responsibility. Also, there may be persons (or job titles) whose responsibilities may directly affect product quality, such as configuration management. These must be listed here, as well. The interrelationships between them are shown in Worksheet 6.1 on page 69.

- Is the organization responsible for software quality assurance required to prepare a software quality assurance plan?
- Must the plan be authenticated by the chief operating officer of organization units with responsibilities defined by the plan?
- Must the organizational structure influencing quality of the software be depicted?
- Must every major organizational element that influences software quality, together with delegated responsibilities, be described?
- Have organizational dependencies and independence of elements responsible to SQA been differentiated from those responsible for software development?
- Have these dependencies (independence) been clearly described or depicted?
- Must tasks associated with portions of the software life-cycle covered by the plan, be described?
- Must task descriptions provide special emphasis on SQA activities?
- Must task sequence be clearly defined?
- Must specific organizational elements responsible for each task be identified?

A Minimal QA Effort

What must be done, when only very little is possible? For instance, when the organization is just beginning to implement quality assurance and there is a learning curve to climb. The quality team must be wise enough to do all that it can with the (normally) minimal resources which have been allotted to it, but at the same time, to achieve as large an effect as possible in order to sell management on the value of the function. (In many companies, the SQA function is the prototypical fig-leaf function used for display to clients. When this is discovered, one needs to be aware that this is not sophisticated management. That means, do not do business with them unless you must, and then only very carefully.)

1. Concentrate efforts for greatest effect

- Historically, most major system failures have been caused by interface problems – hardware/hardware, hardware/software or software/software. Always pay attention to interfaces.
- Early error control (for example tight requirements specifications) is a very effective medical treatment for this problem.
- Search for the critical and risky functions which may cause the most unexpected kinds of problems.

2. Do not become involved in developing new tools or methods

- Your resources are limited and the best thing you can think of is that you need a new methodology? Forget it! Whatever you think you need, you should try to buy, and the cheaper the better. Do not be embarrassed to tell your management that you are buying cheap as part of the learning curve, even though some things may need to be "re-purchased" later on when real needs can be determined.
- The only exception is when a tailored tool is completely and absolutely unavoidable.

3. Encourage developers' cooperation

The SQA group should be actively involved in implementation strategy – in hardware development, QA involvement is a basic expectation of management, users and developers. In software, this must be the same. How is this done?

- Retain emphasis on documents and documentation. The team should expect the amount of documentation to match the size and complexity of the project.
- Provide for a formal hand-over policy for all systems, from development to operations, and audit that the hand-over is carried through according to the declared policy.
- Consider arrangements for exchanging and sharing of information, documentation, expertise and policies, both between projects and even between companies. Make a point of visiting other companies to learn what they are doing. See if you can get to some arrangement that will allow two small efforts (from different companies) to be combined into a larger one, without adding significant resources.

- Make certain that consistent sets of standards and policies have been established across all similar efforts. By "*similar*" we mean devote your efforts to finding the similarities, not the differences.
- Be alert to future growth potential. The history of systems has shown us that many very large projects apparently began as small ones. We can call this creeping growth! This has proven to be one of the prime factors for resource waste in corporations.

Factors Affecting the SQA Effort

There are five factors which must always be accounted for, and which always affect the "amount" of quality assurance which is planned while constructing the SQAP. The term "amount" is meant to infer the portion of the system budget which will be devoted to the quality assurance activities. This portion is measured in terms of a percentage of the system effort as a whole. For instance, if the system effort is expected to be 100 staff-years and the portion for quality assurance has been defined to be 8%, the QA function is being allowed eight staff-years of budget for their activities in the framework of this project.

1. Size of the system

For a large complex system, a **proportionally greater** effort will be needed to achieve success of the quality functions. To what does the term system "size" actually refer? The amount of effort needed to produce the system. Effort means in total from the earliest, most preliminary documents through the "final" system. Table 6.1 gives a viewpoint of the relative kinds of efforts which may be relevant. Effort numbers refer to the number of staff-years. SQA numbers refer, in general, to the **rules of proportionment** for the SQA portion of a software system development, and are expressed in terms of the percentage of the system effort.

2. "Criticality" of the system

How critical is the system? How critical is system performance? How critical is system reliability? Will users merely be inconvenienced by a bug, or could there be irreversible consequences such as loss of life, likely to result from system failure? Can we predict the consequences? For example, many banks have reported (or have had discovered despite them trying to hide it) that financial losses can be very heavy as the result of a system being depended on, but not having been as reliable – or as auditable – as most people thought it was.

See Table 18.1 in the chapter on risk management for a breakdown of the questions of criticality and the dangers that they entail.

3. The cost of correcting errors

When the cost of error correction is especially high, doing things right initially is worth an added effort. An example would be an automotive program in ROM. This requires rigorous quality assurance as mistakes in ROM can be corrected only by replacing the ROM. Replacing 100,000 ROMs distributed throughout the world, is not a cheap process. A company can lose a lot of money by making a habit of this kind of thing. It has happened.

4. Type of release

Is this a new system? Is this an update of an "old" system? If it is an older system, can the previous SQA results still be depended on? (Are there any?)

5. Relationship with the user

Will the implemented software be maintained by the developing organization, or is it a one-time, special project? How nasty is the supplier/customer relationship likely to become when a system is delivered and bugs start crawling out? Some companies use their customers to debug their systems as policy. This is never polite, but it can be acceptable – if the clients agree to this ahead of time. There are situations when there is almost no choice in the matter, such as when the developer cannot have enough information to test the system properly. But always make certain that the customer is aware that he is going to be mistreated, and get his agreement.

Table 6.1 Project efforts represented in staff-years

Total effort[2]	Size	Percentage of QA effort, per system type	
		Data processing	Embedded
Less then 3	Not relevant	1–3	3–5
Up to 15–25	A small system	3–5	3–8
Up to 50–60	A medium-sized system	4–8	5–10
Up to 150–200	A large system	5–10	8–12
Up to 500–600	A very large system	7–12	10–12
More then 1000	Undefined	10–15	10–18

Why these numbers are important:

Why is it so very significant to develop a visceral understanding for the different sizes in systems, and what they mean? In the seminal book by Barry Boehm, *Software Engineering Economics*, some very interesting results were reported.[3] (In any case, this is a book well worth studying. It is certainly one of the "classics" in the field.) Look at Table 6.2. We now know that as society becomes more dependent on the functionality of software systems, and as the machines increase in capacity, software development projects are growing in size, cost and complexity. The really interesting point, is that none of the relationships are linear! By the bye, the capacity of computing power has grown by a factor of two every 18 months, for approximately 100 years. Nobody knows how to predict where that may be taking us, but we do know that the complexity of software systems is not a trivial question to be addressed by trivial means. Particularly by those that are most dependent.

Table 6.2   Software development projects are growing in size, cost and complexity

	Lines of code	Personnel	Schedule	Effort (staff-months)	Project staff
Small	2 K	1.4	4.8	6.5	$27 K
Intermediate	8 K	3.7	8.3	31	$129 K
Medium	32 K	10	14	146	$680 K
Large	128 K	29	24	687	$2.9 M
Very large	512 K	77	42	3250	$13.5 M

Now let's look at where errors occur, or perhaps one should say, how errors occur. Here also, we do not see what most people tend to expect. Most people expect that writing code is the most error prone activity. This simply is not the case. The most error prone activity is trying to understand what exactly is being requested. (So much for the tens of millions of dollars spent on Ada.[4] A bad solution to the wrong problem.) Nearly half of all errors occur in either analysis or in interpretations of the functional specifications. Coding errors are only about 10% of the problems that we need to solve. Look at the graph shown in Figure 6.2.

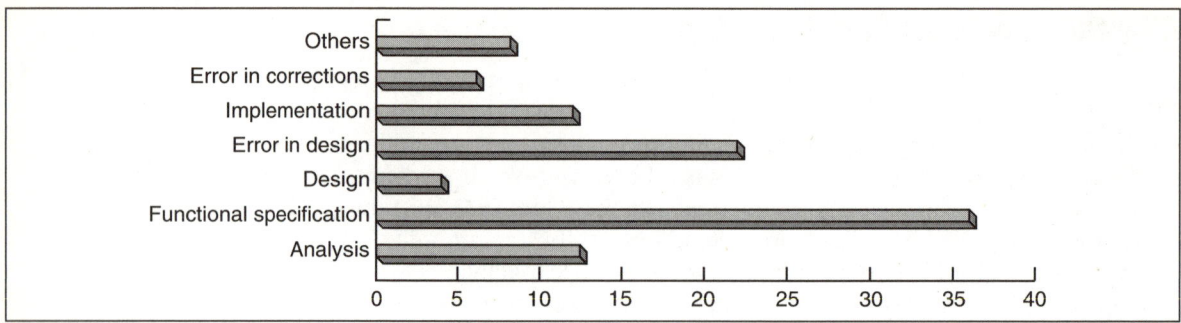

Figure 6.2 Sources of software development errors.

Now, when we couple this with one additional fact, we can complete the picture. Some **75%** of all software projects undertaken are never completed. Now is it clear why it is so important to understand what quality means for software? Now do you understand why the subject is so difficult?

The Critical Personnel Question

Software quality assurance is not a job for just anyone. Neither training for the job nor development experience are sufficient, though both are prerequisites. The successful practitioner must have the right attitude. Look for the person who is always trying to say, "let's find out," and not, "nobody knows." Being an auditor, when a mistake is made, he or she says, "I was wrong;" and not, "it wasn't my fault." The attitude calls for stepping through problems, not around them. The auditor makes commitments not promises; saying, "I am professional, and as such, I must constantly improve!" Perhaps one of the most important attitudes must be that, "there is always a better way to do it, if I can only be good enough to find it!" The excuse, "that is the way it's always been done" is, at best, feeble. It is always unprofessional.

Quality assurance is never a trivial job. To pass quality assurance off to someone because you cannot think of anything better for them to do is always a mistake. Only the very best of people are going to handle the job well. Doing it badly can be far worse than not doing it at all. If no one is readily available, a good practice is to use quality assurance as a stepping-stone for prospective managers.

Seven keys to leadership[5]

Why do some managers simply oversee and others inspire? What makes a manager an exceptional leader? Quality assurance is a management function. It is a management function which needs to understand the use of technologies and techniques for getting its job done. But, in any case, it is a proper stepping-stone to management. Take the following seven guidelines for effective leadership and use them to help you up the next step. Afterwards, look at the next section and at Table 3.3 and you'll see what the direction of **your** growth is.

1. Trust your subordinates

Do not expect them to go all out for you if they are not convinced that you believe in them.

2. Develop a vision

Some executive's suspicions to the contrary, planning for the long term pays off. And people want to follow someone who knows where he or she is going.

3. Keep your cool

The best leaders show their mettle under fire.

4. Encourage risk

Nothing demoralizes the troops like knowing that the slightest failure could jeopardize their entire career.

5. Be an expert

From board room to mail room, everyone had better understand that you know what you're talking about.

6. Invite dissent

Your people aren't giving you their best or learning how to lead if they are afraid to speak up.

7. Simplify

You need to see the big picture in order to set a course, communicate it, and maintain it. Keep the details at bay.

Fundamental Requirements

In 1985, software costs for the US Department of Defense were roughly $11 billion. In the USA as a whole, the total outlay for software was about $70 billion – in the world, the costs for software reached about $140 billion. The present rate of growth in the worldwide software market is about 12%. (As reported by Barry W Boehm, TRW, September,

Table 6.3 Ten fundamental requirements

- Acceptance of the quality process
- Management commitment to the improvement process, as corporate culture
- Belief that there is always room to improve what is being done
- Belief that preventing problems is smarter than reacting to them
- Management focus, leadership and participation
- A performance standard of zero defects
- Participation by all employees, as individuals and as groups
- Focus improvement on processes, not people
- Belief that suppliers work with you when your needs are understood
- Recognition and reward for successes

1987, *IEEE Computer*.) There are certain fundamental requirements for any quality improvement process to be successful. These requirements can be stated quite simply as a list of the ten simple points in Table 6.3.

Think about it. This is what the corporate concept must be based on. This is where the corporate battle-ground is!

The quality professional – and hence, the candidate to be a quality professional – must be prepared to apply simple guidelines. Guidelines which are critical activities for implementation and management of quality for any company, large or small. Notice that both of these lists, though showing the idea from differing viewpoints, really state the same thing. This is, of course, completely intentional.

Table 6.4 shows a synopsis of what the viewpoints need to be. This is not new, but for some reason the corporate community has yet to see them as relevant for software. More is the pity. This oversight has been ridiculously expensive! It is now your job to help them get the message.

Table 6.4 Corporate viewpoints

- Obtain commitment by senior management
- Establish an "improvement council" with director-level participation
- Obtain total management participation
- Secure team participation
- Obtain individual involvement
- Establish system/product/process improvement teams
- Develop and direct supplier involvement activities
- Establish the systems quality assurance activity
- Develop long-range quality strategy and short-range quality plans
- Establish a recognition and reward system

Ways to Kill Quality Assurance

We know of five very effective methods to ensure the failure of software quality assurance. They all concern either doing the wrong job (a very common problem with quality practitioners) or misunderstanding what the right job actually is.

1. The most common of them is trying for too many technical "niceties"

This is usually seen as trying too hard to equate software quality assurance with software engineering. If this is perceived to be happening, the wrong person is doing the job. Replace the staff quickly! Or at least the team leader. That person is frustrated.

2. Another common problem: too much time spent stopping, rather then preventing, defects

This happens when the quality assurance is performed by the developers, rather than for them. Very bad. It is going to cost a great deal before anything real happens. Companies have gone bust from that.

3. What happens when effort is wasted?

When too much effort is wasted on details rather than major problems, that is when we begin to see the developers getting tired of the quality assurance people. This will cause them to stop cooperating. One of the short-term goals of any SQA professional is to get to a point when the developers respect him/her enough to ask for an opinion. They will not do that if you are perceived as more of a dredge than an anchor. Direct the efforts wisely, or get out of the business!

4. Sometimes, management has a problem with the mathematical kid

The perennial academician. What can we do with him? He is very bright but he just does not seem to get by. Placing him in quality assurance will usually lead to too much effort on formal specifications rather then real needs. This is not just useless, boring and always counter-productive. Software quality assurance **must always be practical**!

5. The British are "always complaining about the government, but no one does anything"

Quality is frequently like that. We find complaining comfortable. Sometimes, so much so, that more time is spent complaining about poor quality than motivating developers to perform better. Managers must manage, or there is no hope for any project, not even those "small" ones. The last thing that can be said of software quality assurance, is that it is a magic panacea. That just does not work.

Summary

In summation of this, let us examine two observations resulting from a great deal of software quality assurance experience.

Observation no. 1 concerns "technical writing." Will the author of the document in question be able to understand his own document next month, or a year from now? Few system engineers have had training in prose writing. Yet, that is just what is expected of system engineers engaged in design of advanced products. (In many projects, particularly large ones, 40–50% of development time may be spent in producing documents. In a very large project that one of the authors was involved in, 30% of the engineers' time was wasted because a very bad word processor was chosen.) A professional technical writer is an inexpensive way to vastly improve quality. Use of a few basic rules can improve anyone's writing cheaply. If you can not express it, can you truly be said to understand it?

Observation no. 2 concerns "methodology development." A methodology, devoid of its proper basis, is devoid of effectiveness. We all love to "invent" new methodologies, to discover the best way to show everyone else how to do what they are doing better! It is probably the quickest way for us all to feel brilliant, and it is fun! It is also very expensive. What is certainly at least as important, very few of us have really had the training to do it well. Many methodologies have their basis in mathematics. Can we really be said to understand (to be absolutely certain) the meaning of the "slight" changes to the system? Misguided tools lead to misguided conclusions, always!

Notes

1   Refer to the Glossary for more detailed explanations.
2   As measured in staff years of effort for the entire system development.
3   Using $50,000 per staff year, average.
4   Ada is a trademark of the US Government, Department of Defense.
5   Source: Kenneth Labich, *Fortune Magazine*.

DOCUMENTATION

This chapter identifies all relevant documentation which concerns development, verification, validation, use and maintenance of the software. It states how documents will be checked for accuracy and describes criteria for document distribution.

THIS CHAPTER LOOKS AT CHAPTER 4 OF THE SQAP (ACCORDING to the standard) which describes the documentation to be created by this project. It is axiomatic that every system must have documentation of every step throughout development that leads to its creation. What we need is to understand the minimum set of documentation for any project. Clearly, this minimum changes depending on the kind of system and its criticality. Other factors may also legitimately affect this list. For instance, a specific customer demand (to either add or subtract from the list).

This chapter is matched with paragraph 4.5 in ISO 9001 and paragraphs 6.1 and 6.2 in ISO 9000-3. This is one of the very truly great weaknesses of ISO 9000. Be very careful how you apply it. ISO 9000 does not specify any specific documentation. As a matter of fact, all ISO really discusses is the control of the documents once they have been put in the public eye. That is to say, ascertaining adequacy and versioning of them. This is hopelessly insufficient for any development or long-term maintenance. IEEE 730 is much more applicable and clear.

We begin this discussion here by defining what is the absolute minimum. Afterwards, we describe some of these documents more fully to give you a better feel for what they actually mean to the SQA practitioner.

In terms of the IEEE Std 730, a minimum documentation set must include all of the following:

- Software requirements specification (SRS). A document should be provided which clearly and precisely describes each requirement of the software and interfaces (functions, performance, design constraints and attributes). Remember, interfaces are the single largest cause of disaster. Plan to prevent disaster, not to stop it
- Software design description (SDD). Clearly, all projects must have this document, regardless of their size. A document should be provided describing major components of the software design including databases and internal interfaces. An expansion of this description may also include descriptions of each subcomponent of major components
- Software verification and validation plan (SVVP)
- Software verification and validation report (SVVR). This is required by the standard, but not needed by projects under 35 staff-years
- User documentation[1]
- Software configuration management plan (SCMP) can be part of this plan. However, I do not recommend this for projects larger than ten staff-years
- S/W test plan.[2] Clearly, all projects must have this document, regardless of their size
- S/W test report. Clearly, all projects must have this document, regardless of their size

[Notice that the standard does not stipulate that there be a SQAP. This is an assumption which is implied. Other than (possibly pure) research projects, all projects need a SQAP.] Other recommended documentation products may include the following:

- Software development plan (SDP)
- Standards and procedures manual (S&PM)
- Software project management plan (SPMP)
- Software maintenance manual (SMM)

There is no published standard for the previous four documents that we can really recommend.

Software Requirements Specification (SRS)

The software requirements specification document describes capabilities, states and functionality of all aspects of the system. This includes major components, subcomponents and internal interfaces of the software, and may include databases. It should also include any items specifically required by the user (for instance, a specific computing environment).

Documentation needs to be prepared for each deliverable **and** non-deliverable item of software, firmware and hardware. These nondeliverable items are frequently forgotten, particularly when the developer is not intending to maintain the software. If you are on the purchasing side, there should not be any nondeliverable documents, nor should any item of hardware or software be undocumented, whether deliverable or not. Keep your options open. In the short term, it may cost a little bit more but in the long term you may find that you have saved the company very large sums. Certainly, this documentation should include (at least) requirements, operations and basic design of the item.

Software Design Description (SDD)

The software design description document describes major components and subcomponents of the software, including databases and internal interfaces. One should expect that this process will be carried out according to a standard procedure which has been agreed on. This procedure may include use of a computerized design tool (most commonly mis-named a computer-aided software engineering tool, or a CASE tool). In any case, the design and coding standards to be used in development of both deliverable **and** nondeliverable software items should be properly described. ISO 9000 demands that these procedures be implemented as an integral part of your development procedures and that quality assurance assess, on an on-going basis, their degree of use, as described by the documentation.

Software Interfaces Documentation

Software interfaces documentation describes capabilities and functionality of all interfaces between any two (or more) components of the system. This includes major components, subcomponents and external systems. Both external and internal interfaces of the software should be described.

Software Test Documentation

In the interests of brevity, the test design specification includes test procedures and test case specifications. The test case specifications contain all information directly needed for performing the actual testing of the various software modules. The software test documents include:

- Test design specification
- Test log
- Test summary report

The testing procedures for the nondeliverable software, firmware and hardware items, describe (document) the procedures implemented as described by the documentation.

Software Development Plan

There is no good standard for this. ISO 9000 does not even require it. However, no effective development manager will want to be without it. Whatever format you choose to use, come up with a format, get everyone to agree on it, and stick to it. Consistency is very important.

User Documentation

The user documentation (for example manuals, guides, and so on) specify and describe the required inputs, options and other user activities necessary for the successful use and application of the system. The user documentation has two objectives: a tutorial objective, to train the user to get the most helpful and accurate service from the system and, to provide an efficient on-going reference for usage of the system. Once again, we most strongly recommend IEEE Std 1063. It really is very good.

Document Distribution

Process interface to configuration management

Interfaces between the document distribution function and the system/ software configuration management function, need to be defined, both for code and for purposes of document distribution. It is not correct to think that the code is the more important. We discussed above where our efforts are and where the problems occur. Prevention of error propagation begins here. The specifications are much more important to control. Identification procedures should be established for documents to provide everything with the best professional naming conventions, prior to distribution.

Of course, this control also includes backup procedures, not just the initial release. All of these procedures need to be defined and implemented for all documents before their distribution, including: storage of them off-site, storage in a fire-proof safe and the periodicity of their movements. Have you ever been part of a project that was stored in a building that burned down? We have. It is never pleasant, but if this procedure has been executed properly, it need not be disastrous for the project. Data center managers are accustomed to thinking about disaster recovery, we need to be as well.

Distribution to internal project personnel

The procedures for distribution of system documents to internal project personnel should be clearly defined. Not every project has a need to limit distribution rights, but a lot more projects do, that never get around to thinking about it. Just because your project is not a question of national security, does not mean that everyone's Aunt Harriet should hear about it. Access limitation procedures can be created for project documents very inexpensively and no one needs to be insulted by this. Also, access **traceability** capabilities can be established for documents. This can also prove its cost over time. Are the prerequisites for this distribution clear to all concerned? The prerequisites should be applied to every document which is formally distributed by the project and procedures defined for distribution of documents to nonproject personnel, as well.

Distribution to external project personnel

The procedures for distribution of system documents to external project personnel (whether these are government, client, user representatives or some other external persons) must be clearly defined in written procedures. All of the procedures defined for distribution of documents to nonproject personnel must make clear what the prerequisites are for this distribution.

Security limitations of documents

Distribution procedures should be in agreement with rules set up by the corporate security officer, if one exists. If there is no such function, check to see if there is a need for this. You are only developing a system for data processing of medical data, so why should you need this? Well, if this is your company's main product, this system may be critical to your company's survival. For another, there may be laws concerning data privacy. What is the danger, if you are breaking the law? In some places, this danger may be very nasty. Consider the creation of a *data officer* and see if one needs to be designated for distribution of documents. All this is really superfluous for your development? Fine, but now that you have checked, you **know** that it is superfluous.

Software Quality Planning Worksheet # 7-1

Documents documentation plan

Project: _____   Planner: _____

Date: _____   SQAP: _____

Item #	Development process	Document delivery date	Standard/ procedure	QA control activity	Comments
1	SRS				
2	Design (TLD/DD)				
3	Test plan				
4	Test procedure				
5	Test design				
6	Test results				
7	Users guide				
8	Operations course				
9	Sources				
10					

Notes

1   Only called for by the 1984 version of the IEEE standard. In any case, I strongly recommend looking at IEEE Std 1063. It is excellent.
2   An interesting point here is that testing documents are not really required by the standard, but certainly no real-life project can live without them. In other words, I differ with the standard at this point.

STANDARDS, PRACTICES, CONVENTIONS AND METRICS

This chapter essentially contains a list of the standards and practices to be used for the project. On major projects, this may be a separate volume, in which case this can be indicated here with simply a reference. Certainly, a "software house" should have all of its standard practices in an easily accessible form. This chapter also identifies and defines relevant standards, practices, conventions and metrics to be applied as well as stating how compliance will be assured.

The Control Tower

CHAPTER 5 OF THE SQAP IS AS CENTRAL TO THE CONTROL OF the processes of development and maintenance of all software as the control tower is to aircraft flight. Vast experience has proven that, without the concepts and tools defined by this chapter of the plan, and they need to be very well defined, you are very likely to crash. Whether your plan is discussing a project or the whole company, this is the section which is the primary link to the SEPG in particular and to the capability maturity mode (CMM), in general. This is the section that forms the vital procedural link between the organization which provides for the ways that things happen in the organization (in the case of information systems) or the "look-and-feel" of products, and the general organizational functionality.

At very least, this chapter must include the procedures to be followed by all development and maintenance personnel for all basic technical, design and programming activities involved. This section identifies the standards to be applied by **every** step of product development. Remember, this section does not have to contain the procedures, it must reference them and show their availability. The following information is the minimum requirement:

- Documentation. Discuss the standards to be used for every type of documentation
- Variable and module naming. Some organizations have been sophisticated enough to have computerized their naming conventions (we know of one bank that has the whole process totally computerized, on an IBM mainframe, written in REXX)
- Software programming standards. These must include, at least:
  - logic structure standards, coding standards, both general coding procedures (the more important part) and for the particular programming language you are using (of lesser significance but also recommended)
  - commentary standards
- Software inspection procedures
- Software testing standards and procedure, including test documentation
- Software quality metrics – see below

Metrics

Productivity refers to goods or services produced per unit of labor and expense.

What are metrics and to what are we referring here? Collection and use of data which reflect developers' productivity and the quality of the products that they produce. The questions then arise: What data? How can productivity be expressed? How can quality be expressed? What is productivity? The economists' definition of productivity is usually: "Goods or services produced per unit of labor and expense." In software, none of this is easy to define, to understand or to express. Even worse, there is no industry-wide agreement on any of this – even where standards exist! The basic problems are to define what are units of labor and what is expense.

Metrics refer to the collection and use of data which reflect productivity and quality of the products produced.

Traditionally, the unit of labor was taken to be a line of code (LOC).

Perhaps, if all software were written with a single, identical language and with the exact same methodology, this definition might be able to have some reflection on productivity. Under the circumstances, almost any use of LOC **as a reflection of productivity** is either false, or misleading. It is never a reflection of productivity. (Do **not** look at IEEE Std 1045, "Software productivity metrics," which in these authors' opinion is a complete farce and will be a total waste of your time and effort.) More on this below. They can be used for other purposes, such as planning of preventive maintenance activities or software maintainability, in which case, LOC metrics can be very good. However, that is out of the scope of the present discussion.

According to the standard (IEEE Std 730) software quality metrics must include at least the following list.

- Branch metric
- Decision point metric
- Domain metric
- Error message metric
- Requirements demonstration metric

All of these above mentioned metrics are normative to the standard – that is, the standard demands them as required. By the bye, neither the standard, nor the guidelines to the use of the standard (IEEE Std 730.2) provide precise definitions of what these measurements are. Apparently, interpretation is left up to the reader. We strongly suggest that these measurements are **extremely** insufficient. As a matter of fact, it is by no means certain that they are really helpful. These are essentially LOC metrics **which have been generally discredited** where development is concerned, though they have proven to be useful for maintenance.

One of the significant deficiencies of 730 is this aspect of metrics. The standard does not demand a firm linkage between this chapter (the metrics listed here) and chapter 13 of the plan (see chapter 16 of this book). Besides, why are they here in the first place? They need to be defined in their proper place. The answer is that they were added as an afterthought. This is most unfortunate and is probably the most glaring deficiency of the standard, in its present form. Refer to chapter 13 of the standard for what you do with the metrics and to the appropriate, corresponding chapter of this book (16) to see what metrics you really want to consider. The authors strongly recommend that one avoids LOC metrics whenever possible. If they are to be used, it should only be: (a) via completely automatic tools and (b) only for purposes of software maintenance. However, where that is not possible (i.e. a client demands them) use them sparingly and **never** attempt to equate them with any individual's productivity. It has been proven beyond reasonable doubt that LOC metrics are anti-productivity – that is to say, their usage **reduces** the productivity of software professionals by encouraging the wrong kinds of activities.

As to ISO 9000

This section should be an exact match for ISO 9000-type demands and it turns out that the designers of ISO 9000 – though they were not thinking about software (they were basically against admitting that it existed) and hence they did not address this need in software terms – did a fair job. In any case, it is very broadly covered. Unfortunately, in their desire to be everything to everyone, they are so generic that they sometimes lose the real thread. Paragraph 4.4 of the standard (ISO 9001) states the following:

> The supplier shall establish and maintain documented procedures to control and verify the design of the product in order to ensure that the specified requirements are met.

This sounds good, and they go on to describe a very nice list of sub-paragraphs to further explain what they are referring to. The list includes:

- Design and development planning (4.4.2)
- Organizational and technical interfaces (4.4.3)
- Design input (4.4.4)
- Design output (4.4.5)
- Design review (4.4.6)
- Design verification (4.4.7)
- Design validation (4.4.8)
- Design changes (4.4.9)

Well, this is indeed very broad coverage – better then the coverage provided us by IEEE 730. So, if it is so broad, what is missing? Let's look at Annex B ("Cross-reference between ISO 9001 and ISO 9000-3") of ISO 9000-3 to start to get the picture. First, remember that you are audited according to ISO 9001 and not ISO 9000-3, this is classed as informative "guidelines" not normative. Second, when we look at the entry for paragraph 4.4 we see a list of paragraphs in ISO 9000-3: "5.3, 5.4, 5.5, 5.6, 5.7 and 6.1."

If we then look at Annex A ("Cross-reference between ISO 9000-3 and ISO 9001," the opposite of the previously mentioned table) we see that the match is not exactly simple. Referring to each of those aforementioned paragraphs (5.3 and so on) each one refers to several paragraphs in 9001. Not only is the match not exclusively one-to-one, you need to do some very serious mental acrobatics to comprehend exactly what the demands are. As a matter of fact, this one paragraph seems to cover the entire system life-cycle. So, in summation, what we should say here concerning ISO 9000, more then anything else, is that the coverage is good, but it is difficult to understand and implement.

> Are all standards, practices, conventions and metrics which are to be applied, identified?
>> Is compliance with these items monitored and assured?
>> Are the following standards all provided:
>
> * documentation standards?
> * logic structure standards?
> * coding and commentary standards?

QA Techniques

Following is a (very) brief summary overview of nine techniques used by quality auditors for software. Clearly, there are many others. Once again, as the scope of this quality planning manual has been defined, there is no reason to list more, or to further elaborate the various techniques.

Reviews

There are four reviewing techniques, outlined below. They are all usable and efficient, but as a quality professional, you must be aware when each one of them should apply, and how much. Refer to chapter 9 of this book for more details.

Auditing

"Desk checking" of development documents, for accuracy, clarity and standards conformance, as well as for "errors" by an individual and hence, the least expensive. If performed by a very experienced and talented auditor this can be an excellent way to detect and solve errors. Unfortunately, it is very *talent* dependent.

Inspection

This is a highly disciplined and formal technique of group dynamics used for finding errors in deliverables, such as documents and source code but can also be used for all deliverables. All participants have well-defined roles, while management is specifically excluded from participation. The most expensive of the techniques, but also by far the most effective at finding errors.

Reviewing

This may sometimes be called "peer reviews" or "management reviews" – depending on the method used for selecting participants and is a technique of displaying results of a development process. The audience will usually consist of fellow developers, managers (of various levels) and user representatives. This technique can be very expensive when large numbers of people are involved, but may be an extremely effective means for the participants to learn about the project (content or status).

Walkthroughs

Intermediate deliverables (documents) can be tested for completeness and verified against peer documents. This technique should not be confused with the development testing process (see below). This is sometimes called "document testing" and is always the least expensive. Unfortunately, you also get what you pay for. It is good for keeping the members of the group aware of project content. It also can solve problems cheaply, but do not expect it to be sufficient for a large percentage of the problems.

Standardization

The creation of formal operational criteria that establish a model against which deliverables – and procedures for their production – can be compared and measured. A critical technique for any installation. Absolutely necessary for either ISO 9000 or CMM (and they are both correct). Any attempt to avoid the use of the standards and procedures will force all quality assurance activities to the level of chewing water (i.e. a stupid waste of time).

Simulation

This is the process of studying system behavior through use of **measurable** computer models and is usually performed utilizing specialized tools such as simulation languages.

Testing

Testing is the most commonly used and misused verification method. Experience has shown that approximately 45% of development budgets are spent on testing. The major problem begins by not having created control and completion criteria before the testing process began. Once again, if you do not know where you are going, you will never know when you have arrived. Rigorous testing requires a plan of procedure, including a plan of what is to be done, documentation and an idea of at what stage the effort has been finished/completed. Following are sample test types (there are certainly others, however this is a SQA guide, not a testing guide).

Acceptance testing

This is an overall check of final products at and/or prior to delivery, to ascertain adherence to contractual requirements and is usually judged as more of a legal act then a technical one.

System testing

This is an overall check of final products at and/or prior to delivery and is the final technical survey and evaluation of the viability and quality of the system, as produced.

Functional testing

This is a technique to discover discrepancies between the functional definition of a system and the actual operating (sub)system.

Logical testing

Tests used to discover errors in system computation and logical functions (for example error handling).

Path testing

Technique used to confirm test effectiveness (coverage), based on control topology of the code. This technique demands knowledge of the internal structure of the code, as such, it is a form of white-box testing.

Stress testing

Test to demonstrate at what points the system can be caused to overload – extreme conditions.

Regression testing

This involves "old" tests to be rerun (previously used and archived), and is used to demonstrate that the new release still performs everything the old one did.

Analytical modeling

Analytical modeling attempts to develop mathematical representations of the system – similar to (and frequently a part of) simulation.

Execution analysis

Technique of analysis of an execution. Usually used to find efficiency bottlenecks.

Independent verification, validation and testing (IVV&T)

This form of testing involves the utilization of a **totally independent** agency to find **critical errors** during the development process. A very expensive but very effective technique, used for large and/or critical projects, particularly those involving the danger of loss of life (the most common example is atomic reactor control systems).

Correctness proofs

These are techniques used to formally prove the correctness of programs or algorithms, similar to mathematical theorems, but these are not yet really viable for "real-life" systems.

Planning for Process Improvement

The most important secret to quality planning is not the plan for the present project, it is what are the returns to the organization for the effort. Certainly, we can expect that the project will be better and that productivity will improve, simply because of the SQA effort. However, there can be a much greater benefit, that of continuous quality improvement via process improvement. The first lesson that should be learned from the SQA effort, and applied to the organization, is to create a "road-map" of how, when and where quality is to be improved. What points in the existing development process can be improved for the lowest price with the greatest benefit? Does that sound like standard systems analysis? It is! What you are now asked to do is to perform a systems analysis of systems analysis. Not double-talk, but one of the most difficult and challenging, but rewarding activities you have yet to perform professionally (fun too)!

The basic idea is simply a cost-benefit analysis of all development and maintenance activities. Create a graph of the costs and benefits over time and compare where you get the most gain, most quickly. There is a mathematical technique where one uses a graph shaped like a capital "U", with the Y axis as the bottom, the X axis as the left-hand vertical and the Z axis as the right-hand vertical. This allows a more sophisticated graph (it is called a *three-dimensional graph*). This is an excellent method to show management the results of your analysis and how the organization is going to gain from your efforts to improve process.

A sage told the following story:

A man was walking along a road through countryside which was unfamiliar to him since he had never been there before. However, he had been told that at a certain point he would come to a cross-roads and there he would find a sign-post which would direct his way. After quite some time, he finally arrived at the cross-roads, but he found that the sign-post had fallen! Now which way was he to go? If you have analyzed the problem, you probably know the answer. The solution is to stand the post up and rotate it until the arrow pointing to the place he had come from, points in the correct direction. Then he can use the rest of the information on the post to know where his road lies. Or, in other words, know where you are coming from, and you can know to where you are going.

Notes

1 Refer to the Glossary for more detailed explanations
2 As measured in staff years of effort for the entire system development.
3 Using US$50,000 per staff year, average.
4 Ada is a trademark of the US government, Department of Defence.
5 Source: Kenneth Labich, *Fortune Magazine*.

REVIEWS AND AUDITS

9

The purposes of **reviews** and **audits** are to ensure that the product meets all client needs and requirements, and to find development anomalies as early and as inexpensively as possible.

Overview of Software Project Reviews

THIS CHAPTER IS CONCERNED WITH CHAPTER 6 OF THE SQAP. The objectives of reviewing a software project are two-fold. There is a verification objective known as "are we making the system right?" That is, to reach a degree of confidence (a "confidence level") that the system being produced really is produced the way it ought to be produced. There is also a validation objective, known as "are we making the right system?"[1] In both cases, what we are actually examining are the "deliverables" for the next stage in the development process. The detailed techniques used for each type of review are discussed later.

The purpose of this chapter is to guide the reader in planning what reviews need to be incorporated in the software quality assurance plan (SQAP) that is being developed. The purpose is not to describe in detail all of the techniques for performing the review or to describe all of the different kinds of reviews which may be possible. Certainly, the various standards which describe reviews[2] can supply more information about the possibilities. The principles for the review section are:

- Establishing what reviews are needed by the project – dependent, of course, on size, criticality and complexity of the project.

- What documents/deliverables should each review be examining. That is, what are the contents of the various reviews?
- What should be the results of the review?

Table 9.1 briefly displays the first general categories for the reviews, i.e. which ones are "always" needed, and which ones only for the larger and/or more critical projects. Again, this list does not claim to include all possibilities, only the most common ones. The purpose is for planning.

Table 9.1   Reviews during the project

Critical	Project dependent
SRR	PTR
PDR	CTR
CDR	

The acronyms used in this table are defined and described in detail later in the chapter.

Procedural Description Template

Table 9.2 briefly describes the template used to plan, prepare, and execute any review or audit. Clearly, in many cases, some of these steps may become redundant or may be combined with others. However, management must be aware that, even if a step is not specifically elucidated, it **is** performed.

This is a critical function for ISO 9000 compatibility. While ISO 9000 does not discuss the technologies outlined here (very correctly so), they

Table 9.2   Reviewing description template

1	Objective
2	Abstract
3	Special responsibilities
4	Input (products to which the process is applied)
5	Entry criteria (conditions that must be satisfied before the process can begin)
6	Procedures
7	Exit criteria
8	Output
9	Auditability

are adamant about the importance of management's role in the quality of the final product. Clearly, this is one area where ISO 9000 is particularly strong and where their attitude is to be commended and very carefully adhered to. The basic attitude of management responsibility is the first building-stone of quality. If management is not convinced that they want it, it will be difficult (next to impossible) to achieve. This is where they prove themselves. Management reviews and indeed management reporting of results of other kinds of reviews, are to be taken absolutely seriously. They are the least expensive and the most effective methods of preventing error propagation (now that **is** a wonderful combination).

Action Items

An action item, as its name implies, is something that needs to be acted on. The source of an action item may be a comment during a review or a question raised by the client during a tracking meeting. It is something which has been recorded, perhaps by someone taking minutes of a meeting. Generally someone else needs to take care of it. This taking care may cover the entire range from simply supplying a questioner with some information, up to a radical change of system concept, or anything in between.

Of course, a bug, an anomaly, a defect and a change request are all action items. These are the special cases – except that in our field, the general population is more familiar with the special cases than with the generic.

Software quality assurance is not responsible for recording action items, nor for creating them, nor for performing the work. What they **are** responsible for is making certain that action items **are** recorded and that the work **is** carried out. The questioner must get an answer or the system must be redesigned. That is all. We do not **have** to ascertain that the person is happy with the answer that was received, though certainly, a true understanding and follow-through of the philosophy of quality demands full customer satisfaction.

What is **very** necessary however, is that the action items are recorded, that they are recorded accurately, and that there is a thorough and healthy system to make follow-through both straight-forward and simple. The following worksheet (Action Item Recording Form) should be helpful for their recording. We suggest a computerized log for their follow-through and tracking.

The "natural" place to find an action item tracking system would be the software configuration management system. Unfortunately, most of the systems on the market today still do not indicate that their developers understand the importance of this need. While some of them have "bug

Software Quality Planning Worksheet # 9-1

Action item recording form

Project: _____   Registrar: _____

Date: _____   Audit: _____

Item #	Reference	Description	Action required	Due date	Completion date

tracking" facilities, which is functionally very similar, I have only seen one that handles this requirement reasonably well. That is the "All Change" system from Intasoft, in the UK. *Probably one of the best, most thorough SCM system on the market, at the time of writing.*

CMM Compatibility

Reviews and audits are such an essential part of the CMM approach to software project development that virtually everyone gets to participate. There are many kinds of reviews required at all levels of the development organization from senior management down, and includes anyone who might be affected by the project, both within the organization and outside representatives of end users or of clients. The review and audit requirements are so pervasive that every one of the CMM certification levels requires additional sets of reviews to be performed.

Level 2

Level 2 requires a number of reviews and audits from the early stages of the activity to conform to CMM requirements. Senior management, project managers, the software engineering group and the software quality assurance group are to review and audit the Software Project Planning activities on a periodic and event driven basis. As software projects are brought under CMM discipline, those groups have continuing review and audit responsibilities within the key process area entitled "software project tracking and oversight." The first of these is the specification that senior management review all changes to software project commitments made to anyone outside the organization, regardless of whether they are new commitments or modifications to existing ones. Periodic internal reviews are to be conducted by the software engineering group to track technical progress, plans, performance and other issues connected to conforming to the software development plan. The next requirement fits completely with the theme of this chapter. This is the requirement to hold formal reviews to assess the "accomplishments and results of the software project" at project milestones "according to a documented procedure." Those reviews have to meet the following specifications:

- Formal reviews occur at meaningful points of the software project's schedule, such as the beginning or end of selected stages
- Include affected groups within the organization and customer or end user representatives, as appropriate
- Review materials that the responsible software managers have reviewed and approved
- Check the commitments, plans and status of the software activities
- Document the identification of significant issues, action items and decisions
- Address the software project risks
- Define any refinements in the software development plan as necessary

A major senior management requirement is to conduct a periodic implementation verification review of the activities involved in the key process areas of software project planning and software project tracking and oversight. The objective is to keep upper levels of management aware of software process activities and any possible need for changes. If there are good exception reporting mechanisms, then this type of senior management review may be held at relatively long intervals, provided only that the needs of the organization are satisfied. The activities of this type of review include:

- Technical, cost, staffing and schedule performances
- Conflicts and other issues not resolvable at lower management levels
- Software project risks

- Action items are assigned, reviewed and tracked to closure
- A summary status report to be prepared and distributed to all affected groups

All activities involved in project tracking and oversight are reviewed by the project manager and representatives of all affected groups on a periodic and event-driven basis. Reviews cover:

- Technical, cost, staffing, and schedule performances compared against the development plan
- Use of critical computer resources: current estimates and actual use reported against the original plan
- Dependencies between groups
- Conflicts and other issues not resolvable at lower levels
- Software project risks analyzed
- Action items assigned, reviewed and tracked to closure
- Summary report of the meeting is prepared and distributed to all affected groups

The software configuration management (SCM) key process area has a number of associated reporting and auditing activities. Senior management and project managers are required to review SCM activities on a periodic and event driven basis. The SCM group itself is to conduct periodic audits of baselines to verify conformance to their defining documentation. Finally, the software quality assurance group reviews, audits and reports on activities and work products for software project tracking and oversight and for SCM.

Level 3

Level 3 of CMM requires additional reviews and audits to check on new and extended procedures. Most required review activities are concerned with software development process, although there are some that deal with software project "deliverables" themselves. As in level 2, senior management is required to conduct periodic implementation verification reviews of activities in key process areas. These include reviews of the activities in the key process areas of software process development and improvement, the training program, integrated software management and software product engineering. The activities of senior management reviews are the same as those described for level 2.

Like senior management, individual project managers have an extended set of reviews to conduct at level 3. Project manger review activities have already been described in the level 2 description above. At this level, the subjects of their reviews concern the activities of integrated software management, software product engineering (more commonly known as the software development life-cycle) and intergroup coordination.

The SQA group also have a set of extended responsibilities for level 3. They are to be responsible for reviewing/auditing and reporting on the following subjects. The first of these are activities and work products for managing the software project itself. This includes auditing:

- The process for developing and revising the project's defined software process
- The process for preparing the project's software development and risk management plans
- The processes for managing the project in accordance to defined software process
- The processes for collecting and updating the organization's software process database

The next activity is to review/audit and report on the activities and work products of the software product engineering key process area. The audit must verify that:

- Software requirements are reviewed to ensure that they are complete, correct, consistent, feasible and testable
- Criteria are satisfied for readiness and completion of each task in the life-cycle
- All software products meet their specified requirements and standards
- Required testing is performed
- System and acceptance tests are carried out in conformance to documented plans and procedures
- All tests satisfy planned and documented acceptance criteria
- Tests are completed and recorded satisfactorily

Level 3 introduces a key process area called "peer reviews." This type of review is concerned with examining the software project products or "deliverables" themselves – as opposed to reviewing the activities and managerial aspects of the project. We discuss the most effective techniques for conducting this type of review in some detail in a following section of this book entitled the "Technical Review Process." Review activities carried out as described in that chapter will satisfy the CMM requirements. However, CMM specifications always require that project activities be reviewed. Even in this case, the SQA group is required to audit and report on the peer reviews to ascertain that they have been conducted and documented properly according to the procedure specified for the project.

Level 4

CMM Level 4 has two major key process areas that require reviews and audits. These are called "quantitative process management" and "software quality management." As the reader should now expect, standard senior management implementation verification reviews of the process activities are required. Also, as expected, the project managers are expected to conduct periodic and event driven reviews and the project activities are to be audited by the SQA group.

Level 5

Finally, CMM level 5 has three key process areas entitled "defect prevention," "technology change management" and "process change management." The standard senior management, project management and SQA group reviews and audits are specified. In the case of the senior management implementation verification review of defect prevention, it is worthwhile listing the specific review activities:

- Summary of major defect categories with frequency distribution of defects within each category
- Summary of major action categories and frequency distributions of actions in each category
- Significant actions taken to address the major defect categories
- Status summary of proposed, open and completed action items
- Summary of effectiveness and savings attributable to defect prevention activities
- Actual cost of completed prevention activities and projected costs of planned defect prevention activities

To summarize, the CMM specifications require that work products of software development projects be reviewed/audited by representatives of every group that could be affected by the project. In addition, there are review requirements of the organization's software process group (software engineering), the software quality assurance group, software configuration management group, project management and senior management to check on all project activities – at various levels, maintenance of standards and process improvement activities. It may be a large investment but there are very strong indications that the return on the investment is very positive.

ISO 9000 Compatibility

Experience has shown that, left to themselves, developers seldom find the time to implement review techniques. However, we now know that their use must be encouraged. They are important and effective. We also know today that the activities of reviews and auditing are the most effective error finders that exist. The ISO 9000 attitude is very helpful in this. It does encourage their use and, of at least equal importance, their formal planning and recording. However, the ISO attitude is more a managerial one than a technical one, and we need both.

Paragraph 4.17 of ISO 9001 is called "Internal quality audits" – clearly this is the place for the function. This is a technical issue. While the managerial aspect must not be belittled, the technical aspect must be strengthened as much as possible.

The Management Review Process

Objectives

To provide recommendations for the following:

- Making activities progress according to plan, based on an evaluation of product development status
- Changing project direction or to
- Identify the need for alternative planning
- Maintaining global control of the project through adequate allocation of resources

A formal evaluation of a project level plan or project status relative to that plan by a designated review team.

The review leader is responsible for the administrative tasks pertaining to the review, for assuring that the review is conducted in an orderly manner, and for issuing the management review report.

Management Review Inputs

The minimum input to the management review process includes:

- Statement of objectives
- List of issues to be addressed
- Current project schedule and cost data
- Report from other reviews or audits
- Reports of resources assigned to the project
- Data on the software elements completed

Entry Criteria

Authorization

The need for conducting certain management reviews is initially established in the appropriate project planning documents (for example software quality assurance plan, software development plan).

Initiating event

This would be when the review leader establishes or confirms a statement of objectives for the management review meeting, or judges that the software element(s) and any other documentation or reports are sufficiently complete.

Management Review Procedures

Planning

The review leader, in conjunction with project management, identifies persons to participate, i.e. the review team. In addition, the leader must also schedule the meeting or meetings which will be needed for the review session, making certain that all of the team members are aware of their responsibilities concerning this meeting and their attendance. Finally, the leader is responsible for the distribution of input materials.

Overview

A qualified person from the project conducts an overview session for the review team, when requested by the review leader. This overview walks the team through the materials in a very general sense to make certain that they have the basic understanding needed in order to achieve maximal productivity.

Preparation

Each person on the review team individually studies the material and prepares for the review meeting.

Examination

This includes examination of the project status to determine if it complies with the expected status, and if it is constrained by external or internal factors. This also includes the recording of all deviations from the expected status, accenting risks.

Rework

Plan adjustments or project rework resulting from the review is not considered as part of the management review process, except where needed as additional input to complete the examination process.

Exit criteria

The management review is considered complete when all issues that have been identified in the review statement of objectives have been addressed, and when the management review report has been issued.

Management review output

A management review report that identifies the project, the review team, inputs to the review, review objectives, action item ownership and status, a list of issues and recommendations.

Auditability

The management review report is an auditable item.

Review Process Prerequisites

The objective of reviewing software elements is to evaluate software or project status. The following functions are present to achieve that objective:

- Management
- Development staff
- Development process planning
- Review process planning

Audit Process Prerequisites

The objective of software auditing is to provide an objective evaluation of products and processes to confirm compliance to standards, guidelines, specifications, and procedures. The following requirements are prerequisite to achieve that objective:

- Objective audit criteria must exist
- Audit personnel are selected to promote team objectivity
- Audit personnel are given sufficient authority

All technical and managerial audits to be conducted must be defined. As a minimum, the following reviews are required by the standard:

- Software requirements review (SRR). Clearly needed by any project, though their degree of formality is completely dependent on the project, the company and/or the customer. Generally, this will be more necessary for bespoke software than for product development. (That is not a recommendation, those are the unfortunate facts. The authors strongly recommend that this review always take place.) This review may need to occur frequently during product maintenance.

- Preliminary design review (PDR) [this may also sometimes be called: "top-level design review" – the names are equivalent]. Clearly needed by any project, though their degree of formality is completely project dependent.
- Critical design review (CDR) [detailed-design review]. Clearly needed by any project, though the degree of formality may be project dependent.
- Software verification and validation plan review (SVVPR) .
- Functional audit. Declared needed by the standard, but is useful only for projects larger then 35 staff-years.
- Physical audit. Declared needed by the standard, but is useful only for projects larger then 35 staff-years.
- In-Process Audits. Declared needed by the standard, but is useful only for projects larger then 35 staff-years.
- Managerial reviews. Declared needed by the standard, but is useful only for projects larger then 35 staff-years.
- Software configuration management plan review (SCMPR).
- Post-mortem review.

Other reviews suggested by the standard may include the following:

- User documentation review (UDR).
- Man–machine interface review (MMIR).
- System test review (STR).
- Acceptance test procedure (ATP).

Each of the following sections describes its particular review type in detail. These detailed descriptions include all of the specific items to be reviewed and the time frames.

The Technical Review Process

Technical Review Objectives

The objectives of this review are the evaluation of a specific software element(s) and the identification of any discrepancies from specifications and standards or recommendations after the examination of alternatives, or both.

The following sections contain a lot of material that is repeated, this is because the techniques contain requirements and activities that overlap. At the risk of boring our readers we have chosen to give complete descriptions in order to provide a useful reference. We recommend scanning quickly through the techniques, then studying those you expect will prove the most appropriate for your needs.

Special Responsibilities

Leader

The leader is responsible for conducting an orderly review, and for issuing the review report.

Recorder

The recorder is responsible for documenting findings, decisions, and recommendations made by the review team.

Team member

Each member is responsible for their own preparation, and for formulating recommendations in such a way that management can act on them promptly.

Technical Review Input

The minimum input to the technical review process includes:

- Statement of objectives
- Software element(s) being examined
- Specifications for the software element(s)
- Plans, standards or guidelines against which the software element(s) are to be examined

Entry Criteria

Authorization

Defined by the project planning documents.

Initiating event

This would be when a statement of objectives has been established, the responsible individuals for the software element(s) indicate readiness for review, and when the technical leader is satisfied that the software element(s) are sufficiently complete for a technical review to be worthwhile.

Procedure

Planning

The review leader, in conjunction with project management, identifies the review team, schedules meetings, and distributes input materials.

Overview

A technically qualified person from the project will conduct an overview session for the review team when requested by the review leader.

Preparation

Each person on the review team individually studies the material and prepares for the review meeting.

Examination

This includes examination of the software element relative to applicable guidelines, specifications and standards, or evaluating alternative problem solutions.

Exit Criteria

The technical review is considered complete when all issues that have been identified in the review statement of objectives have been addressed, and when the technical review report has been issued.

Technical Review Output

A technical review report that identifies the review team, software element(s) reviewed, inputs to the review, a list of unresolved software element(s) deficiencies, a list of management issues, action item ownership and status, recommendations on how to dispose of unresolved issues and deficiencies.

Auditability

The technical review report is an auditable item.

Software Requirements Review

A critical review! The software requirements review (SRR) should always be required, for every project. For the very small projects, the review may be quite informal, i.e. (say) three colleagues sitting about the manager's desk discussing the requirements documents. For larger projects, this review should be more formal. The results of this review will determine whether the proposed user of the system will still want it when delivered! To state it another way, while this is clearly needed by any project, the degree of formality implemented for it is completely dependent on the project, the company and/or the customer. Generally, this review is more necessary for bespoke software (projects) than for product development, though that is not a recommendation, those are the unfortunate facts. The first author strongly recommends that this review always takes place, at least in some form. Not only that, but that the results are recorded and retained for the record. This review may need to occur frequently during product maintenance.

> Rule # 1:
>
> Any project larger than three staff-years must be reviewed with a formal reporting procedure to report on review results; larger than 20 staff-years, it must have a formal review procedure with quality assurance participation (document audits by SQA will be the minimum participation) and rigid reporting.

What documents are to be reviewed? The SRR should include at least:

- Software requirements specifications
- Functional performance analysis

- Requirements specifications
- Interface specifications
- Software test plan
- Software development plan
- User's manual (draft)
- Acceptance test plan (draft)
- Software configuration management plan (draft)
- Software quality assurance plan, this plan, at this point in time should include at least the following kinds of information
- All sections of the plan, as per the standard, at least in a skeletal fashion
- Reliability requirements
- Quality requirements
- Risk/criticality analysis
- Maintenance/logistics support requirements
- Trade-off evaluation reports
- Systems safety
- Life-cycle costs (including future maintenance costs)
- Systems security
- Computer environment selection (hardware and operating systems for target and development)
- Programming development environment selection sizing and timing considerations
- Database conceptual design (optional, dependent on system type)

A "successful" requirements review should be the formal entry to the next stage. The next stage in the development life-cycle will be high level (top level) design. However, classifying the review as having been "successful" does not mean that everything is necessarily correct. It certainly does mean that only very few problems remain, that they appear to be known, and that they appear to be clearly under control. **A general "rule-of-thumb" is that no more then 5% of the requirements should have anomalies associated with them, in order to proceed.**

Preliminary Design Review

A critical review! The preliminary design review (PDR) is always needed, for every project. For the very small project, the review may be quite informal, i.e. (say) two colleagues sitting about the manager's desk discussing the high-level design documents. For larger projects, this review should be more formal. This review is technical in nature, and should be discussed in those terms. The results of this review will determine whether the system being produced is really usable in, and by, the environment for which it is being produced.

Rule # 2:

Any project larger than five staff-years must have a review result report of some kind which is reviewed by the proposed user. A project larger than 20 staff-years, or dealing with a technology which is novel to the developing organization, or is particularly critical to the organization, must have a formal review of technical peers, with QA participation.

What documents are to be reviewed?

- An updated software requirements specification
- High-level design document [software design architecture], which should include, at least, all of the following kinds of information, at this point in time
- Modularity (partitioning) analysis and the trade-offs that are involved in this selection
- Executive control (for example, operating system).
- Restart and recovery procedures
- Data and control flow analysis
- Algorithm/equations analysis
- Man–machine interface (MMI) and prototyping plan/design
- Software development plan
- Software quality assurance plan
- Software practices and procedures manual
- Data dictionary specification (optional)
- Software configuration management plan
- Software test plan
- Integration plan [integration test plan]
- Test designs (including scaffolding to be used) updated

The next stage in the development life-cycle will be the detailed design of the project. A "successful" preliminary design review will be the entry criteria in this next step. Again, success means that there are no more than 5% anomalies in the documents reviewed. What does 5% mean? The best recommendation is to use a measure of volume, such as the number of paragraphs (or pages, or requirements, or design objects). The exact unit of measure you choose to use is less important than the consistency of its use and that it be agreed on by all concerned.

Critical Design Review

A very critical review! Frequently, the terms "preliminary design review" and critical design review" have been misunderstood. The terms "*preliminary*" and "*critical*" refer to the review, not the design! This is a significant difference. Management, even more so than others, must have a clear understanding of the issues involved – and their levels of criticality. The final review before calling the design stage complete – and entering the most labor intensive of all "white-collar" activities – is perhaps the most important of all issues management needs to address to attain a reasonable level of confidence in the product being produced.

No corners can be cut on this one!

Rule # 3:

All projects must perform the critical design review (CDR), regardless of size or criticality, and regardless of whether the proposed user is to be an internal (to the organization) or an external user. All review activities must be well documented. SQA must be involved, from the planning of the review through the resolution of its findings.

What documents are to be reviewed?

- Detailed design documents
- Test procedures
- Test case specifications, updated
- High-level design document
- Test designs
- Software configuration management plan

Finally, the next stage – code implementation

Preliminary Test Review

An optional review. The preliminary test review (PDR) is recommended only for critical projects. On all others, this may be undesirable overhead.
   What documents are to be reviewed?

- Code
- Test designs
- Test data
- Test case specifications, updated
- Unit/module test results
- Test incident reports

All code is viewed as documents. All reviewing is performed against standards. The reason for this is that the code as a whole cannot really be effectively **reviewed**, because of the quantities involved and the degree of complexity. Therefore, there is a necessity to find a straightforward method of assessing the degree of care used in production of the code. The only "objective" tool for this has proven to be the coding standards. Almost always, if the coders have been careful in adhering to the standards, they have been careful with other things as well. That does not mean that there will not be errors, of course there will. However, the code will be more maintainable and we shall be able to "perceive" the degree of care used. Remember, this is performed before the real testing processes begin. That is, unit tests have been performed and there are written results of them. Integration has not begun.

Each of the test results are reviewed against the appropriate unit test design, and verified for completeness. Note: this may frequently force changes to the unit test design; and of course, a rerun of the test.

The next stage – integration and system tests.

Critical Test Review

An optional review. The critical test review (CTR) is recommended only for critical projects. What documents are to be reviewed? Whatever constitutes the testing of the system, up to and including the system tests. This also means all of the preparations for that all important task, **the acceptance test**! The minimal list is as follows:

- unit/module test reports
- integration test results
- system test results

The next stage - acceptance test.

Acceptance Test Review

An optional review. What documents are to be reviewed? This review really has only one objective, to avoid embarrassment. The acceptance test is intended to prove to your customer that he is getting what is being paid for. Bad things happening here are always embarrassing (or at least, should be). We review things beforehand to be able to hold our heads up higher. It is like a rehearsal before a performance. The acceptance test is your performance review. The acceptance test requirements (ATR) is your rehearsal beforehand.

- Software requirements specification
- Acceptance test requirements
- Acceptance test procedure

Software Quality Planning Worksheet # 9-2

Reviews and audit plan

Project: _____   Planner: _____

Date: _____   SQAP: _____

Milestone	Configuration items/types	Time frame	Control activity	Expected quantity	Comments
a) SRR	SRS, SQAP				
b) PDR	TLD, Test plan, Preliminary ATP				
c) CDR	DD, Test design, MMI concept				
d) MMIR					
e) SVVPR					
f) SCMPR					
g) UDR					
h) System test					
i) ATP					

The Software Inspection Process

Software Inspection Objective

The software inspection objective is to detect and identify software element defects. It is conducted by peers, typically comprising three to six participants. Defect data shall be systematically collected and stored in an inspection database. The proper use of this formal technique, as originally defined and developed by Michael Fagin, is undoubtedly the most powerful mechanism known for discovering defects in documents and program code.

Special Responsibilities

Moderator

The moderator is the chief planner and meeting manager for the inspection process.

Reader

At the meetings, the reader leads the inspection team through the software element(s) in a comprehensive and logical fashion

Recorder

The recorder is charged with documenting defects detected at the meeting(s) and recording inspection data required for process analysis.

Inspector

The inspector identifies and describes defects in the software element. Inspectors must be knowledgeable of the inspection process, and should represent different viewpoints at the meeting (for example, requirements, design, code, test, independent test, project management, quality management).

Author

The author is responsible for the software element(s) meeting its inspection entry criteria, for contributing to the inspection based on special understanding of the software element, and for performing any rework required.

Software Inspection Input

The necessary input to the inspection process includes:

- Software element to be inspected
- Approved software element specification and inspection checklist
- Standards and guidelines
- Any inspection reporting forms

Entry Criteria

Authorization

Inspections are planned for, and documented in the appropriate project planning documents.

Initiating Event

The software inspection process can be triggered by the following:

- Software element(s) availability
- Project plan compliance
- SQAP or SVVP schedule compliance
- Scheduled re-inspection
- At the request of management

Minimum entry criteria

The software element(s) must conform to project standards of content, and format. All prior milestones must be satisfied, all required supporting documentation must be available, and for a re-inspection, all items noted on the defect list must be satisfied.

Software Inspection Procedures

Planning

The author assembles the inspection package materials for the moderator, who is responsible for assuring that they meet the inspection entry criteria.

Overview

If scheduled, an overview presentation of the software element(s) is conducted by the moderator, and the author makes the presentation.

Preparation

Each inspector must become thoroughly familiar with the software element.

Examination

The inspection meeting follows this agenda:

Introduce meeting	The moderator introduces the participants and describes their roles
Establish preparedness	The moderator asks for individual preparation times and records the total on the inspection report
Review the inspection checklist	The moderator reviews the checklist with the team to ensure that the product has been adequately studied before the meeting
Read software elements and record defects	The reader presents the materials to the inspection team. The inspection team examines the software objectively, and the moderator focuses this part of the meeting on creating the defect list
Review the defect list	The moderator must have the defect list reviewed with the team to ensure its completeness and accuracy
Make exit decision	The purpose of the exit decision is to bring an unambiguous closure to the inspection meeting. Specifically, the inspection team identifies the software element(s) disposition as one of the following:

(1) Accept:
   The software element is accepted as is or with only minor rework
(2) Verify rework:
   The software element is to be accepted after the moderator verifies rework
(3) Re-inspect:
   Schedule a re-inspection to verify rework after revision

Rework

During rework, the author revises the materials, addressing all items on the inspection defect list.

Follow-up

The software inspection process provides follow-up on two levels:

- Verifying rework per inspection
- Reporting inspection data

Software Inspection Exit Criteria

The single exit criterion applied to all inspections is that all of the defects that have been detected are resolved. Each project shall develop its own criteria to meet the needs of its specific products and development environment.

Software Inspection Output

For each software element, the reports produced by the inspection are:

- The defect list, containing the defect location, description, and categorization
- The inspection defect summary summarizing the number of defects identified by each defect category
- The inspection report, containing the number of participants, the meeting duration, the size of the materials inspected, the total preparation time of the inspection team, the disposition of the software element, an estimate of the rework effort and the rework completion date

Software Inspection Auditability

Auditability is provided by the following:

- Documented inspection procedures
- Retained inspection reports
- Retained inspection defect data

Data Collection Requirements

Defects are categorized by the following.

Type

The defect type identifies software element attributes.

Class

Defect class characterizes evidence of nonconformance, and for example, may be categorized as missing, wrong, or extra.

Other classes

Additional defect classes used when inspecting documents could include ambiguous and inconsistent.

Severity

All defects are ranked by severity, such as major severity and/or minor severity.

The Walkthrough Process

Walkthrough Objective

To evaluate a software element for defects, omissions and contradictions, and to consider alternative implementations. The author makes an overview presentation of the software element(s) under review. This is followed by a general discussion from the participants after which the presenter "walks through" the software element in detail. Walkthroughs are useful but have proven much less effective than properly conducted inspections.

Special Responsibilities

Moderator

The moderator is responsible for conducting a specific walkthrough.

Recorder

The recorder is responsible for writing all comments made during the walkthrough that pertain to errors found, questions of style, omissions, contradictions, suggestions for improvement, or alternative approaches.

Author

The author is responsible for the software element(s) being examined, and presents the materials.

Walkthrough Input

The minimum input to the walkthrough process includes

- Statement of objectives for the walkthrough
- The software element under examination
- Standards
- Specifications for the software element(s)

Entry Criteria

Authorization

Walkthroughs are planned for, and documented in the appropriate project planning documents.

Initiating event

A walkthrough is conducted when the author indicates that the software element(s) is ready, and when the moderator is appointed.

Walkthrough Procedures

Planning

The moderator identifies the walkthrough team, schedules the meeting, and distributes all necessary input materials.

Overview

An overview presentation is made by the author.

Preparation

Each participant must review the input materials during this phase.

Examination

During the meeting, the presenter makes an overview presentation. The author walks through the specific software element(s) so that the walkthrough team may ask questions or raise issues regarding the software element.

Exit criteria

The process is complete when the entire software element(s) have been "walked through" in detail, all deficiencies, omissions, and suggestions for improvement have been noted, and the walkthrough report has been issued.

Walkthrough Output

A walkthrough report containing the statement of objectives, a list of noted deficiencies, omissions, contradictions and suggestions, and any recommendations on how to dispose of the deficiencies and unresolved issues. This report should be considered optional. It is a question of the organization's degree of formality of processes. Many times the walkthrough process is completely informal, in which case, no written report is needed.

Auditability

The walkthrough report, meeting minutes, and other materials on which conclusions are based, shall become part of the project documentation files.

The Audit Process

Audit Objective

An audit provides an objective compliance confirmation of products and processes to certify adherence to standards, guidelines, specifications, and procedures. Audits are performed in accordance with documented plans and procedures. The results of the audit are documented and are submitted to the management of the audited organization, to the entity initiating the audit, and to any external organizations identified in the audit plan.

In principle, there are two kinds of audits. There is the individual, desk-check type and an audit performed by a team. The first kind is by far the more common and perhaps, the more favorable. However, there is not a lot to be said about it. Probably every software engineer understands what desk checking means. It is then mostly a question of talent. (How many pieces of data remain in the head while reading the document? While reading section 3.2.5.2.1 does he/she remember that this may conflict with 3.1.2.3.1 in some respect? This is not easy. Very few people really do it well. This is the reason that most authors state that auditing should be almost exclusively checking for standards adherence.)

Most of the rest of this section deals with auditing via a team. It is the responsibility of the audit team leader to organize and direct the audit. The entity initiating the audit is responsible for authorizing the audit.

Audit Input

The following inputs are required:

- Purpose and scope of the audit
- Objective audit criteria
- The software elements and processes to be audited
- Background information regarding the organization responsible for the products and processes being audited

Entry Criteria

The need for an audit is established by one of the following events:

- A special project milestone has been reached
- External parties demand an audit

- A local organizational element has requested the audit
- A special project milestone has been met and, as part of the auditing organization's charter, it is to respond by initiating an audit

Audit Procedures

Planning

The auditing organization shall develop an auditing plan for each audit. This plan will include the following:

- Project processes to be examined
- Software required to be examined
- Reports shall be identified
- Report distribution
- Required follow-up activities
- Requirements
- Objective audit criteria
- Audit procedures and checklists
- Audit personnel
- Organizations involved in the audit
- Date, time, place, agenda, and intended audience of overview session

Overview

An optional overview meeting with the audited organization is recommended.

Preparation

The following preparations are required by the audit team:

- Understand the organization
- Understand the products and processes
- Understand the objective audit criteria
- Prepare for the audit report
- Detail the audit plan

The audit team leader should make the necessary arrangements for:

- Team orientation and training as needed
- Facilities for audit interviews
- Materials, documents, and tools required
- The software elements to be audited
- Scheduling interviews

Examination

The audit shall, as appropriate to its scope:

- Review procedures and instructions
- Examine the work breakdown structures
- Examine evidence of implementation and balanced controls
- Interview personnel to ascertain the status and functioning of the processes and the status of the product
- Examine element documents
- Test the elements

Reporting

The audit team will issue a draft report to the audit organization for review and comments. Audit team rework of the audit report occurs before formal results reporting. The audit team shall conduct a post-audit conference to review with audited organization staff the deficiencies, findings and recommendations.

Audit Exit Criteria

An audit is complete when:

- Each element within the scope has been examined
- Findings have been presented to the auditing organization
- Response to the draft audit have been received
- Final findings have been formally presented
- The audit report has been prepared and submitted
- The recommendation report has been prepared
- All follow-up actions by the auditing organization have been performed

Audit Output

The draft and final audit reports shall contain, as a minimum:

- Audit identification
- Scope
- Conclusions
- Synopsis
- Follow-up

Auditability

The materials documenting the audit process must be maintained by the audit organization for a stipulated period of time subsequent to the audit.

- Can all documentation governing development, verification, use, and maintenance of the software be identified?
- Are documents clearly checked for adequacy?
- Must the review or audit be identified for validating adequacy of each document?
- Must documentation be provided describing methods (for example, inspection, demonstration, analysis or test) to verify that requirements are implemented in the design and code?
- Must each software requirement be defined, such that its achievement can be objectively verified by a prescribed method, such as inspection, demonstration, analysis or test?
- Must methods for inspection, demonstration, analysis and test, to be used to verify that the code, when executed, meets requirements be clearly defined?
- Must a document be provided describing results of executing the verification plan?
- Must this document include results of all required reviews, audits and tests?
- Must technical and managerial reviews and audits to be conducted be defined?
- Must the methods to perform reviews and audits be stated?
- Must a review be held to ensure adequacy of requirements as previously stated?
- Must a review be held to evaluate preliminary design of the software as depicted by a preliminary version of the software design documentation?
- Must a review be held to determine acceptability of detailed software designs, as depicted by software design description, as satisfying identified requirements?
- Must an audit be held prior to software delivery to verify that all requirements specified in documentation have been met?
- Must an audit be held to verify that documents and programs are internally consistent and ready for delivery?
- Must in-process audits of design samples be held to verify consistency of the design, including:
  - Code versus design documentation?
  - Interface specifications (hardware and software)?
  - Design implementation versus functional requirements?
  - Functional requirements versus test descriptions?
- Must reviews be held periodically to access execution of the SQA plan?
- Must these reviews be held by an organizational element independent of the unit being audited or by a qualified third party?

Document Verification

Introduction to Verification and Validation

This section addresses document verification and validation (V&V). This is quite different from the previous techniques discussed. As a process, this is a subpart of the audit. From the point of view of an auditor, the development of software projects is a series of interrelated documents (including the source code listing). As expectations for the proposed system become larger, this model grows more obvious and more painful. Even testing of the actual "working" system will result in a set of documents which form part of the system. Software quality assurance consists of quality analysis of the documents which define and describe the processes involved in defining, developing, testing, operating and maintaining the system.

The development of major systems – whether real-time hardware/software systems, or "pure" software systems based on standard hardware – is not a trivial, easily managed task. The process of developing technologically advanced systems is a continuous, iterative and contingent process of resolving large quantities of uncertainties. For many projects, knowledge-base expansion is a primary (but undeclared) objective. We tend to view everything as a set of individual, discrete problems, rather than seeing the problem of building a system, as a system problem in its own right. From the standpoint of understanding systems, we find what truly connects all aspects of the system – one to each other. This connection should not be linear in nature nor "point to point." It must be as amorphous as the system of creating systems is. It must be all pervasive.

The Verification and Validation Technique

It is the nature of every system that all parts interrelate. These interrelationships are pervasive at all levels, and for all aspects of the system. For this discussion, we call all the various aspects of the system "concepts."[3] A concept is any identifiable "atom" of the system. It might be a data object, a piece of equipment, a process, a module (of software or hardware), an individual (a functionary), an algorithm, a computer room; anything which is identifiable, anything to which a reference exists or may exist.

Data processing professionals commonly use data dictionaries. Sometimes it appears that when we use such a tool, we forget that there are other objects in every system which are not data objects. It is important to identify all concepts/atoms which compose a system. The exercise of concepts identification is a powerful technique for document auditing. (By auditing, we refer to the attempt to quantify the **inherent quality** of a document as it stands alone – without reference to its peers.) Internal document anomalies of all sorts (inconsistencies, interface problems, etc.) are discovered very quickly. Document verification is matching the concepts *between* documents in an attempt to discover inconsistencies or errors which exist between the documents, even if each one (stand-alone) seems quite fine.

We call the various interrelationships between the concepts threads. A thread is an "aspect" of a concept. These aspects (other aspects of course exist) cause a relationship to exist between concepts. These relationships may be hierarchical (the most common of all relationships is that of parent/offspring), sibling, or subject oriented. There are also special kinds of relationships, such as several concepts having common keywords.

The subject relationship has proven to be extremely powerful. It is common knowledge that various participants in a system (developers, maintainers, users, managers) have different viewpoints. This becomes particularly striking when the system is developed by a large organization or a large contracting agency (such as a defense contractor for a military customer). In such cases, the subject classification tool becomes the method of directing attention to subsets of the knowledge-base as they are needed by each serviced group. Subject classification is very useful to the maintenance function.

The process of document audit and verification requires all of the following:

- Acquisition of project documentation
- Analysis of the documents
- Dissemination of information

The quality of the development process will be determined by the accuracy and completeness of its activities. Quality is affected by how and by whom interim products (i.e. documents) are passed through the "process loop." It is very important to recall that this is a cyclical, nonlinear process. This process loop includes:

- Critical examination via audit, verification and validation
- Dissemination of this verified information to other interested parties
- Updating documents as a result of the audit and verification process

The Point

Document auditing, verification and validation are performed by *quality assurance*. Project reviews, formal inspections and structured walkthrough are performed by the *development group*, with quality assurance guidance. The goals of all of these techniques are critical examination of the documents for early error trapping and information gathering. These techniques have shown themselves to be efficient and cost effective for both simple and complex projects, particularly where the quantities of information are larger than can comfortably be managed by a small group of people. As most complex projects/systems are developed over relatively long periods of time, with staff turnover, a continuity of problem/solution sets is frequently lost. This results in information losses, which occur both in the developing and the funding agencies. For this reason, the techniques of reviews, with action item recording and follow-up have been developed. They have consistently proven themselves to be highly cost effective.

Table 9.3 Review types and their formality/cost summary

Review type	Degree of formality	Team composition	Team membership selection criteria	Size/effort
Audit	Semi-formal	SQA	SQA	1
Review	Semi-formal	SQA, management, development, clients	Management	Very large, frequently tens of participants
Inspection	Very formal	Development (no management participation allowed), SQA can act in advisory or viewer capacity	SQA, development	Formally defined at from 5 to 10
Walkthrough	Informal	Development	Development	From 3 to 7

Document Audit and Verification

A Case Study

At the end of chapter 10 is a copy, with minor changes to protect client confidentiality, of a document audit and verification report. This is a real report from a real project. The project is a real-time, embedded system – a flight computer for an aircraft. The size of the project is about 110 staff-months. The company performing the project is a small, but highly skilled, company (of a type called a systems house) with a great deal of experience in this type of application. The first author acts as the head of software quality assurance for the company, in a consultative relationship.

The report is presented verbatim (the text is verbatim, some graphic adaptations have been made to suit the report to this book's format). Where explanations are felt to be needed, these are placed in footnotes.

While reading this, some of the comments may be difficult to understand. Remember that this is a real report and the reader of the original report would naturally read it together with the document which is audited. Some things must be read in context to be really meaningful, in terms of the actual intent of the comment. However, that is not the intention here. What is important is that the reader of this book get an understanding of what a document audit and verification means.

Notes

1   We believe that these questions were first formulated by Professor M. Lehman of Imperial College, London.
2   The most important standard for the review process is IEEE Std-1028. A new version is being processed now and should be going to ballot about the time this book goes to press.
3   A more common term might be object, however, this term has been somewhat over used lately, causing a good deal of confusion. We have adapted an out-of-the-ordinary term to avoid this confusion.

TEST

This chapter identifies and describes the tests to be used on the system and the methods to be deployed for performing them, then recording, analyzing and documenting the results. In the case that a formal software verification and validation plan (SVVP) exists, then this section of the SQAP should contain only those tests not documented in the SVVP. All tests need to be described or referenced.

The Processes of Software Testing

THIS CHAPTER DEALS WITH TESTING (CHAPTER 7 OF THE SQAP contains the testing plans). While testing is an essential part of the quality plan, it should be clearly understood what testing is and can accomplish. Testing is simply a controlled measurement of performance. It cannot be a means to guarantee perfection. Always keep in mind Dijkstra's famous comment that "Testing can only indicate the presence of bugs, not their absence."

The processes of software testing must always begin with an organized plan. This follows logically from the basic concept of software quality assurance being a planned set of activities. In practice, testing is a complex and difficult process. Performed haphazardly, the process is rarely completed well, or on time. As a matter of record, the usual reason for the termination of testing has been poor planning of the budget needed to carry out the activity properly. The major issue to be addressed, both for the test planning and the test evaluation, is a swift and accurate collection of as much data as possible. These data must reflect how the process is to be (or is being) performed. Recent research (usually accredited to Tom DeMarco) indicates that software professionals average about 0.5 to 0.6 defects for every 100 lines of source code during development and about one and a half times that for source code during maintenance. What this means is that for a typical package of a quarter of a million lines of source code (which is not large, certainly not for a Windows environment) we would expect to have some 1250 defects. However, this is *typical*; as systems get larger, the rate of defects grows, geometrically. Of course, not all of these defects are source code problems. From where in the development processes do the problems in the software actually come? We divide the sources of the problems into three categories (see Figure 10.1).

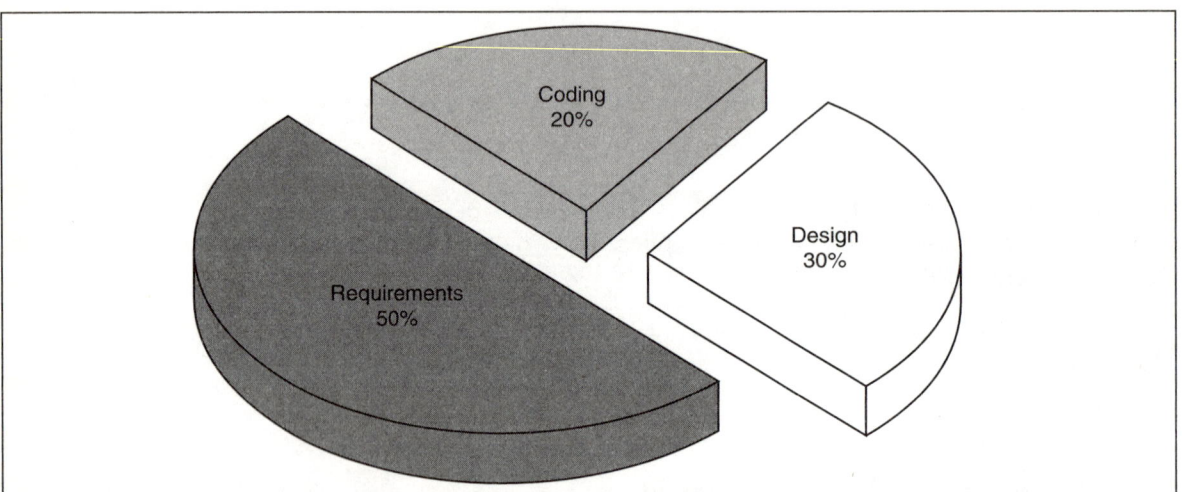

Figure 10.1   From where do problems in software actually come?

Requirements	50%	The requirements were insufficiently understood. Be very careful here about blaming people. Generally, insufficiently understood requirements is the area where users blame developers ("You mean they did not understand **that!**") and developers blame users ("But, why didn't they say so!"). This is never productive. This is an excellent place to avoid errors rather then fix them. These are the most expensive errors to fix and the most divisive.
Design	30%	The design needs were not sufficiently understood or were incorrectly translated from the requirements. Many logic problems are created during maintenance by overly

limited views of systems' design or requirements. The process of making a change in software is a multidimensional process with **nine** definable **states** and many sources of possible error (refer to chapter 11, Problem reporting, for a more detailed explanation of this). We must always assume that every change produces a ripple effect, then fully analyze the ramifications of our proposed change.

Coding   20%   The design was misunderstood at the coding phase. Finally, there are human mistakes made while writing code.

There are actually additional error classifications. These can include documentation errors and errors in the test suite. All of these waste resources and need to be taken into account. However, they are outside the scope of the present discussion. Also, but do not misunderstand this, normal error detection activities (debug, peer reviews and testing) will find the majority of these problems. Most software, of course, does work (if only in the expected situations). Again, what we are talking about is the cost and effort to get them to work. A study made by Microsoft claimed that it may take 12 programmer hours to find and fix a defect.

At most installations, there is a process in place to perform testing. This process is perhaps not the most sophisticated, but it does not always need to be so. Unstructured techniques can frequently work quite sufficiently. However, due to the degree of problems involved, and the historical results of systems having been poorly tested, clearly there *is* room for a more structured approach. The concepts used here allow planning and/or evaluation of the testing of any computerized system, whether information processing systems or real-time. This does not assume the usage of any specific set of test documentation standards (for example, ANSI/IEEE 829 or DoD-Std 2167A) or any specific testing tool or tool set. However, the usage of a standard for test documentation is highly recommended because of the consistency that this will ensure.

Note that this chapter attempts to be complete as to the *possible levels* of testing to be employed. This does not infer or assume that all such levels *should* be employed, certainly not for every system. Realistic test planning must begin with choosing the test levels needed for the system prior to deployment. All testing is based on the satisfaction of requirements. It should be noted that (while not advisable) many systems have informal, unwritten requirements in addition to their formal, written ones. In the testing process, these unwritten requirements must be acknowledged and taken into account, just as the formal ones need to be. They are an inseparable part of the user's **expectations**.

The first difficulty in planning the testing of a system, is discovering what the requirements really are, so that tests may be designed for them. Even when (if?) a formal requirements document exists, and even if this document is "complete" and up-to-date, it usually has not been written with the testing process taken into account. Once the requirements have been discovered, a table of requirements must be constructed and agreed on by all parts of the project's developing and management organization. Then, and only then, can the test planning process begin.

Clearly indicate test applicability for each and every requirement. The primary testing objective is that all requirements should be tested. To do so, every requirement must be clearly identified and labeled. This labeling must index the requirement as to its level in the hierarchy of requirements and should also indicate the source of the requirement. This greatly aids in the efficiency of the testing processes.

ISO 9000 Compatibility

ISO 9001 contains three paragraphs which are concerned with testing. Paragraph 4.10 is concerned with inspecting and testing. Inspecting is covered in chapter 9 of this book, please refer to it there. Paragraph 4.11 concerns itself with control of inspection, measuring and test equipment (notice the difference, 4.10 is concerned with the processes while 4.11 with the equipment and instrumentation). And paragraph 4.12 is concerned with inspection and test status. Let's briefly examine what each of these means to the SQA practitioner.

Both inspection and testing concern themselves with validation of the software product. They are **methods**. Chapter 9 treats questions of the various inspection techniques, so they are not dealt with here. However, we should state that the basic difference (for software) is that inspections (or reviews, and so on) are "in-process" while testing is usually more "final." Testing, being a final validation, is of obvious importance. Let us not misunderstand, final does not necessarily mean at the end, because in software there are always many "ends." Where these sections of the standard deal with receiving inspection and testing of **incoming** software (as well as what is being produced by the organization) this does not concern us here, but rather in chapter 12, Supplier control. Paragraphs 4.10.3 deal with the questions of in-process testing (they also deal with in-process inspection, which we discussed above). That is, this part of the standard addresses unit testing and integration testing.[1] Which are two kinds of "ends" in that they terminate phases of the life-cycle. The most interesting aspect is paragraph "b" where it states that the product will be held until the required (read: planned, in the quality plan, as per paragraph a) reports have been received and verified. I have very seldom seen software projects that could allow that, but it is a nice thought. We can all only hope that this one day becomes practical. The next paragraph, 4.10.4 discusses "final" testing. This states that:

> No product shall be dispatched until all the activities specified in the quality plan and/or documented procedures have been satisfactorily completed and the associated data and documentation are available and authorized.

One can only reiterate the thoughts expressed concerning the previous quote, that they are great ideas, but so seldom do they happen that their practicality must be called into question. What this does mean, however, is that this should be made a corporate goal. Professor Ince[2] evidently agrees with this, as he does not really add anything to the actual text of the standard.

The paragraph dealing with "test equipment" (paragraph 4.11) can be used to imply the kinds of test instrumentation tools used for software testing today. Darrel Ince says here what is probably the most important single thing anyone could say about testing:

> It is important that all testing activities give rise to documentation which demonstrates that the tests have taken place and have been carried out correctly. This directive is not only important for system and acceptance testing, but is important for developmental testing activities such as unit testing.

> Remember what was stated above:
>
> "Testing is simply a controlled measurement of performance."
>
> When this is kept in mind, the importance of this quotation becomes self-evident.

The combination of "controlled" and "measurement" must mean that the process, and its results, are well documented. The only excuse for not doing so, is a desire to hide facts or incompetence. Very harsh words, but then the marketplace can be very harsh. This is a critical legal question, as well. This is the only reasonable way to protect against product liability suits. The standard details a nine step procedure for controlling this (paragraph 4.11.2). With the only exception that "calibration" of test equipment, for software, probably means establishing a corporate baseline for expected results, I strongly suggest that this procedure be adhered to, even if ISO 9001 certification is not a concern.

The final paragraph of ISO 9001 (paragraph 4.12 – Inspection and test status) only really discusses what has already been said, that the results of tests be documented and recallable (that is, one can easily find the document and supply someone with a copy). The only thing worthy of adding here is the question of release of a nonconforming product. At the risk of belaboring the obvious, suffice it to say that the practice of having an appendix at the back of a manual called "known problem" has become quite common. This is terribly insufficient, but certainly the very least that ought to be allowed. We always know where we have *"not quite been successful."*

CMM Compatibility

An organized process of testing is part of the level 3 software product engineering *key process area*. Like all current approaches, CMM recognizes that testing has to be planned and carried out over a number of phases according to a predefined process. The test criteria for acceptance should be developed and then reviewed by the customer or end user. Tests are required to employ effective methods, and testing adequacy has to be determined beforehand according to the employed strategy and the software level to be tested. Strategies may include functional (black box), structural (white box) and statistical. The software levels are defined as unit test, integration test, system test and acceptance test. Coverage is to be defined for each test. The various levels include statement coverage, path coverage, branch coverage, or usage profile. At each level, readiness criteria for testing are established and used. For example, software has successfully completed integration testing before entering system testing. Regression testing is performed at each test level whenever the software or its environment changes. The test plan, test procedures and test cases pass peer review before they are to be used.

Detailed project test planning starts at the requirements stage by the group responsible for system and acceptance testing. Their first task is to analyze each software requirement to verify that it can be tested. Integration tests are planned according to the project's defined software process. System and acceptance tests are planned to demonstrate that the software satisfies its requirements.

During development each code unit is to undergo peer review and unit testing before it is to be considered complete and placed under configuration management. Integration test cases and procedures are to be reviewed with the people responsible for software requirements and design and for the system and acceptance testing. The integration testing is to be performed against the appropriate baselined version of the software requirements and design documents. System and acceptance testing preparations are given adequate resources early enough to prepare testing documentation, schedule testing resources, develop test drivers, and simulators. Test cases and procedures are planned and prepared by a test group that is independent of the developers. Problems identified during testing are documented and tracked to closure. Finally, the test results are documented and used to determine if the software satisfies its requirements.

Software Testing Taxonomy

What is software testing?

What is software testing and why do we need to test software? As one (very bright, but rather narrow-minded) engineer once said to one of the authors, "The software should be written to work, the first time." (Unfortunately, this engineer was the Managing Director of a high-tech aerospace company.) The answer to that is, of course, to define what "... written to work ..." means. Generally, it needs to mean to determine standards of correctness, reliability, robustness and efficiency. As we see from the chapter on planning quality goals, these are not trivial to define, which is why most people simply do not bother – doubt being generally easier to manage than technology. However, as in most complex human endeavors, simply knowing the reasons is a large step forward, but hardly sufficient. The **prerequisites** for establishing an **effective** software testing program are a clear requirements definition for the system, a clear design specification for the software and a clear reliability and quality specification for the final product. As a professional, how many times have you seen any of these, much less, all of them on one project?

How do we go about preparing to test software? Via a test plan which contains clear objectives and well-defined test phases. These phases will almost always include, at least: unit (module) testing, integration testing and system testing; well-defined involvement of software quality assurance (the depth of this involvement is somewhat a matter of opinion, but we shall present some guidelines) and acceptance testing (which is not really testing in the usual sense, but more on that later).

Those who should be involved in the testing, or rather those functions which need to be involved are: analysts/designers; programmers; quality control personnel; quality assurance personnel; project management; sales/marketing management and corporate management. These are all necessary for the product to be an ultimate success. Anything less than this increases the product's level of risk.

One must remember that debugging is not testing. Every developer debugs. Very few really understand testing – even fewer really perform testing. This section contains an *introductory taxonomy* of software testing. It is divided into separate parts, outlining a general classification scheme which is hierarchical – that is, each broad category contains a list of the specific testing classifications, techniques or classes within that particular category set. This is very general and basic by intent. It has been confined to contain only basic outlines of the classifications and their constituent parts, one might say, keywords. Testing, by its nature, must be preplanned, prebudgeted and rigorously controlled. **Testing is always a critical development activity.**

Figure 10.2 is a taxonomy of testing, providing the reader with a testing life-cycle viewpoint. Appendix V is a different kind of testing taxonomy. The appendix provides the reader with a guide-list to testing techniques. Neither one of them is intended to be training guides. If the objective is training in testing techniques, the best books that this author knows of, are those by Dr Boris Beizer (refer to the References). If the objective is training in test planning techniques, such a book is to be added to this series of books, by the same authors.

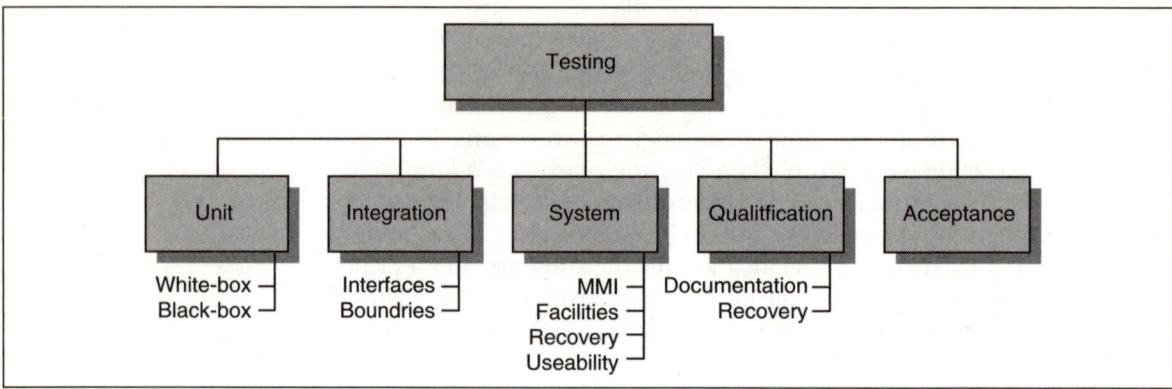

Figure 10.2 A software testing taxonomy, by testing life-cycle phase.

Anomalies

Anomaly and defect counts

In any testing activity, one of the major activities is the reporting of anomalies. An anomaly may be an actual defect in the system or it may reflect some unexpected occurrence which need not be classified as a bug (defect). In any case, some incident has occurred which needs further examination and, perhaps, correction. This activity reflects a large portion of the time and effort spent in testing.

The major rationale for testing should always be to assess the performance measurement of the system. Counting anomalies is one of these measurements. However, simply counting them is insufficient. They must be categorized, prioritized and reported. After that, they must then be converted into the appropriate change requests.

Category and Priority Classifications for Problem Reporting

Classification by category

Problems detected during software operation shall be classified by the following categories:

- Software problem. The software does not operate according to supporting documentation and the document is correct.
- Documentation problem. The software does not operate according to supporting documentation but the software operation is correct.
- Design problem. The software operated according to supporting documentation but a design deficiency exists. The design deficiency may not always result in a directly observable operational symptom but possesses the potential for creating further problems.

Classification by priority

Problems detected in the software or its documentation shall be classified by priority. In order to assign priority, we need an additional concept – that of a goal. **A goal** is the accomplishment of a mission-essential capability specified by a baselined requirement. Of course this also includes operational requirements.

- Priority 1. One of the following:
  - Prevents achieving one or more goals
  - Jeopardizes personnel safety
- Priority 2:
  - Jeopardizes the goals
  - Degrades performance, with **no** alternative work-around solution
- Priority 3. Degrades performance, but an alternative work-around is known
- Priority 4. Produces operator inconvenience or annoyance
- Priority 5. All other errors

Testing Organization

One must clearly indicate the organization(s) responsible for performing the testing activity and the venue of the tests. At the same time, one must also indicate test applicability for each and every requirement (system capability) for which a need has been determined in order for the system to be acceptable.

For the acceptance test procedure, this must be presented in great detail. In addition to the actual detailed procedures of how the test is performed, add to the beginning of the explanation *Entry criteria* and to the end of the explanation *Exit criteria*. These criteria must include, at least, where the system was before the test was invoked (state and/or mode) and where the system is to go to at test exit.

Pass/Fail Criteria

All criteria to be used to determine whether or not the test has been successful must be clearly stated, and agreed on by all sides, *in advance* of conducting the test. This is perhaps one of the most important aspects of testing, in general; and certainly one of the most significant for the acceptance test process in particular.

There are some kinds of systems (for instance, the man/machine subsystem for a larger system) which may not have clear pass/fail criteria. If it is possible, the criteria should be determined. When not practical however, do not attempt to "invent" what really cannot exist.

Requirement Labels

Every identified requirement must be clearly labeled as to its level in the hierarchy of requirements. For the acceptance test plan, clearly indicate the purpose of this test (i.e. verify ...). This is not necessary for the acceptance test procedure, but may be added if it enhances clarity.

All requirements must be labeled as to their source document(s). This indication is a part of the requirement's hierarchy. All labeled requirements shall be tested.

Recovery

A "subsection" of the plan is the question of recovery. Both the system test and the acceptance test should always be conducted under conditions which are as realistic as can be made practical. In real life, systems may sometimes fail because of external events (such as a power outage, and so on). Whatever may be the case, most systems today demand "fail soft" and safe recovery. This means that the system should begin where it left off. Each requirement must be clearly labeled as to:

- whether it affects the recovery capabilities of the system, and;

- whether it leaves trails of data or system states which will need to be recovered.

This information is of greater significance to the acceptance test procedure. It should be added to the acceptance test plan only if it clearly enhances clarity of the plan.

Unit Testing Background

Software unit testing is the process of evaluating the individual modules of a software product. Module evaluation infers measuring a module's performance against its requirements. [For reasons of brevity, the terms "module" and "unit" will henceforward be used interchangeably.]

For the purposes of unit testing, a module's "requirements" means: the requirements of the module, in terms of system needs, performance, etc. These module requirements/needs are defined (identified) by:

- The requirements which are defined by the SRS and have been allocated to this unit.
- System architecture requirements which have, as the result of the architecture analysis, caused derived demands to be placed on this unit.
- Detailed design derived needs.

The addition of the needs and requirements derived from the design stages means that the sum total of all requirements in the general test plan forms will not equal the sum of the requirements in the unit tests. **This is correct.** These totals **must not** be used for the evaluation of this planning process.

"Measuring" means exercising the module, using sample data, and comparing the results of this exercise (actual behavior) with the required and expected behavior. This expected behavior should have been defined prior to the completion of the unit's detailed design. That means the expected behavior must be part of the design verification criteria.

Generally (in most installations), the unit testing task is performed by the developers. Although this is the general case, it is not the optimal one. For best results, unit testing, like all other testing, should be performed by an independent body, albeit in this case within the developing organization. In projects which are not particularly large, these tests can be effectively performed by the developers, provided that the test planning is heavily influenced by QA and the actual testers are not the same people who developed the units being tested. (Notice what was just said: unit tests are to be **planned**. Another surprise, the results need to be reported, not discarded.) A method which may be employed is to divide the developers into (say) three groups: group A tests C's products, group B tests A's products and group C tests B's products. This provides for a minimum degree of independence.

Software unit testing activities include

- Test procedures for conducting tests shall be developed and recorded in the corresponding software unit development files.
- Evaluations of the source code for each software unit, the test procedures, the software unit test procedures and results and a specified percentage of the set of updated software development files.

Unit Test Planning Activities

Planning the general approach, resources and schedule

Inputs:	Project plans
	Software requirements documentation
Tasks:	Specify general approach
	Specify completeness requirements
	Specify termination requirements
	Determine resource requirements
	Specify a general schedule
Outputs:	General unit test planning information

Determine features to be tested

Inputs:	Unit requirements documentation
	Software architectural design
Tasks:	Study functional requirements
	Identify additional requirements and associated requirements
	Identify states of the unit
	Identify input and output data characteristics
	Select elements to be included in the test
Outputs:	List of elements to be included in the testing
	Request requirements clarifications
	Refine general plan
Inputs:	List of elements to be included in the testing
	General unit test planning information
Tasks:	Refine the approach
	Specify special resource requirements
	Specify a detailed schedule
Outputs:	Specific unit test planning information
	Special resource requests

Test Set Acquisition Activities

Design the test sets

Inputs: Unit requirements document
List of software elements to be included
Unit test planning information
Unit design documentation
Test specification from previous testing, if available

Tasks: Design architecture of the test set
Obtain explicit test procedures as required
Obtain the test case specifications
Augment, as required, the set of test case specifications based on design information
Complete the test design specification

Outputs: Unit test design specification
Separate test procedure specifications
Separate test case specifications
Unit design enhancement requests

Implement the refined plan and design

Inputs: Unit test planning information
Test case specifications
Software data structure descriptions
Test support resources
Test data from previous testing
Test tools from previous testing

Tasks: Acquire/obtain and verify test data
Obtain special resources
Obtain test items

Outputs: Verified test data
Test support resources
Configuration of test items
Initial summary information

Measurement activities

Execute the test procedure

Inputs: Verified test data
Test support resources
Configuration of test items
Test case specifications
Test procedure specifications
Failure analysis results, if produced

Tasks:	Run tests
	Determine results; analyze failures and take corrective action
Outputs:	Execution information logged in summary report
	Revised test specifications
	Revised test data

Check for termination

Inputs:	Completeness and termination requirements
	Execution information
	Test specifications
	Software data structure description, if required
Tasks:	Check for normal termination of testing process
	Check for abnormal termination of testing process
	Supplement the test set (acquire additional test data, if necessary)
Outputs:	Check information logged in test summary report
	Additional or revised test specifications, if necessary
	Additional test data, if necessary
	Evaluate the test effort and unit
Inputs:	Unit test design specification
	Execution information
	Checking information
	Separate test case specifications, if produced
Tasks:	Describe testing status
	Describe unit's status
	Complete the test summary report
	Ensure preservation of testing products
Outputs:	Complete test summary report
	Complete, stored collection of testing products

The following sections provide background concepts and briefly outline other types of testing.

Integration Testing – Background

Basically, integration testing means testing the combination of subunits onto an overall unit or system by means of interfacing. This, however, is insufficient as an explanation of the process.

Integration testing means a testing of several modules in order to check that the interfaces are defined and implemented correctly. It is an **orderly progression** of testing in which software components (units and/or subsystems) and/or hardware components are combined in a highly controlled and orderly manner and tested until the entire system has been constructed.

Full integration testing means the testing of the entire system (probably in stages) from the top-level component. This infers performing the integration testing process in a top-down fashion, building up the system from the top-level components on down (utilizing stubs).

Partial integration testing means testing of a set of components (modules) but not the entire set. This form of test is very common when one wishes to validate a build (a subsystem of a product which is to be delivered separately, usually for purposes of user evaluation). There is nothing wrong with this. That is, it can be a perfectly valid testing strategy. Providing that it is not used in replace of the top-down strategy, but rather, to augment it.

System Testing – Background

System testing is the process of exercising an integrated software system (or software/hardware system) with the objective of finding discrepancies between the performance of a system and its original objectives. By objectives, one may mean both those that have been formally defined and others that have not (or perhaps, not yet) been so. This means also, that the process attempts to verify that the system meets the requirements defined for it **and** the expectations of the prospective users.

Qualification Testing – Background

Qualification testing is a very formal test process, usually performed by the developer for the customer. Qualification testing of a system consists of performing a controlled exercise of the product in its deliverable state. A qualification test of each software configuration item (SCI) will usually be conducted on the target computer system or an equivalent system approved by the contracting agency (that means, the people who are footing the bills!). A test environment that complies with the **security** requirements of the contract must have been established.

At the time of qualification testing, the developer/contractor has stated that, to the best of his/her knowledge, all specified functions and requirements of the system, are satisfied. The qualification test must be thoroughly planned and the documentation (test plans and test procedures) must be approved by the client/user before the tests begin. The tests must be performed in the **actual operating environment** (target hardware and software). The client, or the client's duly appointed representative is expected to observe the test and to aid in the recording of the results.

Plans for conducting the formal qualification test should be developed and documented in the software test plan (STP). The testing will include, among other items, stressing the system at the limits of the specified requirements and probably beyond them. The testing may include testing of SCIs integrated with other SCIs and with hardware configuration items (HCIs) that comprise the system. Plans for installation, test, configuration control, and maintenance of each item of the environment must be documented. The persons conducting the testing activities should **not** be the persons who developed the software or are responsible for the software. Every effort should be used to implement refined techniques of requirements traceability, and these should show that all requirements are satisfied or partially satisfied. Each test case which satisfies a requirement should be documented.

For the developing agency, qualification testing is probably the most important of the tests needed during the maintenance phase of the product's life. (Remember Figure 4.1, maintenance is where most of the money goes.) Figure 10.1 shows how this is divided for the various maintenance problems that one can expect to encounter. This may not be identical for your organization, but this is what is happening in the industry as a whole. If you are far from this, I would start by checking my data.

Acceptance Testing – Background

The acceptance test is the set of procedures performed to ascertain a system's readiness for deployment by the intended end users. It is an independent, formally conducted, test to verify that all functional requirements of the tested system have been satisfied. The results of the process determine the acceptability (or reasons for rejection) of the system. Prior to beginning the acceptance test process, even prior to planning the acceptance tests, a set of acceptance criteria must be defined. These criteria shall have clear pass/fail characteristics, which are designed to be readily recognizable. Generally accepted practice is to create two separate documents (or for very small systems, one document with two sections); an acceptance test plan and an acceptance test procedure.

Software Test Description for the Lion Subsystem[3]

Quality Assurance Audit Report[4]
Contract No. XX/XX/2043
Revision No. 02
Dated: 20 August 1995[5]

Audit date: 31 August 1995

Audited by: Mordechai Ben-Menachem

Quality Awareness Ltd.

Documentation control
Index control

This document version # 1.0

Revision #	Paragraph #	Update date	New revision #	Comment

Table of Contents

Executive summary

Audit and verification methodology

1. This report provides the results of an audit and verification of the software test description (STD) document for the Lion subsystem.
2. The audit has analyzed the document in its "stand-alone" mode. The verification process has analyzed requirements traceability and matching of this document with the software requirements specification (SRS), the software development plan and the software test plan.
3. This analysis is being performed at the same time (or slightly after) the actual performance of the test. Therefore, this process has been performed in a formalized manner and a highly detailed report has been produced. The more trivial errors (e.g. spelling, English language usage, and so on) are corrected in the document body, against which we audited, and do not appear in this report.
4. These processes have been performed in accordance with the standard recognized practices for such activities. The audit has attempted to completely cover the document. The verification attempts to cover significantly more than half of the possible areas for error.

Audit and verification results

1. There are a large quantity of errors in the document under analysis. The vast majority of these errors are of types which will not pose significant problems for the quality of the system under test (e.g. spelling errors, typos, English language usage, and so on). Nonetheless, this auditor wishes to express the opinion that they should be corrected to bring this document to the expected level of quality for all deliverables of the system.
2. There are errors which should be corrected in order to ensure the quality of the testing process.
3. It is necessary to correct and re-review (re-audit) the document.

General comments

1. Requirements traceability is sometimes difficult to follow due to differences in wording between the two documents (SRS vs STD). It may be desirable to smooth out some of these inconsistencies by reviewing previously approved documents.
2. Inputs and outputs to the various functions are difficult to trace due to unexplained differences between their expressions in the STD and their equivalent expressions in the SRS. As an example, see paragraph 4.6.16.6. There are four inputs in the STD and only two in the SRS.[6] No indication is provided as to what has caused this discrepancy.

0. Preparation instructions

0.1 Title page

Title page, as required. However in the printout received there is a printer error.
Document control numbers, as required.

0.2 Table of contents

As required

1. Scope

As required

1.1 Identification

As required

1.2 System overview

As required

1.3 Document overview

As required

2. Reference documents

As required
Reference 2.3 c does not seem to appear in the software test plan as a prerequisite for test performance.

3. Formal qualification test preparations

a. This statement seems to conflict with the declarations of Appendix A.[7]
c. [1] Appendix C does not contain the test schedule table.[8]
[2] The schedule, as appears in the software development plan, is out of date and not relevant to this test.
[3] All succeeding paragraphs refer to this appendix, but the appendix is inconsistent with its references.

3.1 MMI general operations

3.1.1 T_MMI_GEN schedule
The required schedule appears to be absent.[9]
3.1.2 T_MMI_GEN pre-test procedures
3.1.2.1 Hardware preparation
As required

3.1.2.2   Software preparation
As required
3.1.2.3   Other pre-test preparation
As required

3.2   MMI forms

As required

3.3   State control test – T_SMM_STL

As required

3.4   Mode control test – T_SMM_MDC

As required

3.5   TSE test and error management test – T_TSE

As required

3.6   RTT GINA test – T_RTT_GINA

3.6.1   T_RTT_GINA schedule
As required

3.7   RTT radar test – T_RTT_RADAR

As required

3.8   RTT SIU test – T_RTT_SIU

As required

3.9   RTT system-A test – T_RTT_SYSA

As required

3.10   RTT other CDU test – T_RTT_OCDU

As required

3.11   SWS drivers test – T_SWS_DRV

As required

3.12   MSN navigation data test – T_MSN

As required

3.13   SWS EEPROM functions test – T_SWS_E2F

Listed not applicable, no explanation found.

3.14   SWS executive test – T_SWS_EXE

Listed not applicable, no explanation found.

3.15   SWS code/data loader test – T_SWS_LDR

Listed not applicable, no explanation found.

3.16   SWS Intel IM-III test – T_SWS_IM3

As required

4.   Formal qualification test descriptions

4.1   MMI general operations test – T_MMI_GEN

4.1.1   T_MMI_GEN_01
Either the test exists or not.[10] At least provide pointers and information for inputs and results. The whole test can not be N/A. Paragraph 4.1.10, while still insufficient, is slightly better.

4.1.2   T_MMI_GEN_02
Either the test exists or not. At least provide pointers and information for inputs and results. The whole test cannot be N/A. Paragraph 4.1.10, while still insufficient, is slightly better.
As a sample, the following test was applied.[11]
This paragraph was cross-checked with 4.2.7.6 (which is part of the T_MMI_FMS_xx). This test uses soft keys.
Using the requirements traceability table (appendix D) to the requirements document (SRS), we found no evidence to support that this test truly reflects all possibilities.

4.1.3   T_MMI_GEN_03
As required
Paragraph 4.1.10, while still insufficient, is slightly better.

4.1.4   T_MMI_GEN_04
As required
Paragraph 4.1.10, while still insufficient, is slightly better.
Possible problem, requirement 3.2.6.1 d lists three keys. The test selects two.

4.1.5   T_MMI_GEN_05
Either test exists or not. At least provide pointers and information for inputs and results. The whole test cannot be N/A.
Paragraph 4.1.10, while still insufficient, is slightly better.

4.1.6   T_MMI_GEN_06
Either test exists or not. At least provide pointers and information for inputs and results. The whole test cannot be N/A.
Paragraph 4.1.10, while still insufficient, is slightly better.

4.1.7   T_MMI_GEN_07
Either test exists or not. At least provide pointers and information for inputs and results. The whole test cannot be N/A.
Paragraph 4.1.10, while still insufficient, is slightly better.

4.1.8	T_MMI_GEN_08

Either test exists or not. At least provide pointers and information for inputs and results. The whole test cannot be N/A.
Paragraph 4.1.10, while still insufficient, is slightly better.

4.1.9	T_MMI_GEN_09
4.1.9.3	T_MMI_GEN_09 test inputs

Why N/A? The table definitely shows input.

4.1.10	T_MMI_GEN_010

Approximately as required. There is room for a better explanation of these requirements as tested.

4.2 MMI forms tests – T_MMI_FMS

4.2.1	T_MMI_FMS_01

As required

4.2.2	T_MMI_FMS_02

As required

4.2.3	T_MMI_FMS_03

As required
Reference 4.2.3.7 in 4.2.3.2 to prevent problems and time wastage.

4.2.4	T_MMI_FMS_04

As required
Recommend reference to 4.2.4.7 in 4.2.4.2 a. to prevent problems and time wastage.[12]

4.2.5	T_MMI_FMS_05

As required
Recommend reference to 4.2.5.7 in 4.2.5.2 a. to prevent problems and time wastage.
Paragraph 4.2.5.2 f. specifies a measurement in meters, 4.2.5.6 1b compares this using feet. Why is this wise?

4.2.6	T_MMI_FMS_06

As required

4.2.7	T_MMI_FMS_07

Paragraph 4.2.7.2 should supply a pointer to 4.2.7.7 to increase clarity.

4.2.8	T_MMI_FMS_08

As required

4.2.9	T_MMI_FMS_09

As required

4.2.10	T_MMI_FMS_10

As required

4.2.11	T_MMI_FMS_11

As required

4.2.12	T_MMI_FMS_12

Paragraph 4.2.12.6 #9 and #10 need clarification – have we powered-off?

4.2.13	T_MMI_FMS_13

As required

4.2.14   T_MMI_FMS_14
           As required

4.2.15   T_MMI_FMS_15
           As required

4.2.16   T_MMI_FMS_16
           As required

4.2.17   T_MMI_FMS_17
           As required

4.2.18   T_MMI_FMS_18
           As required

4.2.19   T_MMI_FMS_19
           As required

4.2.20   T_MMI_FMS_20
           As required

4.2.21   T_MMI_FMS_21

4.2.21.6 T_MMI_FMS_21 - Test procedures
           How does one visually verify that "... bits ... were not sent"?

4.2.22   T_MMI_FMS_22
           How does one visually verify that "... bits ... were not sent"?

4.2.23   T_MMI_FMS_23
           How have we gotten to CDU #2?

4.2.24   T_MMI_FMS_24
           As required

4.2.25   T_MMI_FMS_25
           As required

4.2.26   T_MMI_FMS_26
           How does one visually verify that "... bits ... were not sent"?

4.2.27   T_MMI_FMS_27
           The STD states that the test results are to be visually verified. How
           does one visually verify that "... bits ... were not sent" ?

4.2.28   T_MMI_FMS_28
           As required

4.2.29   T_MMI_FMS_29
           SRS Paragraph 3.2.6.24.6 defines the logic as being in DRS[13]
           3.6.2 and ORS[14] 4.5.5.
           Have these been verified against ORS 6.5?
           This requirement is not traceable, as defined. Comparing this with
           4.2.30.6 #1 suggests that the chapter number might be incorrect.

4.2.30   T_MMI_FMS_30
           As required

4.2.31   T_MMI_FMS_31
           As required

4.2.32   T_MMI_FMS_32

4.2.32.3 T_MMI_FMS_32 - Input
           Inputs listed here do not match those listed in the SRS.

4.2.32.6 T_MMI_FMS_32 - Test procedure
           [#1] The SRS lists 4.5.7 & 5.5.1.

4.2.33   T_MMI_FMS_33
           As required

4.2.34	T_MMI_FMS_34
	As required
4.2.35	T_MMI_FMS_35
	As required
4.2.36	T_MMI_FMS_36
	As required
4.2.37	T_MMI_FMS_37
	As required
4.2.38	T_MMI_FMS_38
4.2.38.7	T_MMI_FMS_38 – assumptions and constraints
	The last sentence of this paragraph is unclear.
4.2.39	T_MMI_FMS_39
4.2.39.7	T_MMI_FMS_38 – assumptions and constraints
	The last sentence of this paragraph is unclear.
4.2.40	T_MMI_FMS_40
	As required
4.2.41	T_MMI_FMS_41
4.2.41.6	T_MMI_FMS_41 – test procedures
	[#1] The SRS lists the reference as 4.6.3.3.
4.2.42	T_MMI_FMS_42
4.2.42.6	T_MMI_FMS_41 – test procedures
	[#1] The SRS lists the reference as 4.6.3.3.
4.2.43	T_MMI_FMS_43
	As required

4.3 T_SMM_STL

As required

4.4 T_SMM_MDC

4.4.2 T_SMM_MDC initialization
[6] IDEA simulator, Not referenced.

4.5 Test and error management test – T_TSE

As required

4.6 RTT GINA test – T_RTT_GINA

This test, as defined, is not a full qualification test as defined by 2167A. The contractor needs to be aware of the inherent limitations.
Other than this aforementioned limitation, this test is defined as required.

4.7 RTT radar test – T_RTT_RADAR

This set of tests (quantity of 34) is defined as required.
However, the tests, as specified, are limited in scope because of the limitations of the simulator being used for them. The contractor needs to be aware of this limitation.

4.8 RTT SIU test – T_RTT_SIU

This set of tests (quantity of 3) is defined as required.

4.9 RTT system-A Test – T_RTT_SSA

As required

4.10 RTT other CDU test – T_RTT_OCDU

As required

4.11 MSN navigation data test – T_MSN

As required

4.12 SWS driver test – T_SWS_DRV

As required

4.13 SWS EEPROM functions test – T_SWS_E2F

As required

4.14 SWS executive test – T_SWS_EXE

As required

4.15 SWS code/data loader test – T_SWS_LDR

As required

4.16 SWS Intel IM-III test – T_SWS_IM3

As required

5. Notes

As required

6. Appendices

References to 4.11.nn are formatted differently from the remainder of the table.
References to several STD paragraphs appear to be missing from the requirements traceability table:

4.12.2
4.12.3
4.12.4
4.12.5
4.12.6

Notes

1   Ince, D (1994) *ISO 9001 and Software Quality Assurance; Quality Forum*, McGraw-Hill. A very small book, but good treatment of the strengths of ISO 9001 *vis-à-vis* software. Sometimes a little too much of an effort is made (to my taste) to show how everything fits nicely rather then really showing where they do not fit. A little bit of constructive criticism does not hurt.

2   Ince, D (1994) *ISO 9001 and Software Quality Assurance*, McGraw-Hill.

3   The name of the document being audited.

4   This report.

5   The identification of the contract and the date of the audited document.

6   The SRS document used for this audit is revision number 2, dated 5 December 1994.

7   Many analysts try to say that a QA audit of a document only checks that the document author has adhered to the standard for this particular type of document. This author believes, after more then 20 years of experience, that this is not only insufficient, it is counter-productive. This statement is a good example of the kind of conflicts that the SQA auditor should try to look for. Clearly, this makes the auditing task more difficult. However, it also makes the audit much more valuable to the document author and to the project as whole.

8   The STD claimed that the schedule was there. However, this was found to be inadequate.

9   Tactful phrasing is always wise.

10   All paragraphs in the STD were listed as N/A – not applicable. The auditor did not accept this as valid or sufficient.

11   The following technique was applied to ascertain the validity of what was written in the STD. This is a good example of the kind of techniques used. This implements the idea of "following a thread."

12   Sometimes the auditor demands, sometimes only recommends. Finding the "right balance" is never easy and the are no hard and fast rules for it. A good auditor needs to "feel" what is right.

13   Design requirements specification – a nonstandard document name used by this project.

14   Operational requirements specification – a nonstandard document name used by this project.

PROBLEM REPORTING AND CORRECTIVE ACTION

11

This chapter identifies and describes the procedures to be used for problem tracking, including all the various forms of corrective actions to be taken for them and the methods to be deployed for performing them.

PROBLEM REPORTING AND CORRECTIVE ACTION IS DEALT WITH in chapter 8 of the SQAP. This chapter of the SQAP is perhaps the most critical one for maintenance of the future software product. That does not mean it is not relevant to the development stages, it certainly is. It just affects the much larger sum of money during maintenance. Remember, corrective action must be taken for any problem found. This applies to the requirements, design and/or testing stages, as well as to the deliverable product. Experience has shown that only about 20% of the time spent on maintenance is to correct coding errors. Most of it is the correction of misunderstood requirements and design faults. Any project larger than a few staff-years and consisting of more than (say) two software professionals needs some formal system for software configuration management. Usually the system will be computerized. In fact, today there really is no excuse for not employing a computer-based package. There are a number of "off-the-shelf" products, most of which are reasonably good and usually inexpensive. Such a formal system should be activated no later than the approval of the first baselined documents. In many projects, these documents may be software requirements specifications. Certainly, organized **change control** procedures must not be delayed to a time later than this. It is strongly recommended that this procedure be activated earlier if possible, for example for storage of, (say) the request for proposal (RFP), contract and final offerings.

Controlling the processes of change is part of software configuration control, which is the second of the four major parts of the software configuration management task (together with: software configuration identification, software configuration status accounting and software configuration auditing). Software configuration control is a mandatory task assignment in the management of any project. In other words, all projects engage in it, there is no choice. Some projects manage the process better, some less so. Occasionally it may be more formal, sometimes less so. The "degree of **formalism**" is not significant. The degree of **control** is of extreme importance.

Requesting a Change

In many organizations, requesting a change may begin with a form, such as an "engineering change proposal" (ECP) form. Note that this statement refers to the beginning of the formal request for a change, but not necessarily the actual start of the process of making a change. This "process of change" may have begun from any of several kinds of formal or informal inputs, such as an error or trouble report (hopefully, also formally reported) or a fresh, original idea from some project personnel. Whatever form is chosen to be used by the organization, the originator of the change request is required to fill in the change request form according to accepted standards. In any case, this chapter of the plan discusses only problem reporting and not all of change requesting. For that area, one should refer to the software configuration management plan (which is out of the scope of this book).[1]

Change Costs

While the whole area of change requests, being part of configuration control and not really quality assurance, is out of the scope of this book, one item is worth spending a little bit of time on – the costs of changes.

All changes cost money. Any manager who forgets that is in need of a vacation. Sometimes these costs can be very high – at least to somebody. One of the authors was involved in a project (as manager of software quality assurance) which was developing a major telephone system (for a specialized application). A contractor had a bidding policy which was designed to *get the project*. They accomplished this by estimating the costs and then bid 70% of the calculated outlay. Afterwards, they would "get them" on the changes. Of course, by that time, the client was a captive slave. In this particular project, the contracting organization happened to have a manager who was very clever. He simply stated: "No changes! None what-so-ever." With no leeway permitted, the contractor lost some $170 million on the contract. (No mistake, $170,000,000.00 – that number came from the person who was their senior executive in charge of purchasing.) From what I saw on the project, the number makes sense. By the bye, that project had another distinction, probably the worst conditions for software development that I have ever seen: from bad chairs through worse lighting to horrid acoustics (every footfall echoed along the corridor). But all that is for a different book about management and productivity.

Any change request should be analyzed for expected costs, before the change is authorized. Project management, and the requester, need to be notified of these expected costs before authorization so that informed decisions can be made. In cases where the need for the change is self-evident (for example resulting from an obvious error/failure in existing software, or an error discovered in a review process) this notification certainly should not obstruct the process of change implementation, and notification may be forwarded after the change has been effected. Information concerning the expected and actual recorded costs of changes should be recorded as part of the project management database. The costs of a change are divided into two parts:

- **Change evaluation cost** – The number of staff-hours needed to evaluate (i.e., analyze) the requested change. This analysis shall always include all ramifications of the proposed change, including, but not limited to, risks to existing functionality. This analysis must be provided to a change control board (CCB) in technical terms and for analysis of possible system-wide effects. One of the important aspects of this analysis is the total expected cost of implementation of the change. This cost is recorded on (updates) the software change request form.
- **Change implementation cost** – The number of staff-hours needed to fully implement the requested change. "Fully implement" means: updating documents, reviews and audits of all new or changed documents; updating source code and fully testing (including regression testing).

Change Traceability

Together with the configuration manager, the CCB validates matching of source items to object items. This matching has two meanings. First, source code to "compiled" object code (this is the simple case) – this usually requires a "continuation trace;" i.e., all relevant documents, back to the ultimate (effected) requirement. Second, a source document to its derived (object) document, e.g., the detailed design which is derived from the top-level design.

The Change Control Board (CCB)

The CCB is usually composed of several permanent members and (perhaps) several ad hoc members. As needs arise, project team members may take part in CCB meetings. In any case, the CCB is empowered to summon other project team members for information gathering purposes. Optimally, the CCB should be composed of four permanent members: A representative of project management and/or technical management (who acts as chair of the board); a representative of the user(s); a representative of product assurance, generally this will be software quality assurance (who may act as the coordinator of board activities); and of course, the software configuration manager.

Some points of clarification may be in order. A representative of the user (or the prospective user) may not be available. In this case, the product assurance representative adopts this additional role. The software configuration management function may frequently be rolled into project development. In this case, the development manager may adopt this role, as well. In certain rare cases, the development manager may act as sole representative of the whole committee (e.g., for a spelling error, when the need for the change is obvious and its costs are minimal).

Generally, good practice is for the CCB to meet monthly. Other meetings may take place at more frequent intervals with partial membership. All meetings must be completely documented and their findings and decisions must be approved by the full board. During development, certain circumstances may call for needed changes at times, or with priorities, that do not allow for the delay inherent in a full committee meeting. In such a case, the software product manager will usually take responsibility for implementation of the change. The product manager is responsible for justifying to the board all actions of this nature. Under no circumstances will irreversible action be taken (such as a change of an approved item for which formal software configuration management has not yet begun). Implemented actions, based on unapproved (by the CCB) change requests will be reversible to their previous state.

CCB Purposes

The CCB is a technical committee which is created with the express purpose of providing both management and development with planned organizational structure specifically designed for controlling processes of change. The context is the proven postulate that this process is the most difficult task in software development and maintenance. Every change request (CR) which is generated is preprocessed by either the software configuration management organization or the customer service organization. Only then is the request forwarded to the CCB for actual processing. This includes allocation of the unique change identifier and a basic validation of the request as to source/authorization (whether the requester is permitted/authorized to request a change, or this particular kind of change) and whether or not the request has been previously processed. Repeated processing of the same change or problem report is a very frequent occurrence, which can cause very large losses.

The first stage is to evaluate and analyze the request. This is similar to systems analysis for any development, but the emphasis is to properly understand, ahead of implementation of the change, what the implementation costs are likely to be. With this stage, the "software change request" form is completed. The second stage is, of course, the actual implementation of the change, with all of its implications. This includes, of course, all standard processes of software quality assurance, testing, software configuration management, and so on. With this stage, the "software change authorization" form is completed when the implementation is begun. This is the "act" that initiates the implementation. The third stage of the CCB's participation consists of the follow-up activities. The "software change notice" form is used at the conclusion of the implementation of the requested change. This form "closes" the CR. (See the figure below for a state diagram of this process.)

> CR processing by the CCB consists of three stages, two of them before implementation. The idea behind this multistaged process is to be able to base the decision making process on an "accurate prediction" as to what the true costs of this development will be. Obviously, this prediction has limits, as does any prediction in software development. The whole picture will not be available from the analysis. The objective of the first stage is, and must be, acquisition of primary information for optimal decision making.

CMM Compatibility

CMM treats problem reports along with change requests as part of the software configuration management *key process area* of level 2. As a key process area, the requirements and activities are defined in a very detailed manner. Among the relevant requirements are a software configuration control board (SCCB), to manage the baselines, the change requests, and coordinate all configuration activities among all the groups involved in a project. In addition, there must be a software configuration management (SCM) group that implements the SCM – that is, it carries out the policies of the SCCB. Despite all the specifications for SCM, level 2 problems and change requests are merely to be "initiated, recorded, reviewed, approved and tracked according to a documented procedure."

In level 3, activity 9 of the *key process area* software product engineering, deals with tracking "defects" identified in peer reviews and testing. Details to be collected and analyzed are to be specified in the project's software process. The set of examples of such details includes: defect description, defect category, defect severity, units containing the defect, units affected by the defect, activity where the defect was introduced, peer review or test where the defect was discovered, description of the scenario being run that identified the defect, expected result and actual result that identified the defect.

Level 5, optimizing, has a *key process area* entitled defect prevention. Basically, the objective of this process is to utilize the history of defects and problems that have been accumulated in the configuration management and defect tracking activities and develop methods to prevent problems. The groups involved in the process relate defects to their identified direct causes, incorporate any other recognized problem sources, and re-examine the software development process. Finally the process undertakes to modify processes and develop activities to prevent defects. An essential part of the activity includes detailed statistics of defects before and continuing measurements after defect prevention processes are implemented.

The authors identify with the goals and most of the processes in the CMM. However, the production of quality software requires that discovered defects and reported problems be treated properly in every viable software development environment. It cannot wait for certification at level 5 or even level 3. Later in the chapter we will address these issues.

ISO 9000 Compatibility

One of the most important strengths of ISO 9000 (ISO 9001) and one of the glaring weaknesses of IEEE 730, is the relative emphasis on on-going maintenance of the product. In ISO 9001 this comes under two headings: paragraph "4.14 Corrective and preventive action" and paragraph "4.19 Servicing." In particular, ISO 9001 states the requirements for corrective and preventive actions separately (in paragraphs 4.14.2 and 4.14.3, corresponding). Not only that, but they go on to state (as part of the *preventive* side):

> ...
> b) determination of the steps needed to deal with any problems requiring preventive action;
>
> and also ...
>
> d) ensuring that relevant information on actions taken is submitted for management review.

What this means, is that a methodology is provided for truly taking care of problems, as a long-term issue. In our treatment of the questions, we attempt to cover all of the items.

On the other hand, 730 does not discuss **preventive** maintenance, at all. The IEEE standard says:

This section shall:

1) Describe the practices and procedures to be followed for reporting, tracking and resolving problems identified in both software items and the software development and maintenance process.
2) State the specific organizational responsibilities concerned with their implementation.

While it is to be highly commended for including " ... the software development and maintenance process ... ," just this is not sufficient. Interestingly enough, the corresponding guide to the use of the standard is no more helpful[2] in this case. In other areas, the guide is much better (that is, its use is more fruitful).

Problem Reporting

Concept

It is very important to make certain, at all times, that all change request procedures are built and maintained in accordance with your corporation's recognized standards, whether internal or external (for example ISO 9000). At the same time, they must also be in accordance with company/corporate specifications. This is true, even when these may be in conflict. What do you do then? Fight! Someone needs to make known to the powers-that-be that such a problem exists. This is not a trivial problem. One of these standards is no longer suitable to the realities of the organization. If management is not made aware of this, it could prove to be very expensive. Also make a point of checking whether these procedures have been implemented as described by project documentation.

Problem Discovering

Software problems may frequently be discovered by various people and under different circumstances. Usually, any valid user of the software is allowed to report the existence of a problem. Unfortunately, the software industry is only too aware that not all users of a software product are always valid users. This forces on all support personnel the existence of a problem of "user validation."

Writing and Verifying the Software Problem Report

All software problems should be reported via a software problem report (SPR). However, as we know, not all problems are created equal. Some problems are going to be reported by a screaming user. (You know, we all have certain kinds of users that when they say "Jump" our only answer is "How high?") When one of these reports a problem, we do not ask them to submit a written report. We meekly say thank you for the information and I shall get right on to it. In other words, write the report yourself. Management is responsible for establishing a clear definition of "user validation" and communicating this definition to the support personnel. SPRs should be verified by ascertaining that the problem which has been reported is reproducible. In some cases, the problem reported is the result of a nonreproducible set of circumstances. This may very well be legitimate. The prerequisites for this type of problem to be processed are:

- a sufficient quantity and detail of documentation has been provided to allow software maintenance to process the problem in a reasonable and efficient manner
- quality assurance has specifically allowed the problem to be processed despite its irreproducibility.

Occasionally, problems are reported as software problems, which are the result of a misunderstanding, by the operator/change reporter, of something which may be unrelated to software. It is imperative to remember that a SPR, once validated and passed to the SCCB becomes a CR. Implementing the SPR is always performed via the procedure for implementation of CRs and it is the responsibility of SQA to verify that this is the way it is done. (Every SPR is, of course, a request to change something.)

Are all change request procedures in accordance with recognized standards (e.g., IEEE Std 1498, IEEE 1074 or DoD-Std 2167A)? And in accordance with company/corporate specifications?

Have these procedures been implemented as described by the documentation?

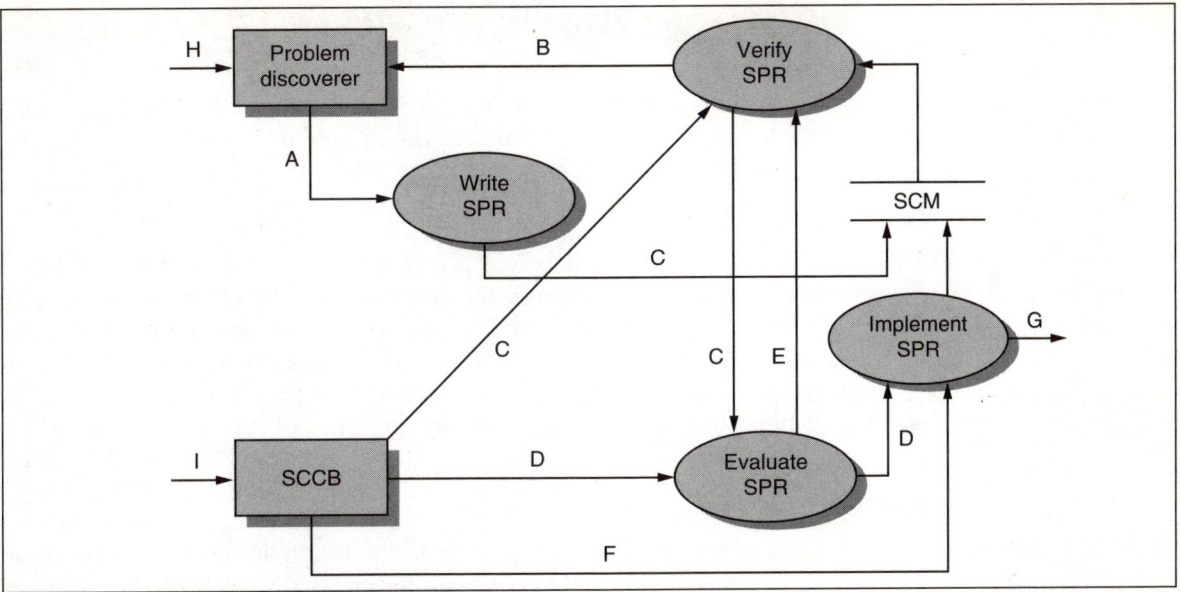

Figure 11.1 Software problem report processing.

Table 11.1 Data Flows in Problem Report Processing

A.	Problem documentation
B.	Invalid SPR
C.	SPR
D.	Change request (CR)
E.	Nonimplementable change
F.	Change authorization
G.	Change/test results
H.	Problems
I.	Change standards

Corrective Action

The concepts of corrective actions are two dimensional. The simple use of the term refers to how a reported problem is to be corrected. The more long-reaching concept is how that problem may be **prevented** from **occurring again** in the future. This implies **process improvement**, which of course, is the golden ring at the end of the race.

The basic issue of how we are to treat a problem that has been reported has been covered by the previous discussion. Issues concerning process improvement are more significant. The most important thing to keep in mind here is that you cannot solve a long-term problem without high quality information as to what really is happening. This means that you need to have a system for ascertaining not only the quantities of defects/anomalies that have occurred, but you must also record where they occurred and where they were discovered (notice that dichotomy, it is very important).

Let's look at a basic example. We know that a life-cycle will contain a series of steps. (Remember, our life-cycle is a model of the way we develop our software.) These steps will generally be performed sequentially with some limited parallel overlaps. A typical life-cycle may have (say) seven steps:[3]

- Conceptualize the problem
- Requirements analysis and specification
- Software architectural (high-level) design and detailed design
- Implementation and coding
- Test – including (at least) unit, integration and system
- Installation and checkout (including porting of data and work culture)
- Operations and maintenance

Correspondingly, we know that in every one of these process steps we can make an error, we can discover an error that has been made or we could have (but did not) discover an error. That is not double talk, we shall illustrate this with an example. An error is made in a requirement. Ideally, we discover the error at that point. This is ideal simply because it is the least expensive. Unfortunately, life is seldom ideal. Not every error is discoverable at the point where it occurred. Some can only be discovered at some later time. We continue with our system and have arrived at the unit tests. We now discover that requirement error. We should, at this point try to learn two things; when the error occurred (say, during requirements analysis) and when the error could have been first discovered (say, during detailed design). We can now learn how to improve our various filters at each step, so that in future projects we shall be more capable of discovering these kinds of errors earlier in the life-cycle.

Dividing the total numbers of defects (anomalies) discovered by the total number of characteristics and multiplying that by 100 gives the **quality level** (QL) of the module or product (in percentage of defects). This measurement may be used in relation to function point counting methods. Taking 100 and subtracting the QL gives the **degree of excellence**. We recommend to plot a graph for each subsystem, with the QL by part number/subsystem. Over time, this will show to management the end results of your work. That is, it will display process improvement.

Figure 11.2 below, depicts a state diagram for corrective actions. A corrective action may result from the need to correct a defect which has been discovered in the product, or the desire to implement a new feature. In either case, there are many states that this may have.

The first state, and the default state at any time we do not know how to attach a better definition, is the **open** state. Every corrective action begins this way. Bye the by, this state diagram is the way that the states of a corrective action should be. We have seen some companies (including one very large company – who will remain unnamed, but one of the biggest) display a different state diagram (see Fig. 11.3). This state diagram is not correct. The differences are not just graphics. Attempting to manage change by this set of states could be a very bad career move.

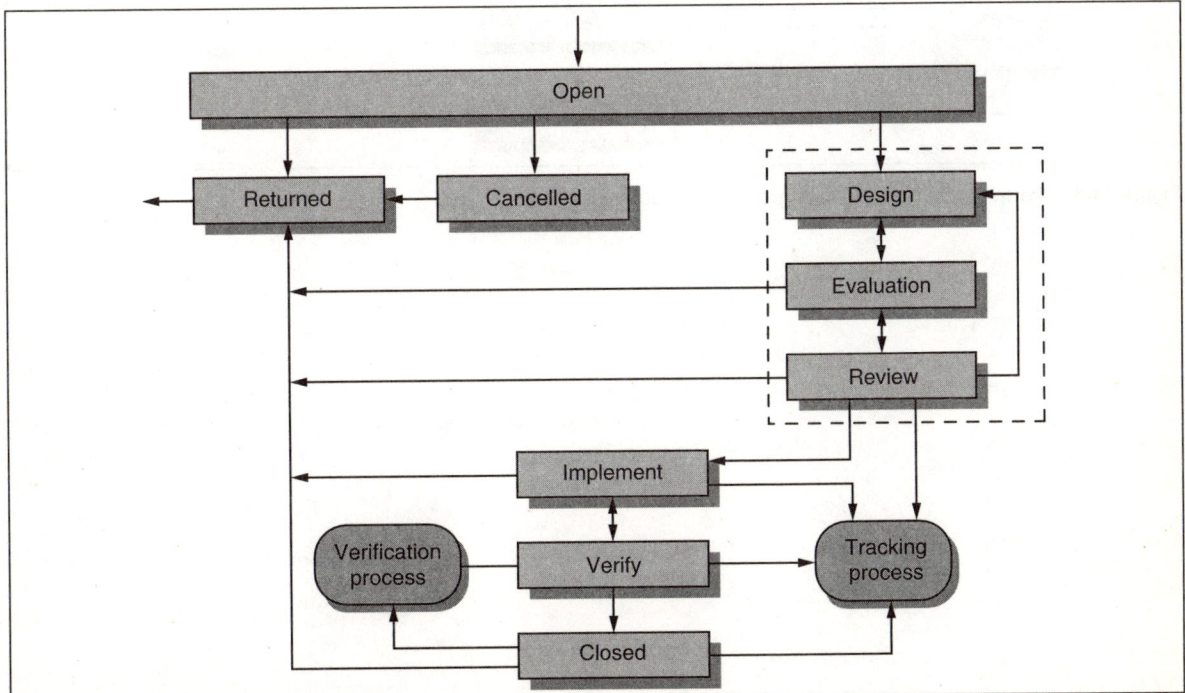

Figure 11.2   A correct state diagram of corrective actions.

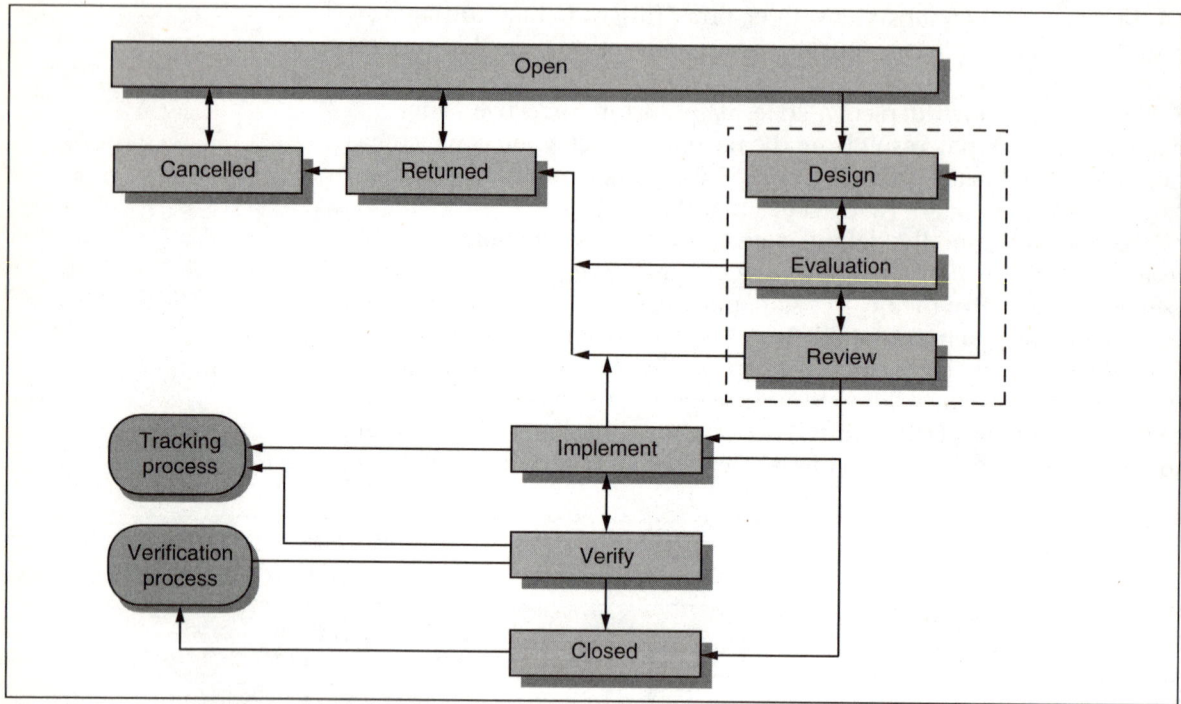

Figure 11.3   An incorrect state diagram for corrective actions.

SQAP planning worksheet # 11.1
Problem reporting and corrective action

Project: _____   Planner: _____

Date: _____   SQAP: _____

Problem source	Required actions	Performed by	Report document	QA control activity
Concept	Action item	Management	AI log[4]	Review
Requirements	Action item	SQA & Management	AI log	Audit & review
High-level design	Action item		AI log	Audit & review
Implementation and coding	Action item	SQA & dev.	AI log	Audit & review
Detailed design	Action item	Develop. manage.	AI log	Audit & review
Unit test	Test incident report	Developers	AI log	Audit & review
Integration test	Test incident report	Technical staff	–	Audit & review
System test	Test incident report	Technical staff	–	Review
Acceptance test	Test incident report	Technical staff		Review
Installation and checkout	Test incident report/ SPR		–	SPR & CCB
Field operation procedures	S/W Problem report			SPR & CCB

Notes

1   See: Ben-Menachem, M (1994) *Software Configuration Management Guidebook*, McGraw-Hill.
2   We are referring here to the as-yet unreleased (but latest) version called IEEE Std 730.2; IEEE Guide for Software Quality Assurance Planning, Draft 5; April 1995.
3   This list of steps will be familiar to you from the discussions of quality goals.
4   Action item log – a journal of all action items.

TOOLS, TECHNIQUES
AND METHODOLOGIES

12

This chapter describes items that support quality assurance functions. These items may be in-house or purchased. They may be software supported, but do not have to be.

IN THIS CHAPTER THE TOOLS, TECHNIQUES AND METHODOLOGIES which are covered in chapter 9 of the SQAP are examined. It details the tools to be used for the software quality program. The standard states that this chapter of the SQAP must identify and describe the tools that support SQA. However, experience has shown that this is frequently the only place where these things are listed in an organized manner (unless your standards call for a software development plan, and that plan is well designed). In such a case, feel free to use this opportunity to document the whole development and maintenance environment. This chapter of the SQAP should also list those organizations which have responsibilities for each of the tools.

Typically in the SQAP this is a short chapter, it is short here as well. Nevertheless, the information needs to be documented. Any tools which are intended to have an effect on the quality of the product produced should be noted (for example, configuration management tools or dynamic/static analyzers). Remember to list the tools with the documentation that is actually in use in the organization, including version numbers of the tool and documentation, along with the tool use environment of platform, operating system, and so on.

Tools aid in the evaluation and improvement of system quality. Typical tools include operating systems, debuggers, documentation aids, analyzers, emulators, simulators and so on. This chapter needs to include all kinds of tools, all types of development and maintenance techniques and all of the methodologies for the use of them. This is for both software and hardware – for both data processing systems and embedded systems.

Software Tools

Note that the relationship between development environments and target environments is significant in the cases where they can be separate. Traditionally there have been different environments for development and use only for embedded systems, but lately even data processing has been making use of different environments.

Hardware Tools

This chapter deals with tools. Clearly, the majority of these are software tools. However, there are many cases where there may also be hardware tools, such as "in-circuit emulators" or simulation devices. These would be typical of embedded system/engineering environments. Even in typical data processing environments, one may find that developers have needs for hardware tools. A banking environment with several thousand workstations may well need protocol checkers and other kinds of communications analyzers in order to completely debug their system. All of these need to be planned.

Techniques

SQA techniques may consist of either (or both) technical and managerial procedures that help evaluate, improve and assure quality of the developing product. Typical examples of such techniques include reviews, standards, inspections, requirements tracing and verification, reliability measurements and logic analysis. All of these may be used in a rigorous and formal manner or in an informal way. These may be equally legitimate, **but they must be defined!**

Methodologies

Methodologies are integrated sets of the above tools and techniques. The methodologies should be well documented. **A description of the *process* which is to be used must be described or referenced.**

For example, if the quality assurance staff uses a formal requirements verification tracing matrix (RVTM) as a method to verify and validate that every requirement is fully traceable from its inception through all design, coding and testing phases, then the plan must clearly state:

- Who is responsible for creating it, in the first place?
- Who is responsible for maintaining it throughout the development and maintenance stages?
- Who is involved in actually tracing the requirements via the table?
- What, exactly, happens when requirements are missed? (A very common error occurs in deciding that a particular something is a requirement.)
- Who resolves open issues?

There are probably many more such questions that can be asked. Expand the list, as you need.

CMM Compatibility

CMM references tools and methodologies at a number of places throughout the defining document. Tools to support SQA rate a single item in the section titled "Ability 2" within the level 2 *key process area* of SQA. This item requires that tools be made available, then lists as examples: workstations, database programs, spreadsheet programs and auditing tools.

The main reference to tools and methods in general is in the requirements of the ability to perform the level 3 *key process area* called software product engineering. This ability is entitled "adequate resources and funding are provided for performing the software engineering tasks." Several lists of generic tools are provided. For general support of software engineering tasks the following are included: workstations, database management systems, on-line help aids, graphics tools, interactive documentation and word processing systems. Support for requirements analysis include tools for requirements tracking, specification, prototyping, modeling and simulation. Software design tools include specification, prototyping, simulation and program design languages. Coding support tools are listed as editors, compilers, cross-reference generators and pretty printers. Finally, support tools for software testing are described as test management tools, test generators, test drivers, test profilers, symbolic debuggers, test coverage analyzers. There is a requirement in CMM to specify the needs for tools, to specify how tools will be selected and how to deliver them to the tool users. At more advanced levels, all tools have to come under configuration management discipline.

If the recommendations of this chapter are carried out, then the requirements for CMM will be met or exceeded.

ISO 9000 Compatibility

Paragraph 4.11 of ISO 9001 states that the supplier needs to control, calibrate and maintain inspection, measuring and test equipment. At first glance, this may sound rather useless for software producers. But this is wrong. This section is actually quite good and a great deal of attention should be paid to it. As a matter of fact, this is probably one of the most typical weaknesses of many developing organizations. It is imperative that for a quality engineering environment it is understood that, even in software, tools need to be evaluated as to their applicability, reliability and usefulness. The fact that a tool has proven very helpful for Project A does not, necessarily, mean that it will be so for Project B. The fact that it has proven helpful for development, does not mean that it will be as good for maintenance.

[We know that some 80–90% of our programming resources are used for maintenance. One of the reasons for this is a lack of tooling and awareness of the importance of "tools calibration" – that is, the tools may need to evolve differently for development and maintenance.] **All tools must be validated for the tasks that they need to perform, and this need not be limited in either time or scope.**

It is true that ISO 9001 directly refers only to testing tools, but the authors choose to understand that all quality management and quality assurance tools are implied.

CODE CONTROL

13

This chapter describes items that support quality assurance functions and methods for recording and controlling changes to software items.

All project configuration management is subordinate to corporate configuration management.

THIS CHAPTER EXAMINES CODE CONTROL, COVERED IN CHAPTER 10 of the SQAP. Actually this is a special case of configuration management. The logic behind the separation is that code is the "final assembly" of the system, so special care needs to be taken to ensure that it is well managed. The title of this chapter "code control" can be interpreted to mean all of those methodologies (tools and techniques) that are to be used to ensure the validity of completed code and to protect this validity, over time. One assumes the existence of a computer program library and some appropriate program library management system.

For data processing environments, this may be also a critical security issue. The question being: have "Trojan horses" and computer "viruses" been guarded against according to the needs of the organization and the vulnerability of the system? For embedded systems, the subtlety of differences between versions can sometimes be very difficult to control without special mechanisms. (We have seen cases where a system worked as specified when compiled under a certain version of a compiler, but stopped working when compiled under the next updated version. Mechanisms need to be created to protect against this happening. Also, there must be a method to roll-back from changes that caused problems that we are not yet equipped to handle.)

All change requests submitted to the project are reviewed by a representative of product assurance or a staff person delegated by the product assurance function. This preliminary review is intended to validate the change request submittal. The product assurance representative performs checks upon the CR forms to ensure validity. All validity checks shall be documented (logged) in the change log. A CR validity check must include, at least, the following: that there is a sufficiency of documentation for the change to be processed and to proceed, and that the author of the change proposal has been authorized to submit change proposals. Authorization to submit the change proposals is frequently limited, i.e., some systems (organizations) allow "anyone" to submit proposals, others limit this function to "qualified" personnel. If the change request began from a problem report, recreatibility of the problem by development personnel must be ensured – this requirement links to the first requirement listed above. That includes ascertaining that this request has not been previously processed (perhaps, from a different source). The log (journal) of the change requests shall be maintained by the product assurance representative. In this way, together with the log, the product assurance representative ensures unique numbering of each change request form and follow up on all activities linked to the change requests.

Emphasis vs De-emphasis

One very difficult part of planning, and management in general, is to know where one must place one's emphasis and where it is of lesser importance. When discussing the control of code we must balance two opposing properties. On the one hand, the code is obviously what makes the program or system function. This is obviously the important part of the project and everything else is subordinate to it, right? Wrong!

The code is obviously important. However, one needs to give it the importance that it has coming to it, but not more than that. Certainly, a mess-up of the code can be disastrous. That is why this chapter exists and that is why it deserves to exist. There can be no doubt about that, nor a belittling of its importance.

However, this does need to be balanced (at least mentally) by a clear picture of the needs of the project during maintenance. Earlier, in Figure 10.1 we saw where software problems occur, however, this is not the whole picture. Look at Figure 13.1 below. There is a certain imbalance between where our problems occur (Figure 10.1) and where we are spending our time and efforts. At the very least, this infers that we need a better balance between what information is stored and saved for later re-use.

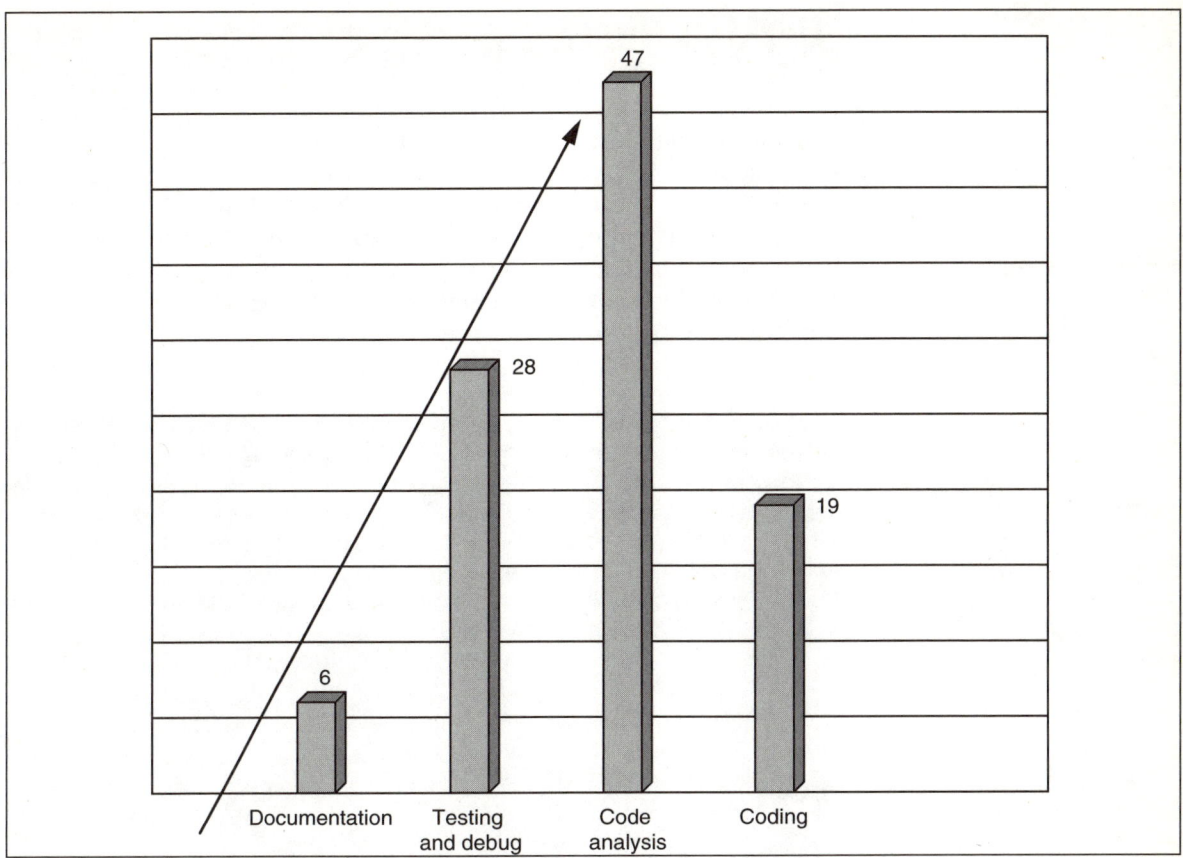

Figure 13.1 Maintenance – where the time is spent.

Notice the arrow? We spend most of our time looking at, and analyzing, the code – where the smallest number of errors are to be found. Obviously, some of this discrepancy is justified by the fact that after we have found a bug in the design, it needs to be fixed by making the code reflect what the design should have been. That is insufficient. If you looked carefully, you may have seen that the last line, the actual coding does not take the majority of time. The code analysis does. Usually this means two things. One is that the upper-level documents (requirements and design) have not been properly maintained. The second is that they frequently are simply not available to be maintained. Again, balance. It is very important. Think about it.

Version Control

Each version has a three position identification number, consisting of: [version] . [edition] . [correction]. The version number is updated for each major revision, where major revisions are determined by the project manager, the product manager or marketing. Edition numbers are updated for each internal release of the part/item. This would normally be performed by the version control software. Correction numbers are updated for every correction entered into the program module. Correction numbers are zeroed with every release.

- Are the configuration management procedures for nondeliverable items of software described and documented?
- Are the configuration management procedures for nondeliverable items of software auditable, as described? Are the configuration management procedures for nondeliverable items of hardware described and documented?
- Are the configuration management procedures for nondeliverable items of hardware auditable, as described?
- Are the configuration management procedures for nondeliverable items of firmware described and documented?
- Are the configuration management procedures for nondeliverable items of firmware auditable, as described?
- Have these procedures been implemented as described by the documentation?
- Are the requirements for version descriptions described in accordance with proscribed standards?
- Have all versions of nondeliverable items been documented upon release?
- Have all version descriptions been written according to these standards?

Archiving

- Are archiving procedures in accordance with recognized standards (for example ISO 9001, IEEE 1498 or DoD-Std 2167 / 2167a)?
- Are achieving procedures in accordance with contract specifications for project freezing and archiving?
- Have these procedures been implemented as described by the documentation?

Nondeliverable Code

The major problem to be addressed for evaluation of nondeliverable software items, for a project and at an installation, is a swift and accurate collection of data (as much data as possible) which reflects how the process is being performed (for example, process quality – does the process need to be improved? Do the performers need additional training?). Well thought-out, informal, manual systems can frequently work quite sufficiently, and sometimes more efficiently. Any documents which relate to the nondeliverable item must be listed by name and number in the managerial documents of the project (for example SDP, SQEP/SQAP, SCMP). The sources of all documents clearly described (government vs nongovernment).

- Have all nondeliverable items which are to be developed as part of the project been identified and clearly labeled?
- Have all nondeliverable items which are to be purchased as part of the project been identified and clearly labeled?
- Have unique names been assigned to each nondeliverable item?
- Do the names of the nondeliverable items clearly imply that they are nondeliverables?
- Has a procedure been established which defines naming conventions for nondeliverable items?
- Have the purposes of the nondeliverable items and their functions been clearly defined?
- Have the criteria for the allocation of requirements to nondeliverable items been clearly established?
- Have these criteria been approved by the user/client representative?
- Does a document exist which summarizes each deliverable and nondeliverable item's purpose?
- Does a document exist which summarizes each deliverable and nondeliverable item's content?
- Does a document exist which summarizes each deliverable and nondeliverable item's design?

CMM Compatibility

CMM does not refer to code control as a specific activity. Code is considered one of the software work products that have to be managed by a configuration management process. The overview section of the CMM document refers to two kinds of configuration management – baselined configuration management with a rigorous change control process, and developmental configuration management. The latter is managed by the developers with the intention that items will be placed under baselined configuration management at predetermined points in the development activity.

Software configuration management itself is defined as a *key process area* for level 2 certification. Like all key process areas, there is a detailed specification of goals, a commitment to perform, a set of abilities (requirements) needed to carry out the functions and a long list of detailed activities that must be performed. The activities specified by CMM tend to be more formal than those specified in this book, but the goals and results are pretty much the same.

ISO 9000 Compatibility

This is really a rather problematic area for ISO 9001. They go to great lengths to discuss both design, and its control; and documentation, and its control. Code is never mentioned because they do not really like software. However, this is one of the instances when we can refer to ISO 9000-3 to see what that standard says about the situation. While code control is not specifically mentioned, the standard does go to quite some length about configuration management, in general (in paragraph 6.1). In this they do actually say that all configuration items need to be controlled.

A great deal more success will be achieved if reference is made to a document issued (we believe) as part of the SPICE project: "Information technology: software life-cycle process. Part 2. Configuration Management for Software."[1] This document is very good.

Note

1   The examplar that we have, and are referring to, is a draft dated 24 January 1995. All of the people involved in writing the document have had prior experience with IEEE 828 for SCM.

MEDIA CONTROL

14

Methods to protect and control access to physical media. This is also a part of configuration management and, hence, is subordinate to overall configuration management.

THIS CHAPTER DISCUSSES MEDIA CONTROL, WHICH IS DEALT WITH in chapter 11 of the SQAP. This chapter includes such "mundane" activities as backup frequencies and procedures, and special facilities (such as fire-proof or off-site storage, or backup sites). There have been projects that "went away" wholly or partially, because of somebody being nasty – or ignorant of proper procedures – and a lack of reasonable, responsible (read: up-to-date or professional) backups. Also, include here any comments about how specialized (i.e., out of the ordinary for your installation or project) media is to be stored and handled. For example, PC diskettes in a mainframe shop or tapes in a PC shop.

This book talks about the software process. That is, the processes which are used to develop software according to the users' expectations, and to maintain this level of software quality over time. One of the parameters of this "maintenance to the level of quality that the users expect" is the distribution of the media containing the software to the user. For instance, a major company (a large chip manufacturer) once distributed a virus on the distribution diskettes of one of its software products. At very least, this is embarrassing. It could also be very expensive. (Consider a manufacturer of medical equipment who distributed a virus with its latest release of the software that drives its machines, and then someone was badly hurt because of this virus.) As we all know, there is a large variety of media on which software can be distributed. It is very important that the interfaces between the corporate configuration management function and the media distribution be defined for the project. A product like "All Change" is eminently suitable to help you over this hurdle.

[Note: In most standard manufacturing concerns, the corporate configuration management systems are generally limited to a hardware orientation. We, the software people, have to match our "outputs" to their needs. It is very seldom that we can demand that they match our needs. Besides, we are more flexible.]

Backup Procedures

Backup is a project critical function. The development library should probably be backed up daily, while the project master library should be backed up weekly. However, in addition to this, the function is project *dependent*, as well. Each project manager should define this function for his/her individual project. For the maintenance project: mistakes in this area can be very bad career moves. Pay a great deal of attention to specifics.

Document Modules

Hopefully, it is superfluous to even talk about these items, but nonetheless, it is still needed for many organizations. Please ascertain that all documents which are significant to the success of the project are formally controlled. In addition, all controlled documents absolutely **must** be stored in the official corporate or project configuration management system, which should be computerized. All changes to the controlled documents must be controlled, just as the changes to the code must be. Backups must be maintained. You have put a lot of work into these things, make certain that this work is respected.

- Are the project documents created via a modern office automation system, allowing reasonable integrity and security?
- Are all documents which are significant to the success of the project, formally controlled?
- Are all controlled documents stored in the official corporate or project configuration management system?
- Is the document configuration management system computerized?
- Does the software for the computerized configuration management system use a known tool, with a significant market share?
- Have all changes to controlled documents been processed through proper channels, using the appropriate engineering change notices and/or change request forms?
- Are backup and master copies of each controlled document stored off-site?
- Can they be accessed within 24 hours in the event of catastrophe?
- Is the document creation process auditable for document security, integrity and efficiency?
- Does the documentation tool set allow workmanship auditing (for example automated spelling checker, automated grammatical checker, complexity analysis, and so on)?
- Has the document creation process been previously audited (i.e., is this audit, not the first audit)?
- Can all documents be readily recreated from the computerized sources?
- Does the configuration management system allow traceability of changes to the documents from previous releases?
- Does the configuration management system allow on-call back-tracking of the documents to previous releases?
- Are document release procedures documented via a software configuration management plan?
- Must methods and facilities used to maintain and store controlled versions of identified software be defined?
- Must methods and facilities used to protect computer program physical media from unauthorized access or inadvertent damage or degradation be stated?

Media Distribution

Process interface to configuration management

The interfaces between the media distribution function and the system/software configuration management function should be clearly defined for purposes of media distribution. All backup procedures should be defined and implemented for all media before their distribution. These procedures should always include aspects of off-site storage and storage in a fire-proof safe. Labeling procedures for the media need to be defined for all media types and implemented rigorously by configuration management. The mechanisms should be as rigorous as those applied to software modules. In addition, one should take into account questions of periodicity of distribution.

Distribution to internal project personnel

For any project larger than small, and even the tiny, if there is a question of secrecy, the procedures for distribution of system media, whether they contain documents or other types of information, should be different between internal and external project personnel. These procedures need to be rigorously implemented and adhered to by all project personnel. It is definitely part of quality assurance to determine that these procedures are strictly followed and that any deviations are reported to management. Certainly, a procedure must exist to enable all distribution of project media to be traced as to sender and receiver.

Distribution to external project personnel

The procedures for distribution of system media to external (client, government or otherwise) project personnel needs to be clearly defined. Of course, this follows from the previous paragraph. Equally obviously, procedures need to be defined for distribution of media (documents, software, and so on) to nonproject personnel.

Security limitations of media

Remember that all cases of unauthorized access have the potential to be problematic. This is true whether the access is malicious are mundane. People playing computer games during work time may not represent a major security problem, but they are using resources that may have been allocated otherwise. (They may also be simply relaxing after preparing for an important meeting, in which case this may be very good. Nothing is ever as simple as it appears at first glance.)

- Are all access procedures in agreement with rules set up by the corporate security officer?
- Have the access procedures been certified (verified) by security?
- Has a data officer been designated for access to media (for example magnetic, optical, ROMs of various types, and so on)?
- Are all distribution procedures in agreement with rules set up by the corporate security officer?
- Have the distribution procedures been certified (verified) by security?
- Has a data officer been designated for distribution of media (for example magnetic, optical, ROMs of various types, and so on)?

CMM Compatibility

Media control is not referenced in CMM. If media are defined as configuration items by an organization or even by a project, then they must be managed under the same discipline that is specified for all such items.

ISO 9000 Compatibility

Unfortunately, this is a more-or-less repeat what was said in the previous chapter about ISO 9001 compatibility. Though here, the writers of the standard are a little more in their natural element – we are concerned here about media, that is a physical object – they still have a bit of improvement to make to suit the mode of thought of this chapter. There is a certain kind of "delicacy" needed in the treatment of magnetic or optical media, which may not be quite typical of other kinds of items. Also, these things need to be performed in coherence with, in parallel with and in constant interface with (software) configuration management. They do not seem to have paid attention to that interface. Here, it is critical.

Once again, if we refer to ISO 9000-3 there is a section on "replication, delivery and installation" (paragraph 5.9) which is certainly the point of reference. However, as said, they seem to have missed something in the building. For instance, while distribution is covered reasonably, interfacing to SCM, security and access rights are weak.

SUPPLIER CONTROL

15

> This chapter describes all methods, techniques and tools used to support and control the suppliers of software products which make up a part of the product developed by this project.

Supplier control is dealt with by chapter 12 of the SQAP, where it describes the provisions for assuring full coverage of the requirements of vendor supplied software – this includes off-the-shelf products and bespoke developments. See also Appendix IV "Subcontractor Quality Auditing."

This supplier control section may need to be adapted for each system's documents/deliverable required by the statement of work (SOW). For previously developed software, see the section below. For software to be developed, the supplier/contractor is required to implement an adequate SQAP, and this chapter of the plan describes the methods to be used to evaluate it and to assure its continued accuracy. Suppliers may mean providers of software to be made-to-order, or off-the-shelf packages. Every supplier of software needs to be controlled! If software is to be made-to-order ("bespoke software"), the absolute minimum demand from the supplier must be the IEEE 730 standard! Anything else is so reckless, that it borders on ignoring the inevitable.

Assuming therefore, that the contractor's quality system is based on IEEE 730, it must obviously include the following three general requirements, as a minimum, along with their additional breakdowns.

The provision of control procedures for:

- Project control of the design process

- Subcontracted and proprietary products
- Support and maintenance of the product
- The production of target, functional, product and maintenance specifications
- Qualification approval of the product
- Configuration control
- Formal procedures for hand-over to the customer
- System development methods
- Use of tools
- The maintenance of tools and standards

B. The contractor shall describe:

- The life-cycle model used, particularly the functions and products (deliverables) of each phase. This also describes how life-cycle products are managed and controlled.
- The methods used in each phase of the life-cycle, their scope and specific products, with a justification as to why they are appropriate to this particular project.
- Tools used which support methods as described above.
- The test strategy used to prove the product. This strategy shall include regression testing.
- The supporting documentation produced and supplied for the software provided.

C. Provision of quality data

The contractor shall provide the quality assurance representative with information relating to the quality of the products released (or deliverables relating to products to be released). This information shall include analysis of defects identified during review and test stages, and also analysis of defects reported from manufacture, installation or in service products and the associated corrective action programs. It must also include provisions for assuring that vendor and subcontractor developed software meets the established technical requirements stated.

What you just read may be nasty. We wrote that the minimum requirement is IEEE 730. Well, what does that mean for a supplier that has ISO 9001 certification? Is that going to be sufficient? We would have to answer in the negative. Unfortunately, ISO is not as demanding as IEEE 730 in terms of the quality system or in terms of the actual techniques for ensuring that the delivered product will indeed be as it was ordered. That does not mean that this particular area of ISO is insufficient. This comment is general. Remember, ISO 9001 provides a general solution for the **whole company**. This is its strength and it is very important because of that. However, it is not specific to software nor was it designed to be so. Do not make unreasonable demands on something which, while very good in its own right, had specific design goals.

Contractor Plans

Controls

- Are the controls described by the contractor's plans used in the development, testing, or acquisition of all nondeliverable software?
- Are the defined controls, as applied by the plans, to be imposed on all deliverable and nondeliverable software, firmware and hardware?

Coverage

- Do the contractor's managerial plans include coverage of all identified deliverable and nondeliverable items?
- In the event of later discovery (definition) of a nondeliverable item, have procedures been defined to add these items to the plans?
- Are the deliverable and nondeliverable items covered by all of the following managerial plans:
  - software development plan
  - software quality evaluation/quality assurance plan?
  - software configuration management plan?
  - software test plan?

Contractor Quality Evaluation

- Are the procedures for quality evaluation of the deliverable and nondeliverable software in accordance with recognized standards?
- Are the procedures for quality evaluation of the deliverable and nondeliverable hardware in accordance with recognized standards?
- Are the procedures for quality evaluation of the deliverable and nondeliverable firmware in accordance with recognized standards?
- Are the procedures for quality evaluation of deliverable and nondeliverable items in accordance with corporate specifications for product release control?

Requirements Assurance

This paragraph of the plan describes the methods to be used to assure that the contractor receives a correct, accurate and complete list of the requirements which have been allocated for the development.

Previously Developed Software

For previously developed software modules, this paragraph states the methods to be used to assure the suitability of the product to the requirements allocated and to the products covered by this SQAP. The supplier control worksheet (SOW) is provided to aid readers to structure their control procedures. Clearly, this worksheet can, and should, be expanded to accommodate any specialized needs that the reader may have.

SQAP planning worksheet # 10

Supplier control

Project: _____   Planner: _____

Date: _____   SQAP: _____

Supplier Name: _____   Contact: _____

Item #	Development process	Delivered document	Standard/ procedure	Supplier QA control activity	QA activity	Comments
1						
2						
3						
4						
5	Acceptance test requirements					
6	Acceptance test	ATP				

CMM Compatibility

SEI defines software subcontract management as a *key process area* for qualification at CMM level 2, Repeatable. The CMM approach requires the appointment of an appropriate person, who commands defined abilities in software engineering, as the software subcontract manager to be responsible for establishing and managing each software subcontract. Basically, the relationships and activities of the contractor and subcontractor as defined by CMM are equivalent to the ones listed above, but CMM defines them in much more detail and specifies a closer contact between the contracting parties during the project period. We would support closer personal contacts as a means to guarantee that both parties maintain their commitments to the other, to ensure that divergences in interpretations of written specifications do not develop over time and to develop the relationship.

On the other hand, CMM has nothing to say about purchasing "off the shelf" (commercial) software. This is not surprising since the entire orientation of CMM is the software development environment.

ISO 9000 Compatibility

This is certainly one of the more applicable of the areas of ISO 9001. Paragraph 4.6 of the standard discusses "purchasing." The subparagraphs of this paragraph consist of the following.

1. Evaluation of subcontractors (4.6.2)

Very few companies really take this seriously. Originally, this is what ISO 9000 was all about. Unfortunately for software, they sort of failed in this respect. What this means is that you must "qualify" your supplier before you agree to buy from them. You must make certain that they really have the capabilities to do the job. The burden of proof is on the supplier, if they want the job.

Examine what their capabilities are. Audit them very carefully and thoroughly. This examination should be similar to the CMM's assessment procedure, though obviously it need not be quite so rigorous or so big. One day should be sufficient. The only companies that we have yet seen that do this conscientiously are "Motorola" and "Elbit." Our understanding is that Motorola even charges their prospective vendors for the audit. The first author has taken part in a SQA capability audit performed by the Elbit Corporation, on one of his clients. It was a very interesting experience. They were very thorough and did it in a manner that **we** gained from the experience. This is wise. **Whatever you do to improve performance of your suppliers benefits you.** Many companies do not realize that they are dependent, that they are one link in the food chain. If their suppliers are better tomorrow than they were yesterday, they all make more money! Elbit are to be commended for their forward thinking.

2. Purchasing data (4.6.3)

The authors would like to suggest that the lessons which can be learned from this paragraph are of extreme importance. [That is not meant as a joke, nor as irony. We have seen projects fail because of a purchased part which never quite worked properly. Usually this is either a problem of a bad definition or a bad interface – in the end this amounts to much the same thing.]

> "Purchasing documents shall contain data clearly describing the product ordered, ... "

If more people took this into account when purchasing software, the job of SQA would be a lot easier. We would have worded this even more strongly. Remember that when you buy bespoke software, the requirements document **must** be part of the contractual relationship and must be legally binding. Not doing this is simply irresponsible. Clearly, this means that SQA needs to be involved in purchasing and the issuance of purchase orders. Generally, this is blatantly lacking in today's environments.

3. Supplier verification at subcontractor's premises (4.6.4.1)

This means that SQA needs to be involved in supplier verification and the issuance of vendor certification. This is another area that is currently sadly lacking. Some of the more sophisticated companies now do this (Motorola is one, see above) but it is still much too rare for the health of the industry. Vendor certification is usually left to the purchasing department who, with all due respect, have not been trained in software technologies.

4. Customer verification of subcontracted product (4.6.4.2)

This section of the standard is well laid out and usable by the software community – not only usable, but applicable and wisely so. I recommend that SQA pay very close attention to its provisions.

ISO 9001 has a paragraph called: "control of customer-supplied product" (paragraph 4.7). This concept is missing from IEEE 730 and the ISO paragraph should be paid attention to. Particularly, the final sentence of this paragraph is instructive:

> Verification by the supplier does not absolve the customer of the responsibility to provide acceptable product.

Need one say any more? This is exactly what we have stated all along here. **This is what vendor auditing/assessment is all about.**

Purchasing Quality Control Methods

The previous section discussed vendor qualification and vendor quality auditing. This section discusses some of the basic techniques for doing it. This whole section is discussed in terms of and in the language of purchasing. Purchasing is a technique and a profession. Many software professionals view this as pure bureaucracy, and use that as an excuse to not respect it. Some projects have paid a very high price for this misunderstanding.

Acceptance quality control

The first technique is "acceptance quality control." This refers to a sort of acceptance test, but the procedure is designed to be performed at the customer site. In purchasing, this is frequently also called source inspection because one is "inspecting at the source" of supply. This refers to performing the whole final test at the manufacturer's site. This would usually not be recommended for a software-only system because of the decreased value of a test not carried out under "real-life" conditions. However, it can be useful for an embedded system as that may be completely independent, or reasonably simulated. This is a very well-understood and well-established method where professional purchasing staff are concerned. This is another advantage to you. Sometimes, you may be able to let them do it.

The advantage accrued from this technique is full control of incoming material at the earliest possible time. This has the potential to save time and effort. This works fairly well for components. Most QA experts would generally state that this is not intended for assemblies. As there really are no discrete components in software – everything is some sort of assembly – this technique is not trivially associable with software. Also, this may be expensive to implement in infrastructure. The generally accepted costs are 10–15%, relative to the material costs.

Incoming Inspection

The second technique is incoming inspection. This refers to performing an acceptance test of the suppliers product, at your site, when it arrives. This is usually the only technique software people know about. It is very brute force and is usually the most expensive technique over the long term. This does not mean that it should not be used. It may frequently be the best option available. However, all too often, it is the only option considered. Not to consider the others is always bad management.

Vendor qualification

Vendor survey and qualification. Relying on supplier quality control after reliance agreement is signed. Companies experts in product and vendor inspection.

Advantages and disadvantages

*   Motivating the vendor to quality by inspection process imposed on supplier, not on product
    A. initial survey and qualifying process
    B. Inspection survey at planned time
    C. Surprise inspection
        – Expected relative cost is 2–3%
        – There is not enough experience yet
        – Additional methods are necessary as usual
    Turning the vendor into an ally. Cooperation based on shared understanding of interests
*   Minimization of uncertainties by open books, open doors and open hearts
*   Special rights to contractor – single source for long time
*   Cost of purchasing QC: 0% to (–)
*   Mutual qualification and strange test element is necessary to improve method

Problems in purchasing quality control

*   Communication of interfaces between vendor and buyer
*   Inflation in engineering documentation during purchasing process (specifications, SOW, WBS, interface control, test plans, changes control, and so on)
*   Change in the skills demanded for purchasing inspectors

Effective Use of Inspection Services

- Test capability to comprise technologies and space.
- Test service quality acknowledgment.
- Inspect capability and versatility in standards and data management.
- Speed of response vs service price in relevant scenarios.
- Economic optimization will be achieved by a sophisticated integration of the four methods, according to **customer test plan policy**.
- Using "ALLY" inspection services. "ALLIES" must be qualified from time to time.

Table 15.1 Comparison of internal quality control to external inspection services

Internal QC	Hired services
Loyal only to our camp	Reliable – independent
No communication problems	Data management
Expensive logistics	Effective in space, time-table and cheaper services
No provisions for temporary overflows	Offers cheaper services for temporary overflows
Difficult to handle timetable and versatile technologies	Needs permanent instructions to personal

The Purchase Order

- Insist on full written information this avoids confusion and increases efficiency
- Avoid telephone deals
- Check for conflicting requirements – clarify with your customer before you start
- Review the shop order for discrepancies with purchase order
- Purchase orders **must** be precise and complete; include all reference documents

RECORDS COLLECTION, MAINTENANCE, AND RETENTION

16

> Axiom: In software, **quality** and **productivity** are inseparable, both as concepts and as results.

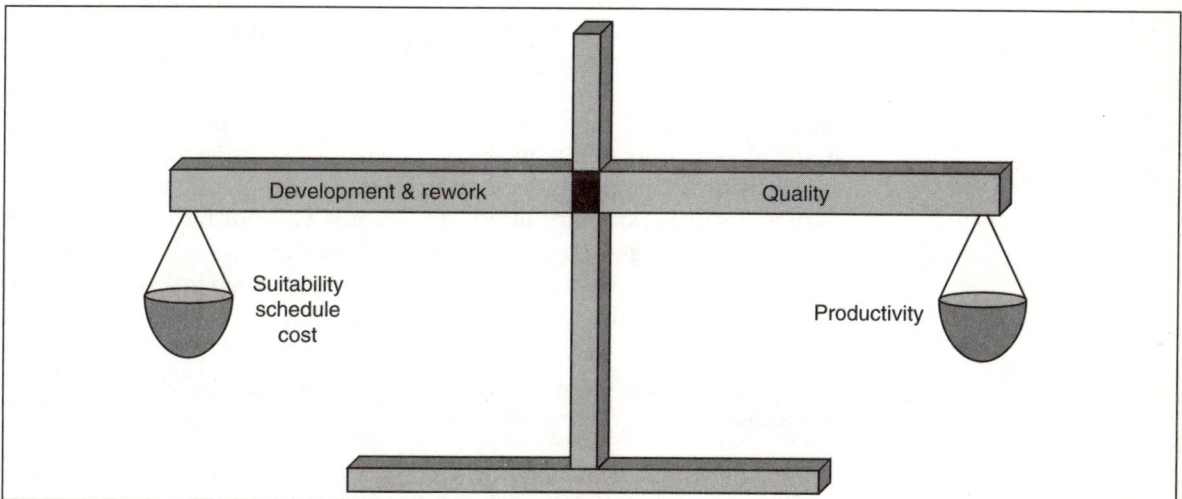

Figure 16.1   The strange balancing of software.

The collection, maintenance and retention of records is dealt with in chapter 13 of the SQAP. The standard says that one needs to record quality information (*records collection*), that you must define how these records are to be retained (*records maintenance*) and for how long (for what period of time) they must be retained and of course, maintained (*records retention*). This section of the plan identifies the plans for the assembly, retention and archival of software quality documentation. This includes all aspects of preparing, maintaining and making available for contracting agency review, records of each activity performed. The methods used to acquire this documentation must be specified or referenced. The archival period must be defined and the methods to be used for safeguarding this information for this entire period must be specified. The formats to be used and the information to be recorded for each type of record should be included. Galileo Galilei was a very smart man. He made a statement which is as eminently suitable for software as it was, at the time, for any science:

> Count what is countable, measure what is measurable, and what is not measurable, make measurable.

That is what this chapter is about. Collecting data, that is, counting and measuring, and then making sense out of what we have then created. Notice the way that is worded: "*...and then making sense out of what we have then created*." More simply put, it would have sufficed to say: "making sense out of what we **collected**." However, one of the very important ideas which we need to think about is the **feedback loop** which is formed as a result of this activity. If you do not measure the quality you are receiving at every step of the process, you are **managing by self-delusion**. Philip B Crosby said "Quality is free." Quality does not cost money, what costs money is the lack of quality.[1] Fifty percent of software costs are directly attributable to error corrections (this finding comes originally from the US DoD, but it has since been confirmed by many investigators). Quality always begins from management and **must** be rigorously managed – more than any other product attribute. If management is not committed, quality just will not happen! The only way to get management involved is to show them how important it is. This is done with numbers. They understand return on investment (what they like to call ROI).

> Fifty percent of software costs are directly attributable to error corrections.

One of the major functions of quality assurance is the collection and accurate reporting of the results of the work being produced. The results mean, the real productivity of the installation. This is not a trivial task. Some installations are still simply counting lines of code, and think they understand productivity! Clearly, if you cannot, or will not, measure it, you cannot manage it. This section contains information about the information to be collected, how it is to be stored and reported and its dates of effectiveness.

Let us keep in mind a few definitions, again the following.

> **Quality**: The totality of features and characteristics of a product or service that bears on its ability to satisfy given needs. (ANSI/ASQC A3-1978)
>
> **Quality assurance**: Planned and systematic pattern of all actions necessary to provide adequate confidence that the item or product conforms to established technical requirements. (ANSI/IEEE Std 730-1984)
>
> **Quality metric**: Quantitative measure of the degree to which the product possesses a given attribute that affects its quality.
>
> **Errors**: An unexpected, undesired state, situation or value.
>
> **Defect**: Imperfection; lack of something essential.
>
> **Fault**: Defect or blemish in object or structure; break in continuity.
>
> **Failure**: An unexpected or unwanted event.
>
> **Maintainability**: Probability of completing a maintenance action in a given time (statistical). "Mean time to repair" (operational).
>
> **Corrective maintenance**: A process of unplanned change to correct the cause of a failure.
>
> **Preventive maintenance**: A process of planned change to prevent failures from occurring.
>
> **Testability**: The ability to perform an accepted series of tests on the system/product which are designed to prove the system's initial or continuous (un)useability. Preventive maintenance is not practical for a nontestable product.

On 3 June 1992 Dr Ernesto Hofmann (of IBM, in Italy) gave a lecture concerning "Mainframe systems in the '90s." One of the most significant items of information which he related was from an article in the Harvard Business Review from August 1990. The article was written by Mike Hammer. The following story was related by Dr Hofmann: "Ford compared a certain business function (purchasing) with one of their Japanese competitors. They found that the Japanese company (of a comparable size) had a department consisting of nine people, while Ford required 435 to perform the same function. They instituted a policy of TQM to "fix" the problem. They considered themselves to have won when they managed to reduce the size to 125. This seems to show an inherent weakness in the thought process. There is still a 1:14 relationship, which is dismal.

Productivity is a measurable item, in any organization, in any environment. Admittedly, this is not always easy to do. Nor is productivity always a simple thing to define. For instance, there is no agreed-upon definition of productivity for software. Even though the IEEE has recently published a standard for software productivity metrics – with which we strongly disagree (see below).

Remember, the creative organization of information creates new information. There are many modes of organization of information. Some of these might be: alphabetical, time, location, category, hierarchy, continuum (cost, color, performance, magnitude, size). These may also be layered ("nested sorting keys").

Investments in quality do not cost, they pay. What costs is nonconformance.

This chapter also describes efforts and resources needed for acquisition of a computerized system for managing quality records collection and retrieval. Such a system could be used as the data processing facility for a corporate software quality evaluation function. Quality evaluation consists of a planned and organized process of recording quality control (this usually means testing results) and quality assurance results in the form of metrics (numerical measurements). These metrics must be gathered from actual development and operational characteristics of the systems and products the organization produces. The data, and the information resulting from the refinements (i.e., the analysis) of this data are then reported to the various "interested parties" for action.

A system of gathering, analyzing and reporting data concerning software, or more directly, concerning the processes used for developing, operating and maintaining software, is a primary control tool for project and corporate management. Through this, management gains true control over the obstacles to system quality and to development productivity, during the overall system life-cycle.

Life-cycle duration of the data in the quality data system is the retention period for the data collected, this parallels project duration but will usually last longer. This must be identical with the life-cycle duration of the system or product which results from the project. In "technical" terms, this begins with the customer's requirements specifications, and ends with "field life" (i.e., operations and maintenance) and finally retirement. The data are retained, at least, until the product is finally retired from service.

Organizational responsibility for retention and storage of the database and realization of data recording, analysis and reporting must reside with the software quality assurance department. If no such department exists, then whatever part of the organization that has responsibilities for productivity and/or quality and/or software engineering activities.

The system creates quality and productivity reports, including error typography and sources, for various management levels and provides tools for relevant analysis needed for future quality and productivity improvements. This ensures the continued productivity and competitiveness of the organization. These tools which must form a part of such a system, must include:

- Statistical division of errors
- The costs of errors (of discovery and repair)
- Evaluation of relative quality of the discovery
- Error clustering analysis
- Error typographical analysis
- Ad hoc findings upon demand by management or by the customer

The system has two major objectives, as follows:

- Aiding in "pin-pointing" processes or subsystems which are "sensitive" to faults; this must also include discovering the "kinds" of faults to which they are sensitive. Sensitive, in this sense, refers to the phenomenon (sometimes referred to as "clustering") in which certain types of errors tend to be more prevalent in certain types of module. No known logical explanation for this has been found, but this appears to be a fact with which we must live.

- Discovering the possible effects of the various types of failure. This is an adaptation of the hardware quality assurance discipline, which is called "failure modes and effects analysis" (FMEA). The system also serves as a collection point for registration of all defects found anywhere in the system, at any time. This supports the (hardware) concept called "failure reporting, analysis and corrective action system" (FRACAS[2]).

The Six Axioms of Quality Management

To repeat again, "quality does not cost money! What costs money is the lack of quality." Fully 50% of software costs are directly attributable to error corrections. Quality always begins from management and – more than any other product attribute – must be rigorously managed. If management is not committed, quality just will not happen! The quality assurance functions must, of course, be linked and interrelated by management controls. These will include standards, training, and measures and methodologies for developing and reporting of progress.

- The process of getting something done is a system
- Quality is suitability of the product to requirements, not abstract "goodness"
- Quality occurs when defects are prevented, not from postmortem appraisal
- There is only one performance goal to be measured against, zero defects. There is no prize for "close enough"
- If you do not measure the quality you are receiving at every step of the process, you are managing by self-delusion
- Investments in quality do not cost, they pay. What costs is nonconformance

The production of software can be controlled similarly to other products. Techniques of interdisciplinary analysis can be used to discover and apply relevant tools. For instance, checklists can be used as a cheap and efficient aid in analysis of any product. They can be simply updated and used to "quantify."

The quality records collection and retrieval software system manages a database of all quality and productivity metrics and simplifies receipt of the various reports of these records, from "the field." The system is a fairly standard data processing system. The only element of the system which is really out-of-the-ordinary, is the nature of the data being processed. It is still quite rare to encounter a software shop which uses the tools it creates to track itself. Any standard hardware, such as an "industry standard PC" is quite sufficient. The system itself must not require any special hardware features. The software must implement an interactive interface with the system user, with on-line update of the database. In most cases, this system should be designed sufficiently simply so that a simple system building tool – an "application generator" – can be used.

Data are **input** in accordance with relevant events. Certain "events" cause reports to be created. These reports certainly include all of the following, and very likely others, for your needs.

- **Change requests** – whether to documents (specifications, designs, user, and so on), to code or to systems/products. This report may be part of the configuration management tools-set. Unfortunately, most popular SCM tools still do not know how to do this
- **Deviations** – from standards or rules of any kind, whether written or simply "agreed upon," also deviations from specifications of any kind
- Documents error reports and updates – these will usually result from technical and/or managerial activities which are intended to evaluate deliverables, such as:
  - Document inspections or reviews
  - Periodic discussions
  - Document audits
  - Action items resulting from client's meetings
- **Test reports** – including all results of unit, subsystem (integration), system tests and acceptance tests
- Software problem reports (STR)

All quality and productivity reports, which refer to software, must be included in the database. Determination of data items and information content to be passed to various representatives of management, is the responsibility of project management and the quality assurance group.

Quality Evaluation Records

The quality records collection and retrieval system is used to obtain information about the productivity, quality and reliability of the software system (or software portion of the system, if it is an embedded system) produced by the organization. This process of records collection should begin with initial specifications and progress through all phases of definition, development and release, through operations, field service and retirement. The system supplies feedback to management about the **quality of**

the processes and tools used for the system's development. Through the use of this kind of system, the developing organization can determine optimization procedures to be used both for present and future developments, such items as the frequency and optimal content of reviews.

Report review findings

- Learn from development experiences, what may be needed for corrective actions required (CAR) for future projects
- Lessen the system maintenance burden
- Improve human engineering and understandability of the system product
- Measure and adapt system performance to client needs

Collecting Quality Data

Clearly, to accomplish the described goals, a practical initial list of data to be acquired must be constructed, and the means for their collection must be defined. In order to report the results of reviews, their (the reviews) data must be acquired. This must include reviews of all types, i.e., document audits, inspections, walkthroughs and both peer and management reviews. These are data which are available from within the organization and simply need to be collected via a form. These data are for internal distribution.

Reports of the results of the various testing processes need to be reported from all levels of testing as aids for improving the testing process. They must include testing performed both during development and the operational phases. This must also include regression test results. These data are not necessarily for internal distribution.

Preparation and Recording of Quality Data

As a minimum, all of the following data must be collected:

- Name of subsystem and/or module
- Error code
- Name of person(s) responsible for correcting the error
- Date of error discovery
- Literal description of error (alphabetical field for summarized description)
- Corrective action required
- Date required by

However, this is truly a minimum. Experience has shown that this is not adequate for the long term needs. We strongly recommend use of the forms in the appendices of this book as a tried and proven method for data collection.

Maintenance of Data Relating to Quality

The following rules reflect the nature of the data in discussion. These data are an important part of any project. The data in the quality/productivity database will reflect the true results of the project in all aspects relating to quality of the software produced and product delivered.

Data collection rule # 1

The data collected must be properly entered into and stored in the database for reporting and distribution to all concerned parties.

> Note:
>
> This may sound trivial, but in software engineering environments, this is one of the most difficult aspects.

Data collection rule # 2

All data must be retained for the entire life-cycle of the product which results from the project. This means, until the product is totally retired.

Data collection rule # 3

Data must be backed up with a frequency not less than once per month and retained off-site. A minimum of three generations of data backup will be retained.

> Note:
>
> Once again, this may sound trivial, but in software engineering environments (where perhaps, one should most expect awareness of the importance of backups) this aspect has proven to be most difficult.

Quality Evaluation Reports

For a system of this nature to function reasonably, to provide real feedback to management and to the developers, at least four types of reports need to be producible, upon demand:

- Reports of review results (as aids for the future performance of reviews). This must include reviews of all types, i.e., document audits, inspections, walkthroughs and peer reviews.
- Reports of test results; test results need to be reported from all levels of testing (as aids for improving the testing process, both during development and the operational phases). This must include regression test results.
- Periodic reports to customer/management.
- System survey reports postmortem.

Software Quality Report Types and Distribution

This procedure recommends that reports are prepared for distribution as defined by the QA database administrator. Reports must be defined for each management level, according to an agreed upon distribution key. A useful distribution key can be *error type/source*. This may be illustrated by a table such as Table 16.1, below. The reporting periodicity (i.e., the frequency of production and distribution) for the various quality evaluation reports must be determined by each project, usually on an ad-hoc basis. The reasons for this result from differences in the needs of the projects being produced. All reporting responsibilities are placed upon the product assurance function.

Table 16.1 Error type/source

Distortion level	Mission failure	System failure	Standard violation	Standards deviation	Errors	
X			X	X	X	Software develop
X	X		X	X	X	Head of team
X	X	X	X	X		Project manager
X		X	X			Client

Software Quality Metrics Analysis

First, let us define what happens with LOC metrics and their use, so that their inherent weakness can be seen. A project is usually organized by a life-cycle model. The model consists of some mix of activities such as those in Table 16.2, below. LOC metrics, by their nature, are only capable of looking at the coding stage of development. In the most difficult of projects, this may reflect 20% of the project's invested effort (in most major projects today, this is closer to 10%). What happened to the other 80 or 90%? Well, even if one attempts to treat them as "fixed costs," and there is some economic justification for this, that is not sufficient. They change too dynamically for that. The requirements, design, testing, documentation and installation efforts are not measured, they are inferred. This is simply not good enough.

Let us assume that one begins a project for the production of a new product. The product is based upon a previously existing product. Indeed, it is because of the existence of this product that you were able to convince your client of your solution's preferability. (In other words, that is how you won the bid.) Eighty percent of the new product is "simply reworking" the existing code of the old product. The other 20% needs to be developed. This is called undercutting the competition by leveraging existing technology. The essence of capitalism, properly used. Now comes the reality. What exactly do we want to measure?. If we only measure the code in the new modules, we have clearly looked at only some 20% of the coding of the project. If we also count the new lines placed in the existing modules, this will still not reflect the effort to find what and where to place them. We know that maintenance of existing code is a difficult and demanding process. Just counting these lines as we have counted the new ones, is unfair. And what about the deleted lines, or the existing lines which were changed? This effort is not small either. Perhaps the different kinds of changes should be counted separately and then "weighted?" Well, then you have a major problem of accurate data acquisition. The simple answer is that no system of counting lines of code is clear enough, or consistent enough, when attempting to equate them

Table 16.2 A possible life-cycle model

Activity	Effort reported accurately	Percentage usually reused
Planning	Never	None
Requirements	Practically never	None
Design	Very seldom	Small parts
Coding	Usually	Major parts
Integration/testing	Usually	Small parts, but growing
Installation and conversion	Very seldom	None

with effort. Another problem is when two, perhaps equivalent, programs are written, in different languages. What happens with LOC metrics is that the user of the "better" language is penalized. Fewer lines are written and hence the "productivity" is reduced. This is, of course, simply absurd. Again, LOC metrics can be useful when comparing existing code with existing code, in the same milieu and in the same languages – but certainly never more then that.

Let's look at what *should* have been in the standard. There are four basic kinds of metrics which this book recommends:

- **Productivity data collection**. Data items reflecting the productivity of the developers and the products that they are producing, over time/effort. They are used to measure costs of production and comparative costs of tool/technique use.
- **Development error data**. Collection and formal recording of data items concerning errors discovered during the development process (such as an error in a requirements document). Important to match the actual error data with the life-cycle stage and milieu in which it occurred. It is important to understand that by error here, we mean any anomalies which may be discovered.
- **Error estimation**. Error estimation (sometimes called error guesstimation, and not without reason) is a set of techniques used to judge the quantity of errors remaining in a system, and via this estimation, to provide a model for level of confidence. It is important to understand that by error here, we mean any anomalies that may be discovered.
- **After delivery error data**. Usually, the only kind of data ever collected. All anomalies discovered after delivery of the product to its users. This may include actual "events" occurred (i.e., problems).

If you have read about software quality metrics lately or you have any real experience in the field, you may be wondering why function points are not added to this list. The answer is two-fold. One is that they are covered by the **productivity data** discussed above. Two they are extremely subjective.

We shall avoid a long dissertation about function points, but saying something about them is appropriate, if for no better reason then that they have become popular (at least to talk about). AJ Albrecht first published the idea of function points in 1979 while working for IBM. The concept was a simple one. Software contains many "fixed" or "inelastic" costs which can be equated with the fixed cost of manufacturing. Albrecht considered that the visible aspects (i.e., the external aspects) is what needed to be examined. In this way, the tools used (such as programming languages) could be isolated from the measuring methodology. His idea was to "measure" by counting, and weighting, five items (it has since evolved to be a bit more complex, more on that below). The items are inputs, outputs, inquiries, updated data files and interfaces to other applications. The weighting factors were developed empirically (see Table 16.3). The idea being, to weight things according to the difficulty of their implementation. The method (the original one developed by Albrecht) consists of the following steps:

- Counting
- Multiplying by the weight
- Adding them together, which results in the "unadjusted total," and finally
- Adjusting by a customer complexity adjustment factor

Table 16.3 Empirical weighting factors

Item	Weight
Inputs	4
Outputs	5
Inquiries	4
Data files	10
Interfaces	7

In 1986 a nonprofit organization was formed called the International Function Point Users Group (IFPUG). This group was formed to encourage the use of this measurement and to further enhance it. In 1987 Britain adapted the methodology as a national standard. In 1990 IFPUG released what is known as release 3.0 of the metric (of the function point practices manual) which contains significant enhancements. Among other concepts, a "language level" was introduced which gives a weight to each of a very large list of languages for their inherent "power." This is meant to provide a way to convert existing software (which, as it exists, can be measured by LOC) into adjusted function points. For each language is also a number which gives an average number of lines needed to implement a function point. For examples, see Table 16.4 below. This concept of language level should not be confused with that developed by Maurice Halstead, though there are some similarities.

Table 16.4 Example levels and weighting factors

Language	Level	Source statements per function point
C	2.5	128
C++	11.0	29
Cobol	3.5	91
Fortran	3.0	105
PL/1	4.0	80

This idea of **source statements per function point** should be taken, perhaps, with a bit of caution. They are admitted to have an inaccuracy of between 25–50%. However, that does not mean that they cannot be a useful tool. They are another cost/effort estimating technique. None of the existing techniques are really any more accurate.

Recently IFPUG has released version 4.0 of the metric. We do not know of any differences which are significant to this forum.

Development Error Data

The collection and formal recording of data items one would expect during development are those which concern errors discovered during the development process (such as an error in a requirements document). Unfortunately, **after-delivery error data**, is usually, the only kind of data ever collected. These are all anomalies discovered after delivery of the product to its users. This may include actual "events" which have occurred (i.e., problems). One of our objectives should be to correct this imbalance. Table 16.5 gives some examples of the kinds of basic data that one should collect and store.

Table 16.5   Data to be collected

Identification data	Module name, references, resources
Size	# "Lines of …[req.; design; code; Doc; …]
Cost/effort data	Total staff-months – TMM
Duration	Total staff-months – TM
Results data	Tools, Req./Design (e.g. PDL), Coding (e.g. Languages)
Testing	Errors, Development Anomalies, Development Errors
After-delivery	

Caveat

The use of an equation like the following is dangerous, use only when languages and tools are identical and then with a great deal of care.[3] Many analysts consider this measurement to be not only anti-productivity but stupid and dangerous. I would tend to agree with that. While this measurement can be useful for comparing task sizes in the maintenance arena, almost any other use is not a good career move.

$$\text{Productivity} = \frac{\text{Lines of code}}{\text{Staff-months}}$$

Sample metric # 1

A model to calculate optimum project duration when the size is estimable, where the following apply: D = duration; E = Effort, in staff-months. This model has the following assumptions: "unlimited' manpower availability, no "loading" problems.

$$D = (1.875E)^{0.33} \text{ (meaning, cube root)}$$

D = duration
E = effort, in staff-months

Average staff size $= E/D$ (effort/duration)

Software reliability

Reliability is a statistical concept, such as mean time between failures. Existing errors are uncovered in a stochastic manner, faults tend to be governed by "whenever the worst can happen, it will." Errors are inherent to the code, failures are events. Where do failures come from? Interaction between "weak" code and unusual events are what causes software/system failures. What this means is that failures are functions of input. Previously unforeseen requirements may cause code to "go weak." Reliability reflects the product's ability to consistently operate failure free, in the environment for which it was designed. The statistical measurement is mean time between failures. This could be interpreted as failures of any kind, at any effect level. In hardware, particularly in electronics, engineers are accustomed to reliability prediction. The following table gives a list of some of the sources used for this. The only really important thing that can be said of this, for software engineering, is that these are statistical measurements of millions of examples of a

Table 16.6 Industry recognized reliability computation models

MIL Handbook 217
MIL Std 756 Reliability Modeling
MIL Std 785 Reliability Program
Bellcore
British Telecom – HRD(4)
IEEE 500
IEC, Canadian, …
Wiebull, FMEA/FMECA, Monte Carlo, …

particular component, over time. There is no way this can be made relevant to software, for the foreseeable future.

A key measure for reliability might be a failure ratio. While a measure for reliability might be the equation: $U = F/N$, where F = number of failed runs, N = total number of runs. Alternatively, a failure rate might be calculated where CPU time is concerned (t = CPU time in seconds). Something like: $U = F/t$. However, both of these are too trivial to be really applied to real software.

Metric rule # 1

A metric has value when its user can readily perceive a relationship between the metric and what is being measured.

How does one "test" a metric?[4] We suggest the three-step process:

- Use the metric to order the cases. Assign new metric values for cases which have yet to be measured and determine accuracy.
- Order the cases based upon the value of the item being measured, for example LOC vs effort. The ordering of one of these may be subjective. This establishes that a link does exist between the metric and what is measured. [In statistics this is a "correlation coefficient of nonzero value."]
- A statistics handbook may be used to calculate distribution, and so on.

To measure – quantifying and classifying the physical world – has always been a basic human trait. The ability to measure has enhanced technological advances by shedding light on pieces of nature's puzzle. JJ Horning, in 1980, made a very interesting prediction. He said: "I am convinced that in the course of the next decade there will be several major disasters that are directly (and properly) attributed to faults in computer programs" (for example airplane crashes, nuclear accidents, major corporate bankruptcies, and so on) Unfortunately, he was largely correct. They all happened, but it only took three years, not ten! Let us look at a couple of well-known example problems.

The first US Venus probe, which was coded in Fortran, was lost in space because of the following coding bug: The programmer thought that he had entered a DO Loop in the source code which would cycle three times, allocating the loop counter "I" the values 1, 2, then 3.

```
DO 3 I = 1,3
```

However, this was not quite the case. What had actually been entered was something visually very similar, but vastly different in operation:

```
DO 3 I = 1.3
```

For those not familiar with the language, in Fortran spaces are ignored. Additionally, variables that begin with the character "D" are "REAL" variables. What this statement actually performed was an assignment of the value 1.3 to the variable DO3I.

One of the authors was asked to maintain some software for a nuclear reactor. The code was written, once again, in Fortran (the version of code was known as Fortran II, this was quite some time ago). The work was done on a machine called an IBM 1130. The project was to convert the code to Fortran IV (that certainly dates me). I discovered a bug in the program, but could not immediately identify what was causing it. It took me more than two weeks of debugging activity to find what it was. (As a matter of fact, the stupidity of this example was what started me on the road to working with software quality in the first place.) What actually happened was that a subroutine was called from various points in the program. This routine had four formal parameters, some of which were intended for input and some for output. The routine assigned a value to one of the output variables (4). This was perfectly all right according to the rules of programming. However, at one point in the program, someone had written a call to the subroutine and had passed a *value*, rather then a *variable* (something like: "CALL S(1,2,3,4)"). What then happened, was that the constant "1" (numerical, one) then had the value of **four**! Every subsequent time that the constant was used (for instance, in a DO loop) the program then misbehaved. The compiler could not detect this. I found this intolerable.

Sample metric # 2
Embedded system empirical guesstimation measure

Development by group experienced with a specific airborne application	0.7 hours per byte of final code.
Not experienced with specific application	1.2 hours per byte.
For ground equipment	0.5 hours per byte.

Sample metric # 3
COCOMO. COCOMO – COst COnstructive MOdel[5]

Estimate lines of code to predict effort, cost and schedule. Compute values for development time and staff effort:

S = lines of deliverable source code (in K)
E = effort
T = time required
m = product of 15 (subjective) cost factors: (15 = "nominal')
$E = a(S)bm$
$T = 2.5(E)M$

Choose values from the following, very subjective, table:

Mode	a	b	
"Organic"	0.38	2.4	1.05
"Semidetached"	0.35	3.0	1.12
"Embedded"	0.32	3.6	1.20

Sample metric # 4
Halstead volume[6]

Maurice Halstead developed a methodology for measuring **computational** properties of a program, as an indication of a module's complexity.

$n1$ = # of unique operators
$n2$ = # of unique operands
$N1$ = # of occurrences of operators
$N2$ = # of occurrences of operands
n vocabulary = $n1 + n2$
N observed Length = $N1 + N2$
$N\char`\^$ estimated length = $n1(\log2(n1)) + n2(\log2(n2))$
V volume = $N(\log2(n))$
D difficulty = $(n1/2)/(N2/n2)$
L level = $1/D$
E effort = V/L

Sample metric # 5
McCabe – Cyclomatic complexity[7]

Tom McCabe developed a methodology to measure **control flow complexity** of a module by drawing a flow graph of the module's logic. Count the following:

e = edges (transfers of control)
n = nodes (block of statements)
p = control paths

Compute:
$C = e - n + 2p$
C = complexity

Sample metric # 6
Function points

AJ Albrecht invented function point analysis (FPA) around 1979 or 1980. FPA is intended to be used for measuring, guesstimating and predicting a system's functionality, in a quantified manner – this is both for development and maintenance. FPA discusses tasks, and their size.

$$\text{Total size of task = intrinsic size of task *}$$
$$\text{environmental factors}$$

$$\text{Intrinsic size of task = information processing}$$
$$\text{size * technical complexity factors}$$

- The criteria for level of complexity needs to be defined, for example, an input with less than n fields will be called "simple."

Table 16.7 Deciding information processing size in a task

	Simple	Medium	Complex	Total
Inputs	3– ?	4– ?	6– ?	?
Outputs	4– ?	5– ?	7– ?	?
Logical files	7– ?	10– ?	15– ?	?
Queries	3– ?	4– ?	6– ?	?
Interfaces	5– ?	7– ?	10– ?	?

- The total arrived at is still "raw material" and is called: "unadjusted function points."
- For establishing the technical complexity (in the second equation), 14 aspects should be used:
    1. data communications
    2. distributed processing
    3. performance requirements
    4. loaded requirements
    5. transaction frequency
    6. on-line input
    7. efficiency of the end-user
    8. on-line update
    9. computational complexity
    10. reusability
    11. installation simplicity
    12. operational simplicity
    13. multisite system
    14. change flexibility.

For each of these aspects one should give a value:

Does not effect it	0
Minimal effect	1
Small effect	2
Medium effect	3
Large effect	4
Very large effect	5

The total will be between zero and 70. This represents the "degree of effect" – impact – (DI).

- To calculate the "internal function point count" – which is the raw function point count – one takes a correction coefficient for the technical complexity:

$$0.65 + 0.01 * DI$$

The result is a number in the range of 0.65–1.35.

- The authors recommend that this be used only after you have gained a great deal of experience in metric application and have gathered at least two years of data from production and maintenance. This quantity will be the minimal amount needed before you can be certain that you have a reasonable handle on what all those coefficients may mean. This methodology is very subjective, and therefore suspect as to whether its results can be experimentally repeatable.

Sample metric # 7
Quality level[8]

Divide the total defects by the total number of inspected items and multiply by 100. This gives the "quality level" (QL) of the product in percentage of defects. Taking 100 and subtracting the QL gives the degree of excellence.

This may be applicable to software, but it is not trivial.

Other sample metrics

Measure quality of textual documents, for example readability. Measure quality of requirements/design, for example consistency checks, completeness checks, readability and standards.

Sample metric comparisons

Compare: an embedded system of 10,000 line (estimated) of new code, developed by an experienced group.

$$E = 3.6(10,000)1.2\ 15 = 3,400,000$$

$$T = 2.5(3.4 \times 106)0.32$$

$$t = [1.875(3.4 \times 106)0.33\ \text{COCOMO}\ T = 308$$

$$\text{QA}\ t = 185$$

Table 16.8   Differences between hardware and software

H/W	S/W
Assumed to be 100% good at supply	The exact quality is not measurable
Errors caused by wear-down	Errors are built-in by the development process
Distinct separation between design and manufacture	Production is via process of step-wise design refinement
Stable once in production	Constant pressure of change forces instability

Reliability

The statistical measurement of mean time between failures (MTPF). This may mean failures of any kind, at any effect level. One of the 11 quality attributes of software. It is user, not developer oriented. The concept is similar to hardware, shows that software is increasingly becoming closer to hardware. It is neither useful nor available in early test stages (when data collection begins). A reliability measure reflects the product's ability to consistently operate failure-free, in the environment for which it was designed.

Sample metric # 8
MTBF

MTBF is the average time (generally, hours) expected to elapse between failures. MTBF is generally calculated by dividing: t, total test hours (for a sample) by f, total number of failures. However, for software, that is clearly insufficient. Hardware MTBF is calculated based upon monitoring all components, in software we can not really do that. For software, by substituting "overage analysis" for "component monitoring" we can approach the hardware concept.

Statement coverage:

$S = \dfrac{\text{No. statements executed}}{\text{Total no. statements}}$

Logic coverage:

$L = \dfrac{\text{No. branches executed}}{\text{total no. branches}}$

$$\text{MTBF} = \frac{t \ [S \cdot L]}{f}$$

An alternate measure uses calculated MTBF to determine a measurement of reliability

$$R = e^{-(t/m)}$$

R being the probability a device will perform for t, target life-time, m is the MTBF. Note that: (a) usefulness for software has yet to be determined; (b) target life-time for software can generally not be predicted, it is always much longer then anyone thought reasonable.

Confidence Level

The probability that the true MTBF of the product exceeds the demonstrated MTBF value.

Reliability activity goal

*   To project software system readiness for acceptance
*   To project reliability in operation
*   To provide the user with a confidence level (this must be based on test results).

"The algorithm" is:

*   Determine audience
*   Define objectives
*   Define data
*   Collect and verify data
*   Analyze and synthesize information content – direct results to audience

Software Quality Metric

A Software quality metric is:

A function which inputs software data and outputs a single value interpretable as the degree to which software possesses an attribute that affects quality.

The activity attempts to develop tools to identify quality characteristics and use them to develop productivity measurements. **Remember that software "units of work" measure a social activity and not production or productivity in the sense of manufacturing.** Remember also that all measures of software "units of work" must be: defined very carefully, compared on an equal basis, and used with great skill, to be of any value. A current assessment of software quality metrics might be that a framework is established with preliminary methodologies. These include those aspects needed for initial application. However, additional validation is required. While the usefulness of their application is clearly established, more tools are needed for this to be really effective.

CMM Compatibility

CMM has no reference to metrics. Level 4, the "managed" level, does specify activities for collecting, storing and reporting quantitative data about a project's software process. There are no specific requirements for the measurements to be taken. At best, there is a list of some examples which include:

- The planned or estimated software size, cost, schedule vs the actual
- Productivity data (no recommendations or suggestions offered)
- Quality measurements as defined in the software quality plan
- Coverage and efficiency of peer reviews
- Effectiveness of training
- Test coverage and efficiency
- Software reliability measures
- Number and severity of defects discovered in the software requirements
- Number and severity of defects discovered in the software code.
- Number and rate of closure on action items

Similiarly, there are no required or recommended analysis procedures. The document does include the following short list of examples:

- Pareto diagrams
- Control charts
- Trend diagrams
- Scatter diagrams

Since we have already commented on the sorry state of the art, nothing more need be added here.

ISO 9000 Compatibility

This entire lengthy explanation that you have received here, is described by ISO 9001 in its final paragraph "4.20 Statistical techniques." This paragraph simply states that one needs to establish documented procedures for measuring process capabilities. We think you have them now.

Notes

1 Crosby, PB Quality is free, the ART of making quality certain! How to manage quality so that it becomes a source of profit for your business!
2 MIL Std-2155; Failure reporting, analysis and corrective action system. This standard describes how one is to systematically record and follow-up on errors in order to find their causes and to prevent them from recurring. While the standard is designed for hardware, it is very instructive for software quality assurance, as well.
3 Jones, Capers (1996) Should the "lines of code" metric be viewed as professional malpractice? 1 November, Software Productivity Research, Inc., private communication.
4 For example, Oakes, M (1986) *Statistical Inference: A Commentary for the Social and Behavioural Sciences*, John Wiley.
5 Boehm, B. (1981) Improving software productivity, in chapter 33, *Software Engineering Economics*, Prentice-Hall.
6 Halstead, HM (1977) *Elements of Software Science*, North-Holland, New York.
7 McCabe, T (1976) Complexity measure, *IEEE Transactions on Software Engineering*, SE-2, No. 4, December.
8 Chacon, SM (1988) All he had to do was ask, *Quality Progress*; May.

TRAINING

17

This chapter identifies the training activities, and the resources required for this training, needed to implement the SQAP.

TRAINING IS COVERED BY CHAPTER 14 OF THE SQAP. THE NEED for an organized program of training should be obvious to anyone dealing in high-technological industries. Unfortunately, it is not. The SQAP, in this chapter, deals with training needed in order to accomplish the defined QA tasks. Once again, if this is the only place where these things may be covered, do not be afraid to include here training for other aspects of the system or organization. If they are covered elsewhere, fine. Someone else has taken care of it. If not, it is your problem to document (and frequently, force people to think about the issues).

Clearly, the first thing that needs to be done is to assess the training needs. Considerations for training needs will include special tools and new methodologies. Also, do not forget that SQA evaluation (self-evaluation) and SQA management must not be neglected. If SQA is to be a stepping-stone to management of the organization, training must be good.

Establish a training plan. Programs may be adapted, purchased or developed to meet the needs. The important thing is to make everyone aware and to show realistic budgets and goals. Remember also to align these needs with the tasks and schedules discussed in chapter 3 of the plan. Finally, if this is a project plan (rather then a corporate plan) remember to update the matrix as training goals are reached. If this is a corporate plan remember that this needs to be reviewed at least annually, and also to update the matrix as training goals are reached.

The following worksheet will allow rapid identification of training needs for each task and individual. Training shall include both task oriented training and tools oriented.

SQAP planning worksheet # 17-1

Skills planning

Project: _____   Planner: _____

Date: _____   SQAP: _____

Supplier Name: _____   Contact: _____

Item #	SQA Task	Skill requirements	Existing personnel skills
1			
2			
3			
4			
5			
6			
7			
8			
9			
10			

CMM Compatibility

CMM refers to training requirements at a number of levels. At CMM level 2, the "Repeatable" level, training needs are described at a number of points as "Abilities." Specifically, CMM level 2 requires that software managers, software subcontract managers, software engineers, the SQA group, the software configuration management (SCM) group and software engineering groups be trained in order to carry out their functions.

For CMM level 3, the "Defined" level, establishing and maintaining a training program is a *key process area* that is required for certification. The defined objective of the training program:

> is to develop the skills and knowledge of individuals so they can perform their roles effectively and efficiently.

The organization is required to develop a written policy on training, set up an adequate budget and to establish a group to be responsible for ensuring that the training needs of the organization are met. Training policies and programs are monitored for compliance and effectiveness and are subject to review and modification. In addition, each software project needs to evaluate current and future skills needs and to determine how additional skills are to be acquired from on-the-job training and informal mentoring to guided self-study and classroom training.

At level 5, the "Optimizing" level, the process of monitoring and upgrading the training program is made even more formal through the employment of a change management procedure. Training objectives and some methods described in this chapter do meet and exceed the CMM requirements for software projects at levels 2 and 3. They do **not** address the level 3 and level 5 general requirements for an organization as a whole. This will require a much larger investment in management organization, people time and money.

ISO 9000 Compatibility

Paragraph 4.18, called: "Training;" discusses the training needs of the whole company. Remember that this needs to be adapted to software. This is not difficult. Other then that, there are no special needs in terms of ISO 9001 or ISO 9000-3.

RISK MANAGEMENT

18

This chapter specifies the procedures employed to identify, assess, monitor and control areas of perceived risk.

R
ISK MANAGEMENT IS DEALT WITH IN CHAPTER 15 OF THE SQAP. It is the final chapter of the plan, according to the standard. However, additional topics are permitted, if desired. As this is a topic which is not well known, we have chosen to discuss it here at some length.

In discussing and examining risk analysis, one cannot limit the concept only to projects or products in development, though that is the most common activity of the risk management discipline. This procedure explains the process of managing risk through analysis. Under no circumstances is this procedure intended to provide solutions to perceived risks or to imply any such solutions. Each risk area (technical, economic, schedule, managerial, marketing) must be identified and this identification must be justified. (Why is this thought to be a risk? With whom has SQA staff consulted? What information has reached SQA to lead them to believe that this is a risk?) The risk factors should be identified, as well as the level of risk. Possible impacts and alternative courses of action should be identified. Every reasonable attempt should be made to quantify the risk.

Caveat

This section must only relate to the risks (presumably technological or technological results) which may occur as a result of the software life-cycle covered by this SQAP.

Risk Assessment

Objective

The overall objective of risk management is provision of a rational foundation on which to base decisions concerning the risks which must be faced. This includes the identification of likely failure points of the project, (or activity) and the risks thereby existing for the organization and/or for related organizations. The process of identification of the risks involved in the software portion of the project, is identical to the process which would be used for any other kind of project. Conceptually, it is similar to fault tree analysis. This is also called failure mode effect and analysis, which is the result of this kind of analysis. Generally, this is used in hardware, but in can be used for software systems, as well, and very effectively. The final objective is, of course, to increase the confidence level of the product.

- When and why can the system, or some part of it fail? Remember, every system created by mankind does eventually fail
- What is the likelihood of such a failure?
- What may happen (to people, to other systems, to the system's mission) when the system does fail?

In typical businesses, the price of nonconformance (PONC) is 25% of **business activities**. If this seems high, remember that in software, PONC is 50% of **everything** that is done! This means that fully half of everything that is done to, with, for or as a result of software, is error correction. Twice what the rest of the world suffers. Clearly software is not really under control. ***Your goal in this activity should be to cut this cost to 40% in two years.*** This is an achievable goal. After that goal has been reached, the suggested goal to strive for is 25% in a five-year time frame.

Risk assessment should strive to quantify the magnitude of every identified risk. Managers should monitor the risks in their assigned areas and develop plans for elimination or reduction of the risks. They also need to report on progress concerning their risks. Every risk assessment item should be documented under headings such as:[1]

- Description
- Impact
- Monitoring
- Mitigation

As risks change during the software systems life-cycle, as indeed they had better, the QA plan should be updated to reflect the new status. Clearly, if the project is not large enough to allow the resources for such an update, then this can be done in the postmortem. I strongly recommend making the effort. It is very cost-effective.

Fault Tree Analysis

A fault tree is an excellent tool for defining problems concerned with the reliability of systems. This is particularly so if the definition of the problem is multidisciplinary, representing professionals having different (read: contradictory) sets of priorities, or who may have conflicting ideas as to what constitutes proper operating and maintenance practices. Fault tree analysis does not need to be expensive or difficult – if it is performed correctly. The tool can be used in a simple or a sophisticated manner, depending on the requirements and experience of the user. Reviewing and structuring of the information assists the analyst in a clear under-standing of the fault tree's logic. Management is usually interested just in the major events and not the details, but the analyst needs to have access to most of the details. A fault tree is based on events, which can be represented by codes.

One main purpose of fault tree analysis is logical identification of factors leading, or contributing, to the occurrence of the top event – the main system-level fault. Numerical evaluation is usually a secondary goal. Cross-links between supposedly independent systems may have very serious, and often surprising, effects on overall reliability. Another one of the primary functions of this reliability analysis technique is to identify cross-links, test for independence and assess their importance. The remainder of the tree will usually be calculated via a simulation technique, such as Monte Carlo simulation. The probabilities for all events can be displayed on the skeleton. This may help in tracing the cause for a too high, or a too low probability. It might be possible to find analysis results by Boolean reduction.

There may be branches with replicated events, but if none of them are used outside, the effect is minimal. Search for independent branches used globally. A tree may also have branches without replicated events. They can be processed separately – self-contained branches can also be analyzed separately. Partitioning of a large tree often simplifies the analy-sis. We recommend an algorithm which searches for independent branches, assuming that after a branch has been identified as self-con-tained, it is removed. Independent branches may be truncated. Trunca-tion is used for simplifying trees for presentation.

Graphical editing can be used for highlighting some aspect of the tree, to better visualize it. If a branch is not self-contained, and the top gate shows events used elsewhere, they can be removed. This may be useful sometimes for plotting. Editing commands should not change the logic of the tree. This reduces possibilities of errors. An experienced analyst may use an overlay with additional capabilities. Event descriptions can be inserted. When a large tree is analyzed, the analyst may wish to isolate two or more branches for a separate analysis. When two branches are defined, they may have a common event. The use of failure rate and restoration time may be helpful. Event names should also be "searchable."

It should be possible to find where events are by looking at a condensed skeleton of the tree. The analyst should be able to tell if a single event, or a combination of two events can cause the top event to occur.

Risk Management Breakdown

The SQAP or the software development plan should identify the possible areas of risk of the project. After **risk identification**, **justification** and **breakdown**, the particular SQA activities in relation to each risk are presented. This presentation should be in a tabular form. The table must clearly list each risk and each and every SQA activity relating to the risk. An example of a SQA activity relating to a risk might be an extra review or specialized documentation. In some projects, the development activities relating to the area of risk may also be listed here. If so, this section must be clearly signed off by the head of development. In general, managing risk implies proper management.[2] It is similar to the management of any other technical issue. Not only that, but the "risk" in risk management becomes quite simple to understand (and manage) when once one understands that it consists of a coherent series of steps.

- Ascertain whether the risks are concerned with technology, implementability, management, marketing or other kinds of risk
- Each risk area or item must be clearly identified – including any and all parts. Risks, particularly technological, frequently tend to a hierarchical nature
- After the risk/risks have been clearly identified, an impact assessment must be performed
- Finally, the risk and its chosen handling procedures must then be allocated to the parties responsible for their application

There must be a follow-through activity to ensure that the risk has been dealt with sufficiently. This is a management/product assurance task, not directly related to the risks. In other words, risk management is the management of the decision-making process, with emphasis on minimizing risk and (hence) maximizing long-term results.

Hazard Identification and Categories

Hazard identification procedures divide into three stages: risk factor identification (by components); justification and categorization. Risks which exist in technological environments, or consist of a technological nature, may be included in one or more of the following six risk categories.

Technical problems

Any and all, technical problems which may relate to the general implementability of the system. An example of this might be unfamiliarity of the organization [read: the development team] with the application or the technologies being used to implement it.

Product stability

Stability of the product and/or the perceived system requirements of the product. These system level and product level requirements are as defined by, and/or for, the final intended user of the product.

Acquisition difficulties

Any and all difficulties which may arise as a result of, or as part of, the systems acquisition process. These difficulties may be directly related to the process of acquisition, such as constructing requirements for technology with which the organization is unfamiliar, or a schedule which causes difficulties greater than normal. Alternatively, they may be the result of the implementation of the system by/for the organization.

Social impacts

Social impacts of the system are similar to the previous risk "acquisition difficulties." They may occur as a result of implementation, or as a result of the acquisition process. The consequences of the social impact of the system might include public or individual safety considerations (for example by the end of 1988, more than 100 persons have been killed or seriously injured in accidents directly relating to software errors in industrial robots.)

This must also include such "purely" social questions as:

- Emplacement of new technology into an organization against the wishes of (some of) the employees or the labor union/organization
- Possible "job obsolescence"
- Displacement of people after system implementation, and
- How the organization is to plan for reassignments

Economic impact

Risks relating, directly or indirectly, to any possible economic impacts to the organization as a result of the system's implementation (read: deployment) of the system. One example of this would include guesstimation of the accuracy of predictions of inflation or currency rate fluctuations. Another aspect of economic impacts of modern systems may be an environmental impact – though this is not commonly a concern of the software. Where this must be accounted for, the economic results of ignoring this factor may be overwhelming.

Failure impact!

The possible impact that a failure to implement, or a failure to implement correctly, the system may have on the organization. This may include, for instance, a lessened ability to compete in the organization's chosen market place. The intention is the impact of failure of the acquisition/development effort on the organization.

Table 18.1 Risk category summary

Item #	Factor
1	Technical problems
2	Product stability
3	Acquisition difficulties
4	Social impacts
5	Economic impact
6	Failure impact

Hazard Identification Procedure

Hazard components

Technological risks are (almost always) composed of several, hierarchical, risk factors. The concept of risk factors refers to the hierarchical decomposition of the risk. That is to say, what the individual parts are and how they are relate to one another. This must be clearly identified, and presented in such a manner that anyone (all involved), within the organization or external to the organization, will be simply and readily capable of understanding the ramifications, to them, of the perceived risk.

The presentation method recommended by this procedure is to display all these risk factors in a semi-formal, hierarchical presentation, such as a cause-and-effect chart (sometimes called a "fish-bone" or "Ishikawa" chart) or a control chart. This may be further augmented (if needed) by a listing of the contributing factors and the relationships between factors, between hazards and, between factors and hazards.

Risk justification

As stated above, the hazard identification procedure is divided into three stages. Once the existence of the hazard has been ascertained, and agreed on, the identification must be justified.

◆ Why does QA (or whoever else is responsible for risk auditing) believe it to be an area of risk?
◆ With whom, of the developing team (identify by job title, not by name) has QA consulted about the risk?
◆ What specific information has reached QA which leads them to believe that this is a risk area?

Categorization

Each hazard identified must be classified according to one or more of the six classes listed in Table 18.1 above. When the risks are complex or complicated, each risk factor must be categorized as well.

The Feedback Mechanism

The hazard identification/auditing process itself poses a risk to the project. This risk exists because the process is generally unfamiliar to both the auditor and the audited (the project team). Also, if the risk analysis process goes awry, serious resource misutilization damage may be caused to the project.

This risk factor can generally be reduced by creating an efficient feedback mechanism. This feedback mechanism utilizes the presentation method presented above. The risks, their component factors and their categorizations are presented for review to all the parties involved in the development process who may have a bearing on the risks. This, of course, includes the users and management.

Risk Evaluation

Each and every identified hazard must be evaluated. The process of evaluation is simplified by use of sorting. All hazards must be sorted in two groupings. That means, they will be listed and sorted twice. The two sorted lists are then displayed "next" to one another – in parallel. These sorts are:

• by the level of danger each perceived hazard presents to the organization
• by the probability of occurrence of each hazard

Risk Dangers

The concept of the danger/dangers which the perceived hazard presents to the organization must be broken down into one or more of the categories presented in Table 18.2. The meanings of the individual categories are self-explanatory.

Table 18.2 Risk danger/criticality categories

Level	Factor	
1	Life threatening or serious injury	High
2	System may be destroyed – such as an air/sea/land vehicle	
3	Mission lost or significant degradation	
4	Theft, misuse or damage to assets	Medium
5	Incomplete mission or selected functional areas of concern	
6	Environmental/social damage	Low
7	Concern for system maintainability	
8	User inconvenience[3]	

Risk Probabilities

Understanding the probability of occurrence of each risk is of utmost importance in understanding the actions needed to be taken as a result of the risk being perceived. Recall the discussion of the dangers inherent in the risk analysis process above. Many times risks have been perceived, but on detailed examination it has been discovered that they are insignificant, because they can never occur. As such, risk probability shall be broken down into three categories, simply:

- High probability
- Medium probability
- Low probability

Significance

It is very important to note the significance of both these lists, for two reasons. First, the lists are interdependent. Their methodical creation has a synergistic effect – one upon the other and on the "author" of the lists. Second, many risks are composed of set scenarios; only when several of them occur in conjunction does the danger to the organization become evident/real.

Reporting

At this stage, it is critical that all parties to the perceived risk be advised of the findings. This reporting is in addition to what has been stated above (in paragraph 4.3). The whole process will prove moot if the feedback loops are not sufficiently clear to all concerned.

A proper presentation of the risk analysis is critical to the overriding success of the process of management of the project. Risk estimates must be expressed in understandable terms. "Understandable" should preferably mean numeric, however, understandability must be the emphasis not toying with numbers. Uncertainties surrounding estimates of hazards (probabilities, and so on) are to be explained in simple and understandable language.

As a minimum, the "risk analysis report" shall consist of at least the following sections:

- Title page
- Executive summary – this section shall include conclusions and recommendations
- Table of contents
- Scope, purpose and objectives
- System identification – this section shall include a brief (say half-page) description of the system under discussion
- Analysis methodology
- Hazard identification results
- Model description (optional)
- Quantitative data obtained (optional)
- Risk estimation results – this section shall include the perceived degrees of uncertainty
- References and appendices

Risk Management

The management of risk is, as has been stated, similar to the management of any other technical issue. That means that it must be carefully planned to be successful. This procedure recommends that risk management be made a part of either the QA plan or the software development plan of the project. A specific section of the plan must be created to deal with the questions of risk, and these questions should be dealt with as has been stated above. The specific section of the QA plan[4] shall identify the areas of risk and their assessments.

After risk identification, justification and breakdown, the particular developer or QA activities – in relation to each risk – are presented. This presentation should be in a tabular form. The table must clearly list each risk (together with its subcomponents) and each and every QA activity relating to the risk. An example of a QA activity relating to a risk might be an extra review or specialized documentation. In any case, all risk-related activities must be evaluated by QA.

In some kinds of projects and/or environments, development activities which relate to specific areas of risk may also be listed in the same table. If this is the chosen method, this section must be clearly signed off by the head of development (in addition to normal QA plan sign-offs). This is to ensure visibility of the process of risk analysis. In no case can the risk analysis and risk management processes be called reasonable, without a high degree of visibility.

CMM Compatibility

CMM takes a restricted view of risks that concern the software project alone. At level 2, project planing activity 13 is defined to identify, assess and document software risks associated with the cost, resource, schedule and technical aspects of the project. The identified risks are to be analyzed and prioritized according to the possible impact on the project. Contingencies are to be identified including schedule buffers, alternate plans for staffing and for additional computing equipment. Project tracking and oversight activity 10 records the aspects identified in planning activity 13 and adjusts the risks and contingencies. High-risk activities are to be reviewed with the project manager on a regular basis. At level 3 the organization is required to establish a procedure for managing software risks of each project.

The techniques specified for risk management far exceed the requirements of the CMM specifications.

ISO 9000 Compatibility

ISO 9001 does not really seem to discuss risk management. However, paragraph 4.3, which discusses "contract review" can be construed to discuss at least a part of the problem. This will not be helpful for an internal project (there is no contract, certainly not a formal one).

Notes

1 Much of the text in this chapter of the book may be similar to that in the IEEE Guide to Software Quality Assurance Planning (the as-yet unpublished draft). This is not plagiarism, the first author wrote them both.
2 Tom DeMarco, in the Keynote address for the eighteenth International Conference on Software Engineering stated that, in his opinion, risk management is the one single activity in software with the highest return on investment.
3 This danger may result in a reduced willingness by the client/user to purchase this or further systems/products from the vendor.
4 Remember, if you are using IEEE 730, it contains a section (15) concerning risks and risk management.

Comparison of the ISO 9000 Model with SEI's CMM[1,2]

19

T HE PURPOSE OF THIS CHAPTER IS TO MAKE YOU ANGRY WITH the authors. (Isn't that a great way to start a chapter? Hopefully it will grab your attention for the entire chapter!) Both models that we want to discuss here deal with methods of assessing the ability of suppliers to meet their commitments. Clearly, the existence of two models with completely different approaches raises some very important questions.[3] If I comply with CMM level n, how does that relate to ISO 9000 certification? If I have ISO 9000 certification for software, what CMM level does that equate to? We shall find the answers to these questions rather surprising.

The "bottom line"

There is very little in common between the two models! Other then the fact that both models deal with methods of **assessing the ability of suppliers to meet their commitments**. Speaking of differences is like comparing apples and doughnuts. Comparisons of this to that, are simplistic and do not really work.

The capability maturity model (CMM) is a five-level framework for measuring **software engineering practices,** as they relate to process. It contains a rating system designed to determine the degree of technological maturity of an organization as determined, in part, by the answers to some 101 questions. A CMM assessment usually takes about five working days and is conducted by a team of about four people. The assessors must be highly-trained professionals, themselves with a great deal of development experience. The SEI takes great care to retain control over who an assessor is and what rights the person may claim to have. It should be emphasized that the questionnaire itself plays only a minor part in the whole assessment. It is used to gather data, but it is certainly not the only source.

ISO 9000, on the other hand is vastly different. ISO 9000 defines a minimum level of generic attributes for a **quality management program**. Thus we see the first dichotomy between the two models. The fact that one is specifically for software development practices/processes while the other is for a generic quality management model. While ISO 9000-3 has cleared up some of the resulting confusion,[4] this is far from a definitive answer, as we shall see below. The set of generic attributes includes 20 areas of activity.

One must also add that the CMM addresses only software, while ISO 9000 addresses the entire organization. Many differences may appear, actually that result from the large difference in the actual **organization** being examined.

In comparing the two models, we have chosen to examine them firstly from the standpoints of where they are lacking. Many people do not like this. The primary concern in this chapter is to make certain that an organization which chooses to use such a model, does so with an open mind and with a full understanding of the advantages and disadvantages inherent in them. Another point which ought to be raised here is why this particular "pair" of models was chosen. Clearly, the ISO model is obvious, quality is the subject of this book. However, the IEEE 1074 model could have been chosen as well as the SEI's CMM. The answer lies in the degree of complexity of the comparison. Though the models are very different, they do have a certain communality of concept, albeit a bit vague.

As an interesting side issue, the SEI is issuing a new model which they call the "people management capability maturity model (P-CMM)," or, for that matter, many others (these three are the most significant today. The P-CMM is an adaptation of the CMM for software, concerned with developing an organization's talent, especially in software and information systems development.[5]

In actually examining the model, the first author saw no reason to link this effort particularly with software. It appears to be applicable to any organization. This may be either good (equally usable by anyone) or bad (too general, too generic, to be really used by anyone). Only time will tell.

The Models' Orientations

The **orientation** of SEI's CMM is the software development process. As stated in their most significant report (CMU/SEI-93-TR-24; ESC-TR-93-177) Capability maturity model for software, Version 1.1 of February, 1993 (authored by Paulk, Mark C. *et al.*):

> The CMM was specifically developed to provide an orderly, disciplined framework with which to address software management and engineering process issues.

The model describes a series of levels, five in number: key process areas (KPA) and their usages. In this framework, software quality is a KPA, as a matter of fact, it is two. Software QA is a KPA of level 2 (that is, an organization must have this in place to be classed as a level 2 organization), while software quality management is a KPA of level 4. Their stated purposes are as follows:

> **Software quality assurance, a key process area for level 2: repeatable.**
>
> The purpose of software quality assurance is to provide management with appropriate visibility into the process being used by the software project and of the products being built.
>
> **Software quality management, a key process area for level 4: managed.**
>
> The purpose of software quality management is to develop a quantitative understanding of the quality of the project's software products and achieve specific quality goals.

Note that both of these definitions are specific to the SEI and do not conform to industry accepted standards. I do not think this is a good thing. An engineering profession grows by building on existing work. (Remember what Isaac Newton said about standing on others' shoulders? Newton was a very smart man.)

The **orientation** of ISO 9000-3 is quality system management! (This is not *exactly*, quality assurance.) Or, to put it perhaps more accurately, the objectives of the ISO 9000 series, in general, is the structure and auditability of the QA function of an organization.

> The purposes of this international standard are
>
> a) to clarify the distinctions and interrelationships among the principle quality concepts, and
> b) to provide guidelines for the selection and use of a series of international standards on quality systems that can be used for quality management purposes ...

The then *more limited* objective of ISO 9000-3 is to provide this auditability for software, where it has traditionally been much more difficult and less obvious. In principle, these both sound very good but both of these models are too limited. Let us examine this **first** by looking at the basic weaknesses with each of these two "wondrous" models.

> This should not be misconstrued to imply that there are only weaknesses, quite the contrary. We must state at the beginning that we are deeply committed to both of these models. They are both very good, and certainly are vast improvements over the past, which totally lacked such methodologies. Although we agree there is a great deal to be said for them, this has been covered by numerous authors. We have chosen the technique of describing their weaknesses because we feel that is the strongest method for comparison.. The objective here is to help you to be able to implement them better by means of understanding where their faults lie.

ISO 9000 Weaknesses

Issue 1: Complexity

ISO 9000 itself is not simply a standard, but a set (a series) of standards, which now includes many documents. As a matter of fact, it includes standards that are not numbered "9000" at all! (see Table 19.1, which contains some of them as well as illustrating the structure of this set of standards). Table 19.1 is, of course, only a partial example! ISO 9004 has some eight parts (this was the last we heard, there may be more now). In addition, ISO 10000 concerns many **auditing** issues which are essential to the successful fulfillment of ISO demands. This complexity greatly increases the confusion, and costs, of implementation.

Table 19.1 ISO quality standards structure

Generic	The model	Guides	Others	Guides to the others
9000	9001 9002 9003	9000-2, 3 ...	9004	9004-1,7 (and more)
10011	10011-1, 2, 3		10012-1	

Issue 2: Repeatability (i.e., reliability of the audit)

One of the most pressing weaknesses is **who audits the auditor**? There are no simple solutions but there are **national** efforts. The most important of these is the British effort, which is called: "TickIt✓."[6] Though this has not been broadly **adopted** by other countries (the British themselves have made this extraordinarily difficult) it is almost *universally accepted*. (Apparently, while most western countries have agreements of mutual recognition, the British national effort seems to be the only effort so far to produce a full methodology (albeit, only really for data processing, not really suitable for real-time).) This is likely to be the reason for its acceptance – it is usually, at least, thought to be the best, most thorough, of the efforts. Among these issues of nationalist pride, this is astoundingly refreshing.

As an example (and one of the reasons TickIt✓ is admired), the TickIt✓ auditor certification procedure places very stringent demands on the auditor: The TickIt✓ office has created the following methodology for certification of a qualified TickIt✓ auditor:

- TickIt✓ course
- Interview
- Auditor certification levels
  – Provisional auditor
  – Senior auditor
  – Lead TickIt✓ certification auditor

There is no universally accepted system for **certifying** an ISO 9000 auditor! ISO itself does not get involved at all in this sort of thing. The international office deals only with national bodies. In the UK there are several companies which are *authorized* to certify organizations – some tens of companies for general certification and some six or seven for software. In principal, anyone can "hang out a shingle" and claim to provide ISO 9000 certification. The only question is when you accept a certifier is whether their certificate will be accepted when someone actually wants to audit you as a possible supplier.

Issue 3: Inherent structure

It is **extremely important** to remember that a software organization is not audited according to ISO 9000-3 but only according to ISO 9001. The quality **audit** is **performed according** to **ISO 9001!**

- The ISO 9000 series was designed to audit the quality processes at a manufacturing/service organization. **Software is *purely* design**, there is no manufacturing stage. Only in ISO 9001 (as opposed to ISO 9002 or ISO 9003) is design even acknowledged (that is the difference between them).

- ISO 9000-3 was intended to bridge this gap, but it is only a **guideline**. This structural anomaly is not solvable under the present methodologies for auditing.

Issue 4: Key audit factors

- Even if we were to look only at ISO 9000-3, the items to be accounted for are very limited.
- Most key process areas are not even really mentioned – at least, not in the same way that they are referred to by software professionals (for example requirements, design, testing, project management, and so on).
- ISO 9001 contains 20 "Quality system requirements." Annex B of 9000-3 claims to show that they are all relevant to software, but some of these references are a bit tenuous. For example, it has yet to be determined why, or at least how frequently, "Handling, storage, packaging, preservation and delivery" are important for a data processing installation. It is certainly true that we can adopt these things to our use – storage might be camouflage for software configuration management – the intentions are very markedly different.
- While certainly one can simply ignore innocuous, obviously irrelevant, requirements, it is clearly better not to have to waste time and effort on them.

There are no **agreed-upon** metrics for any area! Compliance is a "binary" you are either compliant or not. This certainly does not become, over time, conducive to quality improvement. (See issue 5, below.)

- How important is **packaging** to software quality? Usually not very.
- **Software configuration management** is separately handled by several different clauses while in software this is an absolutely critical technology, with whom a lack of success is almost ensured.
- **Software product maintenance** is essentially not covered.
- *Software* **project control** is quite different from building houses, or anything else!

Issue 5: Processes/product improvement

The concepts are essentially nonexistent!

- Internationally
- Broadly accepted and known
- Has become a **very important** marketing issue

CMM Weaknesses

Issues 1: Granularity

The defined granularity is much too small. There probably should be a granularity of (say) 10 and allow some sort of "*shading*" for instances when a site excels in one technology but lacks in another.

- Motorola uses a *bar graph* showing a score of 0 to 10. Not binary in each KPA. You can see where you are per process area. This is clearly more productive.
- The CMM is now changing. Apparently, in CMM Version 2.0^7 one can look at "other level KPAs" even though you are at level n, you can look at a KPA of level $n + 1$.

The score is a by-product. **The objective of the process is to identify opportunities for advancement.**

Issue 2: People/process/technology

The CMM is based on a premise that software is: *people/process/ technology*. This is insufficient. What is demanded to produce software which is:

- High **quality**
- **Useful,** and
- On **time** and within **budgets**

is much more than just these simple items. We need to see reference to facilities and premises, customer's view, interfaces, cataloging of software items and several other items.

In other words, the model is too simplistic!

Facilities and premises

Research has repeatedly shown that a badly designed site is not conducive to productivity. Lighting, distractions, noise, work-place design, and so on – all have adverse effects on the costs and accuracy of the process.

Customer's view

Without this, everything we do is valueless. A methodology which attempts to understand what construction of software is all about needs to address the prospective user of the system being developed. Customers do not understand its importance until it is too late.

- **Commitment** 5: common features of a KPA – implication of dual commitment.
- Project planning phase has explicit references to the customer (see SQA KPA). They are to be in constant contact with the customer.

Interfaces

We have repeatedly seen that this is the most difficult part of the software development process. Productivity measurements cannot be relevant if this is not examined. It is not simply another piece of the puzzle. It is intrinsic to the productivity of the activity

- Inter-group coordination – level 3 KPA

Cataloging

The model lacks clear concepts of "*cataloging*" of items for reuse. If the model is "a productivity model" then it must include cataloging as **the** cheapest method to enhance productivity. Auditing the existence of SCM is not sufficient. The concepts are there, but they are hard to find.

Issue 3: CMM Focus

The focus of the CMM is still on technology, not problem solving. What this is all about is: **systems analysis** of the **system** used to **develop systems** (the overall picture).

- There is the **SEPG** whose job this is. This does not solve the question of determining whether a particular problem is **solvable by us**.

Issue 4: Site Comparisons

"The proof of the pudding is in the eating." How reliable are comparisons between sites? What is the correlation between graduating to the next level, and improvements in productivity, quality and customer satisfaction? These must be proven for validity of the CMM to be implied.

Issue 5: Objective measurements

The model does not sufficiently include objective measurements (i.e., independently repeatable) of real things. The model defines a stage called "repeatable" – is it? Does a level 3 really mean that there is **always** more productivity than level 2? It seems to me that this is the really basic question. If the answer to this is anything less then absolutely always then this assessment process is not repeatable. Which means that it is not yet good enough.

- The assessment process can be choreographed
- The assessment is *probably* repeatable
- There are flaws in the accuracy of the assessment, particularly if there is intent (assessors have been misled). This is not very difficult

The Capability Model Enjoys Some Important Strengths

- First, they have retained very strong control over the auditors who are allowed to issue a certification which has the appellation CMM certification. This is significant. (Remember what was stated above about TickIt✓? That was one of their strengths also.)
- The SEI is maintaining a "public database" of the data collected by its accredited auditors. Unfortunately, this is not really complete, because the auditors who are accredited as part of corporations (for instance, Motorola has its own internal auditors) are not required to update the database (it is optional). Also, the results on the database are not quite as public as the good of our profession would seem to demand.

SPICE – Software Process Improvement and Capability Determination

SPICE is a slightly silly acronym which stands for **S**oftware **P**rocess **I**mprovement and **C**apability d**E**termination. A mostly European (unfortunately) effort.[8] One of the very nice things about this venture, is that the SEI is making a point of participation. This is healthy. This effort is sponsored by the ISO – Working Group 7.21 (ISO – WG 7.21). The SPICE project is intended to create an agglomeration of:

- SEI CMM
- ISO 9000-3
- TickIt✓
- Trillium
- IEEE 1074
- "All" of 1074 and a whole number of other things. Tailoring and adaptation; acquisition; baselines; process transforms; defines structure; process ownership; defines software quality assurance as a development process

Table 19.2 A chart to compare the standards

	Orientations	Metrics	S/W vs systems vs item	Ethics	Self-assessment capability	CPI	Organizational issues
2167/1498	Product	None	Major emphasis	None	No intention		Weak
CMM	Process	Subjective		None	Guardedly, SEI is not always happy about it	Major emphasis	Very strong
Trillium	Combined process and product	Subjective		None		Major emphasis	Strong
1074	Combined process and product				Designed in		Weak
9000-3		None	Not relevant		Talked about		Major orientation

Worldwide, **quality system certification** is becoming increasingly important for information technology systems as well as for all others. *ISO 9000*, its European equivalent, EN 29000 and its various national versions (Q90 in the USA) are strategic goals for an increasing number of organizations. This is particularly true now, as public procurement authorities are basing their purchasing decisions on certification of ISO 9000 compliance.

> Remember, once ISO 9000 certification has been achieved, the job is not completed! Certification must be maintained and renewed, usually on a yearly basis.

The emphasis of the 1990s is on global competition. This has caused a tremendous increase in the awareness of quality as a prime strategic weapon of competition. The unprecedented speed at which the ISO 9000 series of standards has become **the** status quo ante of quality is the best possible proof of this statement. *Quality systems certification* is a concept that the industrial world is ripe for. Anyone not doing is simply being left behind.

The concept of standards for quality is not new. Historically, we can find extensive development of quality standards by the Chinese emperors of 2000 years ago and equally extensive discussion of the ethical and commercial ramification of standards of quality in the Talmud, also from some 2000 years ago. However, this is the first time in history that we are viewing such a tremendous grass-roots revolution which is making quality the *primary* criterion for competition.

> The ISO 9000 series has quickly been adopted by many nations and regional bodies and is rapidly supplanting prior national and industry based standards. It has been adopted by the European Committee for Standardization (CEN). One of CEN's purposes is to harmonize quality standards and eliminate trade restrictions within the EEC.
>
> *Quality Progress*, May 1991.

Experience has shown extensively that applicability of advanced methodologies is not practical without automated tools. Software projects are becoming increasingly competitive and precarious. Customers and suppliers seek to shift the burden of risk-taking on to others. On the other hand, risk-taking can potentially be very profitable. Indeed, some argue that managing risk is what makes project management different from general management. Project management must have an active role in managing the project, and adopting a professional approach to analysis and management of risk has become essential. A good model ties assessment methodologies to strategic organizational alternatives, via an assessment framework. Significant long-term benefits result from the assessment report, which aids management in pointing towards recommendations and action plans. This framework provides a general description of the process, based on predefined principles. These are necessary for execution of an organization/installation process assessment.

The assessment is the management basis for controlled change and engineering process group. This group is the basis for software development processes, software quality assurance, software configuration management, software tools, software metrics, standards and software engineering training. This integrated view was first called software quality management in an article presented at an IPO conference, by the first author in 1980. Continuous process improvement (CPI) cannot be mandated. It must be made to happen. This begins from management. Managers, at every level, must clearly define that CPI is a high organization priority. They must begin by demanding to improve their processes. This is the only certain way to enlist motivation of practitioners to embrace CPI.

Notes

1   This chapter of the book is based on a paper presented by the first author to the Second Israeli Software Quality Assurance Conference and also an article by Bamford, Robert C. and Deibler II, William J. (1993) Comparing, contrasting ISO 9001 and the SEI capability maturity model, *IEEE Computer*, October.

2   Both of these models were first publicly published in 1987.

3   Actually, there are more then two models. IEEE 1074 is another model. IEEE 1489 may be one as well. Trillium is another. The SPICE effort, discussed elsewhere, is still another. There are many more. These two are the most important in the market.

4   There have been several versions of this. At the time of writing, another version is in process. The group is trying very hard, but they have a difficult time of it. Remember who votes on the acceptance of the standard – those with an economic interest in the process of certification. As this may imply, it makes it more difficult.

5   This definition is the formal definition supplied by Judah Mogilensky, one of the developers of the model, in a talk at the July, 1995 ISPIN (Israel – Software Process Improvement Network) meeting in Tel-Aviv, Israel.

6   TickIt' is only for software. ISO 9000 is generic.

7   If CMM Version 2.0 ever comes out. It has been in process for a very long time.

8   There are Americans on the committees, but many US groups seem to be trying to "boycott" the effort.

APPENDICES

······················

If we have gone too far (for some) or not far enough (for others), We apologize to one and all. In any case, I sincerely hope that you find this useful. A great deal of work went into it.

Appendix I – Software Quality Program Evaluation

This appendix serves as a tool for the evaluation of the software quality program for a project and/or at an installation. This checklist augments those partial checklists embedded within the text. The embedded checklists are intended to help the text to be more understandable and to be immediately applicable. While this checklist is intended to be used to actually perform a detailed evaluation. Evaluations of this sort may usually be performed for either or both of two purposes:

- auditing that the proper procedures are being carried out at a contractor's or subcontractor's installation; or
- when beginning the processes at an installation which has not previously had experience with this sort of formalized activity.

The major problem to be addressed in both of these cases is a swift and accurate collection of data (as much data as possible) which reflects how the process is being performed. In most installations there is, of course, some process in place to perform the task of storing and releasing software. Frequently, this process has developed over time and has never been formally audited. The process is perhaps not the most sophisticated, and is likely not computerized – it does not always need to be computerized. Manual systems can frequently work quite sufficiently.

Scope

Identification

- Have the requirements for the establishment and implementation of the project software quality program been defined and made public knowledge?
- Do these requirements include planning for and conducting assessments of the quality of the software?
- Do these requirements include planning for and conducting assessments of the quality of the documentation?
- Do these requirements include planning for and conducting assessments of the quality of workmanship of all contractors (and subcontractors) for the software?
- Do these requirements include planning for and conducting assessments of the quality of all work which will need to be performed for the on-going maintenance of the software?
- Have all deliverable and nondeliverable items which are to be developed as part of the project been identified and clearly labeled?
- Have all deliverable and nondeliverable items which are to be purchased as part of the project been identified and clearly labeled?
- Does the project include client-supplied items which will need to be verified?
- Does the project include client-supplied items which will need to be included within another object (item) which will need to be validated and/or verified?
- Have the system's boundaries, as regards the items to be stored and/or released, been clearly defined?

Purpose

- Have the purposes and functions of all deliverable and non-deliverable items to be developed been clearly defined?
- Have the purposes and functions of all deliverable and nondeliverable items to be purchased for this development been clearly defined?

Introduction

- Does a document exist with a summary of the purpose and contents of all deliverable items and each nondeliverable item?
- Does a procedure exist for the storage, handling and release of software items?

Referenced documents

- Are any documents which relate to the quality program, listed by name and number in the managerial documents of the project?
- Are any documents referenced by the documentation, listed by name and reference number?
- Are the sources of all documents clearly described (government vs nongovernment)?

Applicability

Software quality program

- Does the statement of work specify a formal software quality program (SQP) or any form of software quality assurance?
- Have the techniques which are needed for the SQP been acquired and put in place?
- Have the tools which are needed for the SQP been acquired and put in place?

Other development items

- Is the SQP specified to apply to both software and firmware items?
- Is the SQP specified to apply to both deliverable and nondeliverable items?

Contractors

- Has the SQP been defined to include all developing groups within the contractor's organization?
- Has the SQP been defined to apply to all contracting organizations?
- Is the SQP applicable to contractor's of the project, who are not involved, or are indirectly involved, in development?

Maintenance

- Is the SQP specified to apply to both development stages and postdevelopment (maintenance) stages?

General requirements

Establishing the SQP

- Has the contractor established a SQP?
- Is this SQP in accordance with the established standards?
- Has the SQP been initiated by formally informing all personnel of management's quality commitment?

- Has the management's quality commitment been declared in writing?
- Does this SQAP include all of the following:
  - Software quality planning
  - Software quality assessment (measuring)
  - Software productivity measurement
  - Software quality/productivity reporting.
- Is the SQAP formally defined as an on-going activity, fully integrated with the development?

Objectives of the SQP

- Have the software quality objectives been defined in a measurable form?
- Have measures been defined for all software documentation deliverables?
- Have measures been defined for all software code deliverables?
- Have measures been defined for all software nondeliverables?
- Have measures been defined for all processes used to produce software deliverables?
- Have measures been defined for all products produced using software deliverables or nondeliverables?

Responsibilities for the SQP

- Does the SQP oblige all contractor organizations, functions and personnel, involved in software related activities?
- Have the organization responsibilities for performing the SQP been agreed upon and assigned?
- Have the necessary training times which are needed for the SQP been budgeted and scheduled?
- Does the SQP define and describe all resources needed for software quality responsibilities?
- Are the people and/or organizations responsible for corrective actions defined by the SQP?
- Is a formal distinction made between persons responsible for development and those responsible for software quality assessment?

Software quality planning

- Has a review of the contract requirements been performed to identify software quality needs?
- Have provisions for timely acquisition of SQP needs (resources, skills and/or tools) been planned?
- Has a software quality assurance plan (SQAP) (or SQP plan) been developed by the contractor?

- Has the contractor insured that every subcontractor will provide a SQAP which is functionally equivalent to the contractor's SQAP?
- Have all client-owned and client-furnished equipment, software and facilities to be used for the SQP been included in the SQAP/SQPP?
- Have all organizational structures and personnel, and their corresponding quality oriented responsibilities, as they are to be used for the SQP, been included in the SQAP/SQPP?
- Has the schedule for all quality assurance activities been included in the plan?
- Have all tools which will be needed for all quality (or quality assurance) oriented activities, been provided for in the SQAP/ SQPP?
- Does the SQAP/SQPP include descriptions of quality program activities and quality oriented products?
- Can the SQAP be confirmed to be consistent with all other plans of the contract (for example development plans)?
- Has the SQAP been verified that other plans' provisions are not unnecessarily duplicated?
- Has the client reviewed the SQAP/SQPP and signified approval?
- Can the developing organization demonstrate how the SQAP/ SQPP will accomplish the declared quality objectives?

Quality plan updates

- Has the contractor (and subcontractors) provided for periodic SQP plan updates?
- Has the contracting agency (the client) been notified of all SQAP/ SQPP updates within 30 days of their occurrence?

Software quality records

- Has the developing organization provided for the creation and maintenance of accurate and timely records of all quality activity assessments?
- Has the developing organization provided for the creation and maintenance of accurate and timely records of all product assessments, for products which are under direct control?
- Has the developing organization provided for the creation and maintenance of accurate and timely records of all product assessments, for products which are under indirect control?
- Do these quality records provide input to a management direc-ted, corporate-wide, quality improvement program?
- Do these quality records provide input to the project corrective action program?
- Has the developing agency provided for client review of these quality records, on a periodic basis and upon demand?

- Has the contractor provided for the existence and continuous update of the quality records throughout the life of the product (i.e. including the maintenance phase)?

Detailed software quality program requirements

Assessment of software development plans

- Has the contractor assured that all software development plans (main and subcontractors) have been documented?
- Are all software development plans kept up-to-date for the whole length of the project?
- Do all software development plans comply with the contract?
- Are all software development plans (main and subcontractors) consistent with one another?

Assessment of software development documentation

- Have all documents which are called for by the contract been provided for?
- Can every development document be confirmed to adhere to the required format?
- Has the contractor performed the necessary verifications and validations upon each document, before its delivery to the client?

Assessment of software development processes

- Have all system requirements been allocated to software requirements?
- Can this be shown to be correct (verified) for each and every case?
- Have all software requirements been allocated to architectural design entities?
- Can this be shown to be correct (verified) for each and every case?
- Have all architectural design entities been refined into detailed module designs?
- Can this be shown to be correct (verified) for each and every case?
- Have all detailed module designs been converted into code?
- Can this be shown to be correct (verified) for each and every case?
- Has a technical procedure been defined for each of the development life-cycle stages, which are defined by the SDP?
- Have all project personnel been made aware of these technical procedures and have they been adhered to by all project personnel?
- Does the structure and organization of the software development library (SDL) comply with the contract requirements?

- Does the SDL comply with the current version of the SDP and the configuration management plan?
- When the SDL is routinely accessed, are the readily available versions the most recently authorized versions?
- Are all authorized versions under configuration control?
- Are all library modules clearly identified and labeled?
- Are all module version labels clearly relative to those (versions) which preceded it?
- Have all software development files required by the contract been established?
- Have all software development file formats been described in the SDP?
- Do all software development file format adhere to the formats described by the SDP?
- Are technical evaluations of all deliverables (products, by-products and documents) provided for by project planning?
- Has every deliverable document been audited and verified, prior to delivery, for each of the following:
  – Standards adherence?
  – Technical correctness?
  – Interface matching to its "sibling" documents?
  – Requirements allocation?
  – Derivation matching to the "parent" documents (in the document hierarchy)?
- If a repeat-submission, has the document been reaudited for verification with all of the above?
- If a resubmission, has the document been reaudited to insure continued matching with its "off-spring" documents?

Assessment of development management processes

- Have the controls for all deliverable media been assessed, prior to media distribution?
- Has the client been notified of the results of this assessment, prior to media distribution?
- Have the controls for all deliverable documentation been assessed, prior to media distribution?
- Has the client been notified of the results of this assessment, prior to documentation distribution?
- Is all document and media distribution control by the configuration management plan?
- Has the contractor put in-place the proper controls for storage, handling and release of deliverable:
  – Documentation?
  – Media?
  – Computer program configuration items?

Assessment of configuration management

- Has a software configuration management plan been produced for the project (either as a separate document or within another plan)?
- Is all corrective action to deliverables controlled by the SCMP?
- Where warranted, are corrects to nondeliverables controlled by the SCMP?
- Are all problems (errors, anomalies) detected in products under control reported promptly and corrective actions initiated?
- Are all detected problems classified by category and priority?
- Is analysis performed for each problem detected to identify error trends and error clustering?
- Are all change requests, whether resulting from corrective action or initiated by client or project personnel, tracked and reportable?
- Are all changes in deliverables verified before resubmission to the configuration control system?
- Is the software configuration management system computerized, using an up-to-date product?

Assessment of testing

- Can all informal tests and testing processes of deliverable software be assessed by the contractor?
- Can all formal tests and testing processes be assessed by both the contractor and the client?
- Are records kept of all test assessments which can be retained for test traceability?
- Are all tests and testing processes in compliance with:
  - The software development plan; and
  - The software test plan?

Assessment of nondevelopmental software

- Has all support software been evaluated and acceptance tested?
- Have all software tools which are to be used for this development been defined, including acquisition dates?
- Does all nondevelopmental software comply with the contract?
- Has all nondevelopmental software been placed under configuration control?

Assessment of nondeliverable items

- Does all nondeliverable software comply with the contract?
- Has all nondeliverable software been placed under configuration control?

- Has all nondeliverable software been tested prior to operational use?
- Is all nondeliverable software maintained after release?

Project management

Assessment of subcontractor management

- Have all subcontractor development procedures been assessed for compatibility with main contractor procedures as precontract award policy?
- Are all subcontractor development procedures documented, baselined and common knowledge of all developers?
- Has the subcontractor's SQP been assessed for compatibility with that of the main contractor?
- Are all applicable SQP requirements included as part of the contract with the subcontractor?

Acceptance, inspection and delivery

- Have all deliverable products been scheduled for acceptance testing?
- Have procedures been defined for the acceptance testing of all subcontractor and main contractor deliverables?
- Have all relevant procedures been performed, for each deliverable product, before delivery?
- Have records been kept, and delivered to the client, with the results of each acceptance test?
- Have all contract required configuration audits been performed and documented?

Formal reviews, audits and inspections

Note:

All deliverables to be reviewed must be quality audited before submission to review and submitted sufficiently prior to the review, to allow the reviewers to study the material.

- Has a list and schedule for all formal reviews been included as part of the SQAP?
- Has a list and schedule for all audits been included as part of the SQAP?
- Has a list and schedule for all formal inspections been included as part of the SQAP?
- Have all deliverable software products been audited and verified before review?

- Have all deliverable software products been delivered to the client's reviewers, at least five working days before each review?
- Has a project status report been presented at each formal review and has this report been submitted before the review?
- Have all review generated action items been allocated for developer reaction?

Product certification

- Has the contractor submitted evidence of compliance with all software related requirements?
- Has the contractor submitted evidence that the submitted software source code matches the tested object code?
- Has the contractor submitted evidence that the version of software delivered matches that which was formally tested?
- Has the contractor submitted evidence that all nondevelopmental software performs as per related requirements and is documented?
- Has the contractor submitted evidence that every module of software delivered to the contracting agency relates to the system configuration into which it is installed?
- Has the contractor submitted evidence that all physical media used to deliver software to the contracting agency contains:
  - An authorized copy of the correct version?
  - Only that, and nothing else?
  - The version submitted is from the proper development library?

Postdevelopment project follow-up

- Have all problem reports submitted to the contracting agency been resolved?
- Have all change requests submitted to the contracting agency been resolved?
- Have all corrected, rereleased products been tested and validated to ensure continuing requirements compatibility?

Appendix II – Ready-to-use Forms

Module production checklist and evaluation

This is the basic form for collection of information pertaining to the module. The form serves both as a method for collecting information (and storage on the database) and as a "tickler" as to the basic information which needs to be collected.

Source/code module level

This is a three-part, two-page, form which is designed to aid in the analysis and measurement of module quality. Part I consists of a checklist/form, for measuring code aspects of reliability, maintainability and testability. The measures are used to assess quality of the code's structure. Part II of the form consists of a checklist for measuring aspects of the code for maintainability of the software module, This analyses and measures the conciseness of the code. This part is based upon the Halstead techniques for code analysis/volume (see 1.4 6). This part is to be used for modules which are primarily computational. This should not be used for modules which are primarily logical/control in nature. Part III measures the module's self-descriptiveness. The primary use of this measurement is towards the future maintainability of the software.

Inspection – module summary report

This form/report is designed to display, at a glance, summary results of analysis of a module. This may be used to report results of code analysis using any or all of the previous forms, or as a result of a module inspection.

Module evaluation form – subjective evaluation

This form is designed to be used for surveying the opinions of programmers about their peers' work. It can provide a framework for a subjective evaluation which, given a sufficiently large statistical sample may provide the evaluation team with a significant amount of information concerning the quality of the modules being examined.

• •

Module production checklist and evaluation

Title: _____   Revision No.: _____

Author: _____   Requester/Project: _____

Date requested: _____   Date released: _____

Scheduled date: _____   Original release: _____

Purpose of component: _____

Formal design: Designer: _____

                  Location: _____

Environment: Development machine: _____

                  Development O/S: _____

                  Target machine: _____

                  Target O/S: _____

Algorithm reference: _____

External components: _____   Quantity: _____

Internal components: _____   Quantity: _____

Files: _____

Screens: _____

#	Input Parameters			#	Output Parameters		
	Name	Type	Source		Name	Type	Target
1 2 3				1 2 3			

Error source correlation

The following two forms have been found to be very useful in quantifying anomalies in a design document or in a code module (respectively). With very trivial changes – the list of error types down the left-hand side of the table – one may adapt this form for other areas to be inspected (requirements, testing and so on).

Corporate cultures do not change rapidly. The development culture of an organization affects the quantities and kinds of errors that one may expect to find. Based upon this, we know that there is almost always a direct correlation between module size and the number of anomalies one can expect to find in a given module of type x. In a report published in the *Communications of the ACM* for January 1984 (p. 43) this correlation was displayed for lines of code. (This is a very limited view, but researchers find this easier to check than the more complex views.) Generally, about 5% of all modules with up to 50 lines of code can expect to have errors. If they have 100 lines, we should expect about 15% of them to be erred. When we get up to 400 lines, about 78% will have problems. One would assume that there would be differences depending on the language used. However, this is only one dimension of the problem.

One must also examine error sources. We know today that all programming activities tend to be error prone. There have been many studies to determine the industry averages. It is very instructive to measure your organization against those averages. However, to do so you need first to have collected this information, over a reasonable period of time.

- The most error prone of all programming activities is ***program maintenance***. In the text body of the book we have discussed what errors are caused and how one needs to plan for them. In this area, about 50% of our activities are error correction activities.
- In development, about 15% of our errors stem from incorrectly understood requirements. About 35% come from poorly conceived functional specifications.
- Actual coding errors only account for about 15–20% of the errors encountered.

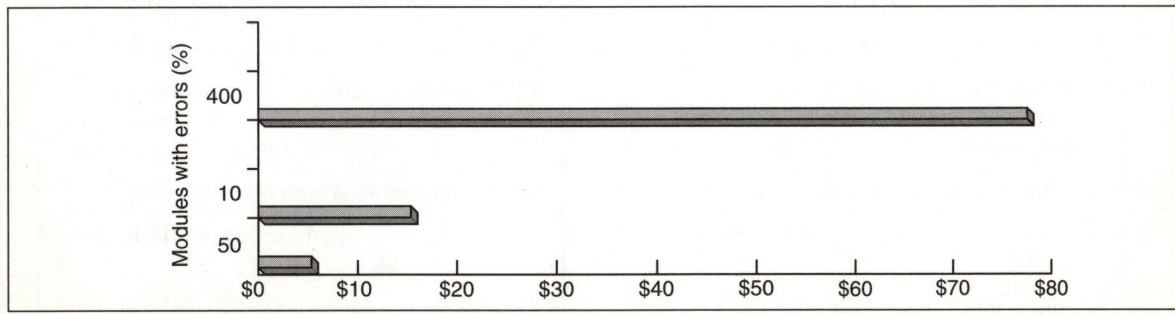

Figure A2.1   Modularity creates smaller modules, which means fewer errors.

Source code module level

System name: _____   Date: _____

Module name: _____   Inspector: _____

I Structure (reliability, maintainability, testability)

1	# lines of code		11	# of decision points	
2	# lines excluding comments		12	# of conditional branches	
3	# machine language statements		13	# unconditional branches (e.g. GOTO)	
4	# data manipulations		14	# loops (WHILE, DO)	
5	# statement labels		15	# of loops with jumps out of loop	
6	# entrances to module		16	# of modified loop indices	
7	# exits from module		17	# module modification (e.g. ALTER) constructs	
8	Maximum nesting level		18	# of negative/compound Boolean expressions	
9	# of decision points (IF, WHILE, REPEAT, DO, CASE)		19	Is a structured language used (Y/N)	
10	# of declarative statements		20	Is flow top-to-bottom (Y/N)	

II Conciseness (Maintainability)

1	# of operators		3	# of operands	
2	# of unique operators		4	# of unique operands	

III Self-descriptiveness (maintainability, flexibility, testability, portability, reusability)

Please provide quantitative answers to the following checklist. Yes/no questions should be answered with a zero if no, or a ten if yes. Other questions may optionally have their answers converted to percentages.

1	# of lines of comments		7	% nonstandard statements commented	
2	# of non-blank comments lines		8	% of commented declared variables?	
3	Prologue describes purpose, author, version, date, inputs, outputs and assumptions?		9	% variable names mnemonic and self-descriptive?	
4	Satisfied requirement indicated?		10	% comments which are informative	
5	% commented decision points and control transfers.		11	% code logically blocked and indented.	
6	% commented machine code		12	# of lines with more than one statement.	

These forms should be used for analyzing the numbers of errors found and for creating your own calculations of where **your** organization makes errors and what kinds of errors they are.

Initial inspection – design module summary report

Project:		Registrar:		
Form date:		Inspection date:		
Audit type:		Module:		Component:

Problem type:

	Major			Minor			Total	
	M	W	E	M	W	E	No	Percent
LO: Logic								
IR: Interface requirements								
DU: Data usage								
TU: Tool usage								
AD: Algorithm design								
DM: Design maintainability								
MA: Module attributes								
DE: Design error								
ES: External specifications								
SC: Requirements traceability								
DT: Design for testability								
ST: Standards								
OT: Other								
Total								

Re-inspection required?   **Y**   **N**

Staff-hours for inspection:		Total staff-hours:		
Staff-hours for rework:		Inspection No.:		
Implementor name:		Signature:		
Moderator name:		Signature:		

Key: M = missing; W = wrong; E = extra

Code Module inspection summary report

Project: _____   Registrar: _____

Form date: _____   Inspection date: _____

Audit type: _____   Module: _____

Component: _____

Staff-Hours for Inspection: _____   Total staff-hours: _____

Staff-hours for rework: _____   Inspection No.: _____

Implementor name: _____   Signature: _____

Moderator name: _____   Signature: _____

Re-inspection required?   **Y**   **N**

Problem type	Major			Minor			Total	
	M	W	E	M	W	E	No.	Percent
CL: Code logic								
LR: Linkage requirements								
DD: Data definition								
LU: Language usage								
PE: Performance								
CM: Code maintainability								
MA: Module attributes								
DE: Design error								
ES: External specifications								
SC: Specification clarification								
CP: Code prologue								
ST: Standards								
OT: Other								
Total							100	

Key: M = missing; W = wrong; E = extra

Module evaluation form subjective evaluation

Module: _____   Evaluator: _____

This form is used for subjective evaluation of the program module being evaluated. The form is based upon a checklist which has proven useful in industrial/production environments. The checklist is designed to be used at code evaluation level, by the auditor of a module. Please make any comments after each question or on a separate sheet.

		No				Yes
1.	Are all variable names used reasonable and mnemonic?	1	2	3	4	5
2.	Are sufficient and useful comments provided?	1	2	3	4	5
3.	Are lines and spaces used clearly and consistently, giving the module a comfortable and readable format?	1	2	3	4	5
4.	Is the high-level design apparent?	1	2	3	4	5
5.	Is the low-level logic comprehensible?	1	2	3	4	5
6.	Are you satisfied that the algorithm was a good choice?	1	2	3	4	5
7.	Is the algorithm implemented well?	1	2	3	4	5
8.	Is the module understandable?	1	2	3	4	5
9.	Would this module be reasonably easy to modify?	1	2	3	4	5
10.	Is this module compiler independent?	1	2	3	4	5
11.	Is this module machine independent?	1	2	3	4	5
12.	Would you have been proud to sign your name to this module?	1	2	3	4	5
13.	Are the data structures used in sensible way?	1	2	3	4	5
14.	Would you find it hard to improve this program?	1	2	3	4	5

Software Problem Report

Date: _____

Distributor Data

Distributor: _____   Contact: _____

Telephone: _____   Fax: _____

User Data

Company: _____   Contact: _____

Telephone: _____   Fax: _____

Product Name: _____   Ver.: _____

Impact of problem on customer:

_____

_____

_____

_____

Detailed problem description:

_____

_____

_____

_____

_____

_____

Supporting documentation attached:

_____

_____

_____

_____

_____

_____

Sample code inspection checklist

1. Are compilation errors avoided?	
2. Is unexecutable code avoided?	
3. Are all declared data items used?	
4. Is redundant code avoided?	
5. Are endless loops avoided?	
6. Are references to undefined data items avoided?	
7. Is argument passing compatible?	
8. Are unnecessary branches avoided?	
9. Do all branches point to locations with mnemonic names?	
10. Are all alternatives of conditional execution correct?	
11. Is initialization for all program states correct?	
12. Is common storage correct, verifiable and protected?	
13. Are constants defined with the correct values?	
14. Are mathematical algorithms implemented properly?	
15. Are buffer sizes adequate for present and future use?	
16. Are margins for min/max data values adequate?	
17. Is the program logic correct and have assertions been added to allow it to be verified?	
18. Are comments clear and concise?	
19. Are comments consistent and sufficient?	
20. Have coding standards and conventions been followed?	

Appendix III – A Template for Software Quality Program Plans

This template is based on a former United States Department of Defense standard for software quality programs. This standard is now obsolete. However, the format of this is quite good and may prove useful for those with projects for specific systems in a contractual relationship.

Purpose

The software quality program plan (SQPP) identifies the organizations and procedures to be used to perform development activities for this military project.

Preparation instructions

Title page

The title page shall contain the information identified below in the indicated format:

[Document control number and date: Volume x of y]

[Revision indicator: date of revision]

SOFTWARE QUALITY PROGRAM PLAN

FOR THE

[SYSTEM NAME]

CONTRACT NO. [contract no.]

System/Subsystem Sequence No. [Date of document – day month year]

Prepared for:

[Contracting Agency Name, department code]

Prepared by:

[Contractor name and address]

Approved by:

[Contracting Agency Representative]

Date

Table of contents

1.   Scope

1.1.   Identification

Contains the approved identification number, title, and abbreviation, if applicable, of the system and CSCI to which this SQPP applies.

1.2.   System overview

1.3.   Document overview

1.4.   Relationship to other plans

2.   Referenced documents

3.   Organization and resources

3.1.   Organization

Describe the organization responsible for fulfillment of, and for ensuring compliance with, the SQP requirements. Include the authority and responsibilities of each organization and its relationships to other organizational entities (for example, the organization(s) responsible for performing configuration management). A chart should be used to illustrate the structure of the organization(s) performing SQP activities and their position within the project management system.

3.2.   Resources

3.2.1.   Contractor facilities and equipment

3.2.2.   Client furnished facilities, equipment, software, and services

3.2.3.   Personnel

3.2.4.   Other resources

3.3.   Schedule

For each activity, indicate activity initiation, dependencies on other events (such as availability of draft documents), and activity completion times. Include key development milestones, such as formal reviews, audits, and key meetings.

4. Software quality program procedures, tools, and records

4.1. Procedures

The procedures to be used in the SQP and each of the requirements to which they apply.

4.2. Tools

The tools to be used in the program, including the tool's name, identification number, version, development status and role in the program.

4.3. Software quality records

Plans for preparing, maintaining and making available for contracting agency review, records of each program activity performed. Include the formats to be used and the information to be recorded for each type of record.

5. Notes

6. Appendices

Appendix IV – Subcontractor Quality Auditing

Company name:

Address:

Location (mail stop):

Contact:

Phone:

Fax:

Product/Project:

Audit date:

Auditor name	Signature	Company sign-off responsibility	Signature

SQA planning

Table 1 of 6	Yes	No	NA	Comments
1. Is a SQAP available?				
2. Does the SQAP identify quality requirements?				
3. Is the SQAP in accordance with the standard?				
4. Have all SQA tasks been identified?				
5. Have all SQA responsibilities been assigned?				
6. Has SQA independence been established?				
7. Does the SQAP identify quality characteristics?				
8. Does the SQAP identify quality goals?				
9. Have all SQA activities been scheduled?				
10. Has a life-cycle plan been established and agreed upon (including development management)?				

SQA inspection

Table 2 of 6	Yes	No	NA	Comments
1. Has a software development plan been established?				
2. Has the software development plan been agreed upon?				
3. Have software development methods been established?				
4. Have all software development personnel been trained in using the established methods?				
5. Have programming standards been established?				
6. Have testing standards (including documentation) been established?				
7. Are all action items recorded and tracked?				
8. Have action items tracking methods and tools been established?				
9. Have audit, inspection and review procedures been established?				
10. Have all audits described by the procedure (until this time) been performed?				
11. Have all inspections described by the procedure (until this time) been performed?				
12. Have all reviews described by the procedure (until this time) been performed?				
13. Have all performed inspections been according to procedures?				
14. Are formal verification methods used?				

SQA control and acceptance

Table 3 of 6	Yes	No	NA	Comments
1. Have review procedures been established?				
2. Are sessions held to review phase results?				
3. Are review results reported formally?				
4. Does the schedule account for these reviews?				
5. Are all reviews performed in accordance with the established procedures?				
6. Have all reviewed documents been audited by SQA prior to the review?				
7. Does a control cycle exist for utilization of review and inspection results?				
8. Does a test plan exist?				
9. Do test designs and descriptions exist?				
10. Is there a formal hand-off procedure?				

Configuration management

Table 4 of 6	Yes	No	NA	Comments
1. Does an SCMP exist?				
2. Is the SCMP written to a recognized standard?				
3. Have configuration control procedures been published?				
4. Have all team members been trained to follow the SCM procedures?				
5. Is SCM system documentation in accordance with requirements?				
6. Are all development events controlled by the SCM procedure?				
7. Are all maintenance events controlled by the SCM procedure?				
8. Have SCM personnel been identified?				
9. Do all deliverables have unique project names?				
10. Do all non-deliverables have unique project names?				
11. Have SCM systems parameters been established?				
12. Is change monitoring guaranteed?				
13. Are all baselines accounted for?				
14. Are all development resources under SCM control?				
15. Are all testing resources under SCM control?				

Nonconformance

Table 5 of 6	Yes	No	NA	Comments
1. Does the contractor have a nonconformance procedure?				
2. Does this procedure include defect reporting and corrective actions?				
3. Are review action items tracked and solved?				
4. Are interprocedure interfaces (SCM, nonconformance and change control) clearly determined?				
5. Have persons responsible for nonconformance been identified?				
6. Do all responsible parties have clearly designated responsibilities?				
7. Is a clear change procedure established?				
8. Has a Software Problem Reporting procedure been established?				
9. Is the SPR procedure activated from testing?				
10. Is the SPR procedure activated by users?				

Software procurement

Table 6 of 6	Yes	No	NA	Comments
1. Do controls exist for S/W tools procurement?				
2. Do controls exist for materials procurement?				
3. Do controls exist for S/W building blocks procurement?				
4. Is there a formal acceptance procedure for subcontractor supplied items?				
5. Does this include documentation?				

The Quality Audit Report

The following form is to be used for the auditing of additional functions, not covered by the preceding forms. The above tables/forms are used to audit for the standard software quality assurance items – this is seldom sufficient and is intended to be an initial baseline from which you may create the audit that your organization needs. Certainly, this form must be used for, at least, the auditing of the technical issues.

page: ___ of: ___

#	Item description	Does the requested item exist?	In what language is the item?	Has an English translation been prepared?	Comments
1					
2					
3					
4					
5					
6					
7					
8					
9					
10					

Appendix V – Testing Taxonomy

Testing techniques

Path testing

White-box testing
Loop testing (is a special case)
Path predicates
Error guessing
Test coverage
Static analysis/static-flow analysis
Dynamic analysis tools
Symbolic testing/symbolic evaluation
Program instrumentation
Input space partitioning
Environmental simulation
Virtual machines
Predictive modeling/bebugging
Complexity measuring
Mutation testing
Failure prone module analysis

Transaction flow testing

Database testing
Data-flow testing
Fault-tree analysis (Chapter 18 on risk management provides a detailed explanation of fault tree analysis)
Timing constraint testing

Input validation and syntax testing

Nondeterministic program constructs
Predicate transformation
Threads
Data-flow testing

Logic testing

Black-box testing
Logic coverage testing
Equivalence partitioning
Boundary value analysis
Cause–effect graphing
Decision table
Boolean algebra based testing/bebugging/error guessing

Ambiguity testing
Fault-tree analysis
Interrupts, priorities and reentry testing

State testing

State transitions
State-table representation
State bugs
Transition error tracing
Functional program testing
Algebraic program testing
Random testing
Grammar-based testing
Fault-tree analysis
Interrupts, priorities and reentry testing, timing, constraint testing

Data driven testing

Semantic shifts
Clustering
Representation changes
Data-flow testing

Regression testing

Defects taxonomy

Requirements defects
Design defects
Documentation defects
Coding defects
Test defects
Replication checks
Timing checks
Reversal checks
Reasonableness checks
Structural checks
Diagnostic checks

Static analysis vs dynamic testing

Maintenance testing
Testing resulting from defect reporting

Tool testing

Compiler testing

Life-cycle based testing

Unit testing

Input validation and syntax testing
Error guessing
Incremental testing
Top-down vs bottom-up testing

Higher-level element testing

Logic testing/logic-based testing
Decision table
Boolean algebra based testing
State testing
Decision node/path testing
Syntax-directed testing
Clustering analysis
Function testing

Integration testing

Top-down vs bottom-up testing
Logic testing/logic-based testing
Decision table/Boolean algebra based testing
State testing
Threads
Clustering analysis and error trends

Subsystem testing

State testing
Function testing

System testing

Cross-reference
Requirements trace test
Specification trace test
Design object trace test
Database
System functional testing

Qualification testing

Functional testing
Environment testing
Requirements trace verification

Acceptance testing

Functional testing
Environment testing
Requirements trace verification
GUI/MMI validation
Pass/fail criteria testing
Recovery testing/recoverability verification, system readiness testing
Acceptability testing
Performance testing
Quality-of-service testing

System status tests

Configuration testing

System states
Permutation tests
Degradation tests

Recovery testing

Restart
Redundancy
Built-in-tests testing (an automatic test procedure programmed into a device and stored inside, usually for real-time systems)
Accountability

Security testing

Attacks and attack methods
Tiger teaming

Stress testing

Risk testing

Performance testing

Performance objectives instrumentation

Reliability testing

Response time
Multiple displays

Bug taxonomy

Functional bugs

System bugs
Process bugs
Data bugs
Coding bugs
Logic bugs
Testing bugs
Clustering bugs

Installation test

Documentation validation
GUI/MMI validation
Firmware configuration matching validation

Useability testing

GUI
Vision, color, control, response time documentation
Training
Protection mechanism validation
State restoration validation
Concurrent process testing
Competing/cooperative process testing

GLOSSARY

Archive
: The module archive file in which all evolutionary history of a workfile is retained. (see logfile).

Audit
: An independent evaluation of software products or processes to ascertain compliance to standards, guidelines, specifications, and procedures.

Auditing
: Desk checking of development documents for clarity, standards adherence and errors.

Baseline
: An agreed upon release of a product.
1. "A specification or product that has been formally reviewed and agreed upon, that thereafter serves as the basis for further development, and that can be changed only through formal procedures."

2. A document or set of such documents formally designated and fixed at a specific time during the life-cycle of a configuration item." IEEE

Branch
A variant development path that diverges from the primary (trunk) of software development.

CCB
A change control board is a committee whose function is to govern the process of change in a project.

Change evaluation cost
The number of staff-hours needed to evaluate the requested change, both in technical terms and for possible system-wide effects.

Change implementation cost
The number of staff-hours needed to fully implement the requested change. In this case, "fully implement" means updating of all documents and source-code files and full testing (including regression testing) of the updated system /subsystem.

Configuration control
"An element of configuration management, consisting of the evaluation, coordination, approval or disapproval, and implementation of changes to configuration items after formal establishment of their configuration identification." IEEE

Configuration file
A text file that governs the operation of the software configuration management system via configuration parameters and operating conditions.

Configuration identification
"An element of configuration management, consisting of selecting the configuration items for a system and recording their functional and physical characteristics in technical documentation." IEEE
[There is a second definition, but it is not relevant in the present context.]

Configuration management
"A discipline applying technical and administrative direction and surveillance to: identify and document the functional and physical characteristics of a configuration item, control changes to those characteristics, record

and report change processing and implementation status, and verify compliance with specified requirements." IEEE

Configuration status accounting
"An element of configuration management, consisting of the recording and reporting of information needed to manage a configuration effectively. This information includes a listing of the approved configuration identification, the status of proposed changes to the configuration and the implementation status of approved changes." IEEE

Defect
Imperfection; lack of something essential.

Delta
The set of differences between one revision of an item and another. Delta reports are usually taken from an archive.

Deviation
1. A departure from a specified requirement.
2. A written authorization, granted prior to the manufacture of an item, to depart from a particular performance or design requirement for a specific number of units or a specific period of time. IEEE

Errors
An unexpected, undesired state, situation or value in the document or code.

Fault
Defect or blemish in object or structure; break in continuity.

Failure
An unexpected or unwanted event.

Hardware
The "touchable" tactile part of a system, usually meant to include the electronics and the mechanical parts of what we are looking at.

Hazard
1. A condition which is accompanied by the potential for causing one or more undesirable consequence(s), which may or may not be reversible. (An example might be an anomalous or erroneous data or state of a system.)

2. The potential for causing such adverse (side) effect(s) at various levels of use of the product, process or service.

Hazard identification   Recognition that a hazard exists and that its characteristics and constituent parts have been defined – and agreement concerning them has been reached – among those concerned with the product, process and/or service.

Inspection
Item   A unique object, to be identified and managed.

Lock   A semaphore-like marker placed on a particular revision of an item in a archive. If the locked revision is accessed by anyone, a warning is issued and access is prevented. Locks are generally applied when a revision is extracted for updating.

Logfile   The module archive file in which all evolutionary history of a workfile is retained (see archive).

Makefile   A text file (program) used by the make utility to govern the actions needed to be taken by the make utility to rebuild the system.

Maintainability   Probability of completing a maintenance action in a given time (statistical). "Mean time to repair" (operational).

Maintenance, corrective   A process of unplanned change to correct the cause of a failure.

Maintenance, preventive   A process of planned change to prevent failures from occurring. Preventive maintenance is not practical for a non-testable product.

Make utility   A part of the usual set of configuration management tools used to automatically and accurately build (and rebuild) a software system.

Physical configuration audit (PCA)

The physical configuration audit is a management audit, at the end of a development cycle, that verifies the physical presence of all items.

Quality – 1

1. The totality of features and characteristics of a product or service that bears on its ability to satisfy needs. ISO/TC 176; International Organization for Standardization.
2. The degree to which a system, component or process meets specified requirements. [2.b] The degree to which a system, component or process meets customer or user needs or expectations. (ANSI/IEEE Std 610.12; see section 2 [9]).
3. A system of production methods which economically produces goods or services meeting the requirements of consumers. Modern quality control utilizes statistical methods and is often called statistical quality control. The Japanese Industrial Standards.

Quality – 2

The following definitions of quality have been applied in various forums by some of the most prominent leaders in quality assurance during this century. They are supplied here for context and informational purposes. (If you do not know these names, you should find out more about them. These are the people (with the addition of Dr Deming) that have really mattered in QA in the 20th century. None of these people deal or dealt, in software)

Dr JM Juran
Fitness for use

Philip Crosby
Conformance to requirements

Dr Kaoru Ishikawa
To practice quality control is to develop, design, produce, and service a quality product which is most economical, most useful and always satisfactory to the consumer.

Quality assurance	1. A planned and systematic pattern of all actions necessary to provide adequate confidence that an item or product conforms to established technical requirements.
	2. A set of activities designed to evaluate the process by which products are developed or manufactured.
	(ANSI/IEEE Std 610.12; see section 2 [9]).
Quality attribute	A feature or characteristic that affects an item's quality. Note: In a hierarchy of quality attributes, higher level attributes may be called quality factors, lower level attributes called quality attributes. (ANSI/IEEE Std 610.12; see section 2 [9]).
Quality control	Note: this term has no standardized meaning in software engineering at this time. Candidate definitions are:
	1. A set of activities designed to evaluate the quality of developed or manufactured products (contrast with: quality assurance [2]).
	2. The process of verifying one's own work or that of a coworker.
	3. Synonym for quality assurance. (ANSI/IEEE Std 610.12; see section 2 [9]).
Quality factor	See: quality attribute. Note: In a hierarchy of quality attributes, higher level attributes may be called quality factors, lower level attributes called quality attributes. (ANSI/IEEE Std 610.12; see section 2 [9]).
Quality metric	1. A quality measure of the degree to which an item possesses a given quality attribute.
	2. A function whose inputs are software data and whose output is a single numerical value that can be interpreted as the degree to which the software possesses a given quality attribute. (ANSI/IEEE Std 610.12; see section 2 [9]).
Review	An evaluation of software element(s) or project status to ascertain discrepancies from planned results and to recommend improvement.

Reviewing	A technique of displaying results of a development process. The audience will usually consist of fellow developers, managers and user representatives.
Revision	An instance of a module (or workfile). Each time a workfile is checked back in to its archive, its revision number is updated.
Risk	A measure of the probability and potential severity of adverse or anomalous effects to health, property, assets, society, mission, security or the environment. For purposes of this procedure, risk is estimated by expressing expectation of an adverse or anomalous effect.
Risk analysis	Estimation of potential effects of occurrence of a hazard to: individuals, populations, organizations, property, environment or mission.
Risk assessment	The complete processes of Risk analysis and risk evaluation.
Risk control	The process of management of perceived risks, via risk assessment, evaluation and estimation.
Risk estimation	Determination of the extent and probability of hazards. The purpose is feedback to management of levels of exposure.
Risk evaluation	An explicit value judgment of exposure to economic, social and environment consequences of hazards, with the express purpose of identifying and choosing from a range of alternatives for management of the risks.
Risk factors	The hierarchical decomposition of the risk. That is to say, what the individual parts are and how they are relate to one another.
Risk management	The complete processes of risk assessment and risk control.
Software	Computer programs and all their constituent parts; e.g., code, requirements and design specifications, user documentation and tests definitions and results.
Software element	A deliverable or in-process document produced or acquired during software development or maintenance.

System	A bounded physical or logical entity, with a known identification, a defined operational environment and objective(s) obtained via interaction of constituent parts. A system must possess a clear method of being referenced (bounded) and its purpose must be known to its "public." A system's objectives are achieved via planned interaction of all its parts (a system is more than the sum of its parts).
Tip	A tip revision is the most recent revision on the trunk of the revision tree or the most recent revision on a branch of the revision tree.
Testability	The ability to perform an accepted series of tests on the system/product which are designed to prove the system's initial or continuous (un)useability.
Trunk	The primary development path of a workfile, as stored in the archive.
Variation	An alternate form of a module.
Version	An instance of a (whole) system. May consist of an "arbitrary slice" through the revisions of the various archives.
Workfile	A copy of the module for editing or viewing.

Acronyms

The following list of acronyms are likely to turn up when looking at questions relating to configuration management. Though this list is far from exhaustive, it will be helpful to all those who normally speak the English language or to those who use English as a foreign tongue. This list attempts to include most of the acronyms relating to both hardware configuration management and software configuration management.

It will probably be not needed for those whose major language it DoDese. For those who actually wish to communicate, we recommend to use acronyms sparingly.

ATP   Acceptance test procedure
ATR   Acceptance test requirements
AB/L   Allocated baseline

BoM   Bill of "materials"
BOC   Bell Operating Company (USA)

CA   Configuration auditing
CA   Configuration audit
CAD   Computer aided design
CC   Configuration control
CCB   Change control board
CDR   Critical design review
CFE   Client furnished equipment
CI   Configuration identification
CM   Configuration management
CPCI   Computer program configuration items, outdated US military term, sometimes still used.
CSC   Computer software component (DoD-Std 2167/2167A), outdated US military term, sometimes still used.
CSCI   Computer software configuration item (DoD-Std 2167A), outdated US Military term, sometimes still used.

DD   Detailed design
DPM   Downtime performance measurement
DPU   Defects per unit

ECP   Engineering change proposal

FB/L   Functional baseline
FCA   Functional configuration audit
FMEA   Failure modes and effects analysis

GFE	Government furnished equipment
H/W	Hardware
HLD	High-level design (see top-level design; used interchangeably)
ICB	Interface control board
ICWG	Interface control working group
IDD	Interface design document
IPQM	In-process quality metrics (a set of quality metrics defined by Bellcore for use by the RBOCS).
IRS	Interface requirements specification
KPA	Key process areas (this is a term from the SEI's CMM. It has lately become popular in other forums, as well).
LC	Life-cycle
MGMT	Management
MMI	Man–machine interface
MTBF	Mean time between failure
MTTR	Mean time to repair
MoU	Memorandum of understanding
NA	Not applicable
O&M	Operation and maintenance
ODC	Other direct cost
OS	Operating system
PB/L	Product baseline
PCA	Physical configuration audit
PCI	Product configuration audit
PCR	Program change report
PDR	Preliminary design review
PTR	Program trouble report
QA	Quality assurance
R&M	Reliability and maintainability
RBOC	Regional Bell Operating Companies (in the USA, this was the name applied to the various companies formed as a result of the breakup of the Bell/AT&T system).
RDW	Request for deviation/waiver

RQMS   Reliability and quality measurements (developed by Bellcore for use by the RBOCS. Usually, the phrase "... for telecommunications systems" is added to the end of this definition, but that does not invalidate its relevance to other types of software)

S/W   Software
SCCB   Software change control board
SCCS   Source code control system (a subsystem of the UNIX operating system).
SCM   Software configuration management
SCMP   Software configuration management plan
SDD   Software design description
SDL   Software development library
SDP   Software development plan
SDR   Software design review
Spec   Specification
SQA   Software quality assurance
SQAP   Software quality assurance plan
SQE   Software quality evaluation
SQP   Software quality program
SQPP   Software quality program plan
SRR   System requirements review
SRS   Software requirements specification
SSDD   System/subsystem design definition
SSS   System/subsystem specification
SVVP   Software verification and validation plan
SVVR   Software verification and validation report

TC   Test case
TD   Test design
TLD   Top-level design (see High-level design; used interchangeably)

TP   Test plan
TPr   Test procedure
TR   Test review
UDF   Unit development folder

VDD   Version description document

WBS   Work breakdown structure

REFERENCES

As has been stated, this book is intended, among other things, to help you gain a working knowledge of software quality assurance and software quality management. The magic word there is **working**. None of this is of any value if you cannot make it work, **for you**! We have not covered all possible aspects of quality assurance or of managing for quality, nor did we at any point intend to. We have therefore included here a very extensive list of references. If you do not need it, then we have, perhaps, been better authors than we were capable of predicting.

While there is no shortage of material in the literature, there is certainly much less than what one might expect to find on such a critical subject. Most published literature contains information designed for specific needs or application or to demonstrate a specific idea (such as large military-like projects or another domain).

These lists are certainly not exhaustive – they are meant to be representative. Generally much of the "chaff" (read: useless junk) has been eliminated. Those items which the authors' experience has shown to be somewhat useful, have been included.

Standards

The first thing that you, the reader, should notice, is the unbelievably large quantity of standards that we have had to include here. Some 70 standards, directly relating to software quality and software management (and there are more). Clearly, this is absurd. Now the question is, what do you need to do with this list – obviously one cannot reasonably be expected to be familiar with them all. The answer is that one needs to be aware of the problem (the quantity) and to have the tools to choose what you **do** need. The authors have been involved in creating many of them, and has always made a point of trying, very forcefully, to make them as compatible with one another as possible. On this point, we have usually failed. It seems that every group that writes a standard wants it to be an island with no bridges to any other standard (even if many of the same people are involved). We think this is not only bad, but counterproductive, but we have been outvoted.

Institute of Electrical and Electronic Engineers (IEEE)

The following standards are sponsored by the Software Engineering Subcommittee of the Technical Committee on Software Engineering of the IEEE Computer Society and American National Standards Institute. Note that IEEE standards are updated or reaffirmed every five years.

ANSI/IEEE Std 1002-1987, IEEE Standard Taxonomy for Software Engineering Standards, IEEE, 1987; reaffirmed 1992.

ANSI/IEEE Std 1008-1987, IEEE Standard for Software Unit Testing, IEEE; 1987, reaffirmed 1993.

ANSI/IEEE Std 1012-1986, IEEE Standard for Software Verification and Validation Plans, IEEE; 1986; reaffirmed 1992.

ANSI/IEEE Std 1016-1987, IEEE Recommended Practice for Software Design Descriptions, IEEE; 1987; reaffirmed 1993.

ANSI/IEEE Std 1028-1988, IEEE Standard for Software Reviews and Audits, IEEE; 1988; reaffirmed 1993.

ANSI/IEEE Std 1042-1987, IEEE Guide to Software Configuration Management, IEEE; 1987; reaffirmed 1993.

ANSI/IEEE Std 1058.1-1987, IEEE Standard for Software Project Management Plans, IEEE; 1987; reaffirmed 1993.

ANSI/IEEE Std 1063-1987, IEEE Standard for Software User Documentation, IEEE; 1987; reaffirmed 1993.

ANSI/IEEE Std 610.12-1990, IEEE Standard Glossary of Software Engineering Terminology, revision and redesignation of IEEE Std 729-1983; February 1991.

ANSI/IEEE Std 730-1989, IEEE Standard for Software Quality Assurance Plans, revision of IEEE Std 730-1984 and redesignation of IEEE Std 730.1-1989; January 1991.

ANSI/IEEE Std 828-1990, IEEE Standard for Software Configuration Management Plans, IEEE; 1990. This standard supersedes: IEEE Std 828-1983 Standard for Software Configuration Management Plans, Institute of Electrical and Electronic Engineers; 1983.

ANSI/IEEE Std 829-1983, IEEE Standard for Software Test Documentation, IEEE; 1983.

ANSI/IEEE Std 830-1993, IEEE Guide to Software Requirements Specifications, IEEE; 1993.

IEEE Std 982.1-1988, IEEE Standard Dictionary of Measures to Produce Reliable Software, IEEE; 1988.

IEEE Std 982.2-1988, Guide for the Use of IEEE Standard Dictionary of Measures to Produce Reliable Software, IEEE; 1988.

ANSI/IEEE Std 983-1986, IEEE Guide for Software Quality Assurance Planning, IEEE; 1986. Presently classified as obsolete. May be redesignated 730.2-199? when the balloting process is completed on the new draft.

ANSI/IEEE Std 990-1987, IEEE Recommended Practice for Ada[1] as a Program Design Language, IEEE; 1987; reaffirmed 1992.

IEEE Std 1016.1-1993, Guide for software design descriptions, IEEE; 1993.

IEEE Std 1044-1993, A standard classification for software errors, faults and failures, IEEE; 1993.

IEEE Std 1044.1-1995, Guide to standard for classification for software anomalies, draft version, not yet released; IEEE; March 1995.

IEEE Std 1059-1993, Guide for software verification and validation, IEEE; 1993.

IEEE Std 1061-1992, Standard for a software quality metrics methodology, IEEE; 1994.

IEEE Std 1062-1993, IEEE Recommended practice for software acquisition, IEEE; 1993.

IEEE Std 1074-1991, Standard for developing software life-cycle processes, IEEE; 1993.

IEEE Std 1074.1, Guide for developing software life-cycle processes, IEEE; unapproved draft; February 1993.

IEEE Std 1175-1991, Standard reference model for computing systems tool interconnections, IEEE; 1991.

IEEE Std 1209-1992, Recommended practice for the evaluation and selection of CASE tools, IEEE; 1992.

IEEE Std 1219-1992, Standard for software maintenance, IEEE; 1992.

IEEE Std 1220-1995, Trial use standard for the application and management of the system engineering process, IEEE; 1995.

IEEE Std 1298-1992/AS 3563.1-1991, Software quality management system, part 1: Requirements, Australian Standards Society, 1991.

IEEE Std 1420.2, IEEE standard for information technology, Software reuse, Data model for Reuse library interoperability: Basic interoperability Data Model (BIDM), un-approved draft, D2.0, IEEE; January 1995.

IEEE Std 1498 and EIA IS 640, Standard for information technology, Software life-cycle processes, Software development, Acquirer-Supplier agreement, unapproved draft; IEEE and EIA, March 1995.

United States Department of Defense (US DoD)

US DoD standards are, or have been, used by all NATO countries and many other states which extensively use military equipment manufactured by the USA. Other countries may also have military standards relating to the subject but they are used almost exclusively by their developers. As such, they are "in-house" standards and not commonly known outside. There did not seem to be any reason to go to the extreme of providing details.

This is a much abbreviated list. The full list of US DoD Standards relating to software management is several pages long. All the following documents were developed and are published by the US DoD – most of them are probably obsolete. It is important to be aware that, in principle, all US DoD are to be replaced by "civilian" standards, therefore these are presented as examples and for completeness. There have been many other US DoD standards for software, however most of those have been superceded by the following list.

DoD Std-2167A Defense System Software Development, 29 February, 1988; United States Department of Defense. (including relevant DIDs). Update and redesignation of 20 DoD Std-2167 Defense System Software Development, 4 June, 1985; United States Department of Defense. (including relevant DIDs).

DoD STD-2168 Military Standard; Defense System Software Quality Program,

DoD STD-480 Configuration Control, Engineering Changes, Deviations and Waivers,

MIL Std-2155 Failure Reporting, Analysis and Corrective Action System, United States Department of Defense.

MIL STD-1521B Technical Reviews and Audits for Systems, Equipment and Computer Programs, Military standard; 1985.

MIL STD-483 Configuration Management Practices for Systems, Equipment, Munitions and Computer Programs, 1 June, 1971.

MIL STD-490, Specification Practices, 1 February, 1969.

International Standards Organization (ISO) and International Electrotechnical Commission (IEC)

The following documents have been developed by the International Standards Organization (ISO). It should be noted that various versions of these documents exist under different numbering conventions, particularly by various national committees – for instance the American version of ISO 9000 is called Q90. However, the "parent" document, and the **one** that is always most relevant, is the original document as published by the ISO.

The ISO 9000 series of standards was not originally designed for software, but for manufacturing processes (ISO 9001 covers manufacturing processes which have design aspects). The document referenced above, even though it describes how ISO 9001 is to be used for software, barely mentions Software Configuration Management (paragraph 6.1). The discussion of SCM is less than two pages long and very minimal. ISO 9000 and ISO 9001 – the actual standards – do not mention either software or configuration management. In software there is no manufacturing process – software is all design. At the time of this writing, the applicability of the ISO 9000 series to software has not been proven.

International Electrotechnical Commission, Requirements and guidelines for analysis of technological risks, second draft; International Electrotechnical Commission; May 1989. (As this is a draft, no document number exists. This author was not able to ascertain whether a final document had been issued as of this publishing date.)

ISO 8402, Quality management and quality assurance vocabulary, 1986.

ISO 9000, Quality management and quality assurance standards – Guidelines for selection and use, 15 March 1987.

ISO 9000-2, Quality management and quality assurance standards – part 2: Generic guidelines for application of ISO 9001, ISO 9002, ISO 9003; 25 July 1991.

ISO 9000-3, Quality management and quality assurance standards – part 3: Guidelines for the application of ISO 9001 to the development, supply and maintenance of software, 1 June 1991.

ISO 9001, Quality systems – Model for quality assurance in design/development, production installation and servicing, 15 March 1987.

ISO 9002, Quality systems – Model for quality assurance in production and installation, 15 March 1987.

ISO 9003, Quality systems – Model for quality assurance in final inspection and test, 15 March 1987.

ISO 9004, Quality management and quality system elements – Guidelines, 15 March 1987.

ISO 9004-2, Quality management and quality system elements – part 2: Guidelines for services, 15 March 1987.

ISO 9004-7, Quality management and quality systems elements – part 7: Guidelines for configuration management, February 1994. This document is generic and not specific to software (see ISO 10007, below).

ISO/IEC 7.23-2, Information technology: Software Life-Cycle process, part 2: Configuration management for software, ISO/IEC SC7, WG8 project 7.23; 24 January 1995. This document is part of the ISO 12207 process (an accompanying document) and sort of "competes" with 9004-7. The document contains a table to map this with ISO 9004-7. The authors believe that this is significantly more relevant to software.

ISO/IEC 9126 Information technology – Software product evaluation – quality characteristics and guidelines for their use, ISO and IEC.

ISO/IEC 12207 Information technology – Software life cycle processes, ISO and IEC.

ISO 10005, Quality management – Guidelines for quality plans, ISO. This document is part of an alternate ISO process and sort of "competes" with 9004-7. This document is generic and not specific to software.

ISO 10007, Quality management – Guidelines for configuration management, ISO. This document is part of an alternate ISO process and sort of "competes" with 9004-7. This document is generic and not specific to software.

ISO 10011-1, Guidelines for auditing quality systems – part 1: auditing, ISO.

ISO 10011-2, Guidelines for auditing quality systems – part 2: qualification criteria for auditors, ISO.

ISO 10011-3, Guidelines for auditing quality systems – part 3: managing audit programs, ISO.

ISO 10012-1, Quality assurance requirements for measuring equipment. Part 1: Management of measuring equipment, ISO.

For the following, we use the British Standards numbering because this seems to be more well known. These all are ISO standards, as well.

BS 6143 Part 2: Guide to the economics of quality – Prevention, appraisal and failure model; 1990.

BS 7165 Recommendations for Achievement of quality in software; 1991.

BS 7850 Part 1: Guide to management principles; 1992.

BS 7850 Part 2: Guide to quality improvement methods; 1992.

Other standards

ESA PSS-01-101 Software quality assurance plans, Issue 1; European Space Agency; February 1983.

ESA PSS-01-20 Quality assurance of ESA spacecraft and associated equipment, Issue 1; European Space Agency; April 1981.

ESA PSS-01-21 Software quality assurance of ESA spacecraft and associated equipment, Issue 1; European Space Agency; February, 1983.

ESA PSS-01-30 Reliability assurance of ESA spacecraft and associated equipment, Issue 1; European Space Agency; May 1981.

ESA PSS-01-40 Safety assurance of ESA spacecraft and associated equipment, Issue 1; European Space Agency; April 1981.

Technical reports

Bell Canada (1994) Trillium, model for telecom product development and support process capability. Release 3.0; Bell Canada; December.

Ben-Menachem, M *The PATRIARCH Software Quality Assurance Handbook*, MIV-Meda, Catalog No. 2000.

Ben-Menachem, M *The PATRIARCH Quality Planning Manual*, MIV-Meda, Catalog No. 2110.

Ben-Menachem, M *The PATRIARCH Quality Analysis Manual*, MIV-Meda, Catalog No. 2120.

Ben-Menachem, M *The PATRIARCH Quality Review Manual*, MIV-Meda, Catalog No. 2130.

Ben-Menachem, M *The PATRIARCH Management Procedures Manual*, MIV-Meda, Catalog No. 3200.

Bryan, W and Siegel, S (1984) Software configuration management (SCM). Grumman-CTEC Publication No. 84-ISD-034; Grumman-CTEC, Course Workbook.

Butler, RA Integrated logistics support, implementation and management. Technology Training Corporation, Course Workbook.

Cherkovsky, D (1988) Software change control procedure. Report No. B-D110.0010.01.20-4.01, Israel Aircraft Industries, TAMAM, September.

Cherkovsky, D (1988) Software problem reporting and corrective action procedure. Report No. B-D110.0010.02.20-4.00, Israel Aircraft Industries, TAMAM, July.

Craig, R (1990) Software practices and measures benchmark study. Software Quality Engineering; December.

Dean, JW (1983) Advanced configuration management. Technology Training Corporation; Course Workbook.

Dean, JW Advanced configuration management II. Technology Training Corporation; Course Workbook; October.

ESA software engineering standards, Issue No. 1, 1984.

Fowler, P and Rifkin, S (1990) CMU/SEI-90-TR-24, ESD-90-TR-225, Software engineering process group guide, Software Engineering Institute, Carnegie Mellon University; September.

Gartner Group (1991) Change man takes on a challenging endeavor. Report Number P-420-540, Software Engineering Strategies, Gartner Group, 5 April,.

Holmes, D Boeing embedded software standards system. Boeing Military Airplane Company; lecture notes.

IBM: Problem and change control at the state of Washington Data Processing Service Center. Report No. GK20-1073-0; Installation Management series; IBM; undated.

IBM (1976) Problem and change management in data processing, a survey and guide. Report No. GE19-5201-0, IBM, August.

IBM (1978) Inspections in application development, introduction and implementation guidelines. Report No. GN20-3814, IBM; August.

IBM (1982) Change management workbook. Report No. G320-8013-0; IBM, May.

Israel Association of Electronics Industries (1992) A guide to total quality management. Israel Association of Electronics Industries, May, in Hebrew.

Israel Association of Electronics Industries (1993) A guide to the quality circle facilitator. Israel Association of Electronics Industries, February, 1993; in Hebrew.

Israel Association of Electronics Industries (1993) Simplification of processes, a performance folder. Israel Association of Electronics Industries, February, in Hebrew.

ITT Programming Education Center (1982) Principles of program testing. ITT Programming education center, Stratford, CT, November.

Kreuter, KF (1979) Reliability of software. European Space Agency (ESA) July.

Paulk, MC *et al.* (1993) CMU/SEI-93-TR-24, ESC-TR-93-177, Capability maturity model for software, version 1.1, Software Engineering Institute, Carnegie Mellon University, February.

Pratt, TW, Knight, JC and Gregory, S (1983) NASA-CR-170012, On the engineering of critical software, February.

Presson, E (1984) RADC-TR-84-53, Software Test Handbook Software Test Guidebook, Vol. II (of two); March.

Reifer, DJ and Reifer Consultants Israel Aircraft Industries, Hardware/software configuration management. Training seminar, Course Workbook.

Reifer, DJ, Knudson, RW and Smith, J (1987) Final report: Software quality survey. American Society for Quality Control (ASQC); 20 November

Rolls, C. *et al.* (Working Group Chair) (1989) WME/89-173/JB Hood reference manual, issue 3.0, European Space Agency (ESA), September.

Springman, M (1990) Incremental software test approach for DoD Std-2167A Ada projects. TRW Systems Engineering & Development Division; February.

Stanghellini, E (1984) *Quality Improvements Process*, Honeywell Information Systems Italia, November.

Thompson, K and Ritchie, DM (1975) *UNIX Programmer's Manual*, 6th edition, Bell Telephone Laboratories.

TickIt (1992) Guide to software quality management systems construction and certification using EN29001. British computer Society and the UK Department of Trade and Industry; February 1992. Notes: (a) This document *belongs* also to the section on ISO documents. However, it is a publication of the UK Department of Trade and **not** of the ISO. (b) This document is accurate for the previous version of ISO 9001. It has not yet been updated for the latest version.

Ziegler Jr, K (1978) Improving stability in large systems (a management system). DAPS Code 0933, GG22-9051-00, IBM, June.

Articles from Professional Journals

Legacy articles

Some may dismiss these articles as "philosophy," while we are dealing with technology. This would be a vast mistake. In a seminal article for *IEEE Computing*,[2] David Loge Parnas, one of the most important names in the field, made a very quotable statement: "The wheel is reinvented so often because it is a very good idea; I've learned to worry more about the soundness of ideas that were invented only once." The concept here is very important. Too often, in western culture, we expect only the newest of ideas to be good and useful. This is incorrect and counter-productive. There have been a lot of marvellous ideas developed in the past that are quite applicable to what you are doing today. The problem is to find them. This list provides you with some of the better, more useful, ones.

Bachman, CW (1973) The programmer as navigator. ACM Turing Award Lecture, *Communications of the ACM*.

Backus, J (1977) Can programming be liberated from the von Neumann style? A functional style and its algebra of programs. ACM Turing Award Lecture, *Communications of the ACM*.

Cook, SA (1982) An overview of computational complexity. ACM Turing Award Lecture, *Communications of the ACM*.

Dijkstra, EW (1972) The humble programmer. ACM Turing Award Lecture, *Communications of the ACM*.

Floyd, RW (1978) The paradigm of programming. ACM Turing Award Lecture, *Communications of the ACM*. [An interesting note. This seems to be the first time the word "paradigm" was used in this meaning. If you check dictionaries, its meaning is related only to grammar. It has since become quite fashionable.]

Hoare, CAR (1980) The emperor's old clothes. ACM Turing Award Lecture, *Communications of the ACM*.

Iverson, KE (1979) Notation as thought. ACM Turing Award Lecture, *Communications of the ACM*.

Perlis, AJ (1966) The synthesis of algorithmic systems. ACM Turing Award Lecture, *Communications of the ACM*.

Richie, DM (1983) Reflections on software research. ACM Turing Award Lecture, *Communications of the ACM*.

Santamaria, NC (1990) The pragmatism of wisdom – an interview with Dr Edward Teller. *A&DS*, May.

Thompson, K (1983) Reflections on trusting trust. ACM Turing Award Lecture, *Communications of the ACM*.

Wirth, N (1984) From programming language design to computer construction. ACM Turing Award Lecture, *Communications of the ACM*.

Current articles and proceedings

Here, in general, we have avoided including articles more than ten years old, except in the case of quite extreme utility or note. An article may be quite excellent, and old, and utilitarian, but still not belong to the "legacy" category. These would be those that deal very specifically with software quality and do not have any general appeal. Examples of these would be the special issue of the *AT&T Technical Journal* of March 1986 (just within the limit) specifically devoted to quality; or articles by an author whose work we particularly recommend (for example Fletcher Buckley).

Agrawal, LN (1985) *The COLPCA Model*, Agora.

Amster, SJ and Hooper, JH (1986) Statistical methods for reliability improvement. *AT&T Technical Journal*, **65**, 2, special issue on quality; March–April.

Avizienis, A (1987) On the achievement of a highly dependable and fault-tolerant air traffic control system. *IEEE Computer*, February.

Bamford, RC and Deibler II, WJ (1993) Comparing, contrasting ISO 9000 and the SEI capability maturity model, *Computer*, October.

Basili, VR and Perricone, BT (1984) Software errors and complexity: an empirical investigation. *Communications of the ACM*, **27**, 1, January, 42–50.

Bazelmans, R (1985) Evolution of configuration management. *ACM SIGSOFT Software Engineering Notes*, **10**, 5, October.

Ben-Menachem, M (1991) A procedure for risk management with reference to software. *Proceedings of the Fifth Israel Conference on Computer Systems and Software*, IEEE.

Bersoff, EH, Henderson, VD and Siegal, S (1979) *Software Configuration Management, Problem Management Series, Project Scheduling and Control*, Auerbach.

Bersoff, EH (1984) Elements of software configuration management. *IEEE Transactions on Software Engineering*, **SE-10**, 1, January.

Blum, J (1984) Computerized software configuration management system, an ORACLE relational DBMS implementation, *Israel Software Quality Assurance Conference*, October.

Boehm, BW (1976) Software engineering. *IEEE Transaction on Computers*, **C-25**, 12, December.

Boehm, BW (1984) Verifying and validating software requirements and design specification. *Software*, January.

Booch, G (1986) Object-oriented development. *IEEE Transactions on Software Engineering*. February, 211–21.

Buckle, JK (1983) Software configuration management: an approach to project organization.

Buckley, FJ (1991) Do standards cause software productivity problems? *IEEE Computer*, January.

Buckley, FJ (1984) Software quality Assurance. *IEEE Transactions on Software Engineering*, January.

Carpenter Jr, CL (1988) Software quality assurance. *ASQC Professional and Technical Development*, April.

Chacon, SM (1988) All he had to do was ask. *Quality Progress*, May.

Collins, F (1983) *Change Management Strategies*, Systems Management Series, Auerbach.

Cottam, ID (1984) The rigorous development of a system version control program. *IEEE Transactions on Software Engineering*, **SE-10**, 2, March.

Davis, AM (1985) Customized automated configuration management. *Joint STARS Business Practices Workshop*, US Department of Defense.

Dawood, M (1994) Companies' agencies should seek ISO 9000 certification. *Computer*, March.

Deines, G (1993) Automating the ISO 9000 compliance process. *ASQC Quality Congress Transactions*.

Dunn, RH (1988) Software quality assurance: a management perspective. *Quality Progress*, July.

Eckel, EJ (1986) Quality in AT&T network systems. *AT&T Technical Journal*, **65,** 2, special issue on quality; March–April.

EDP Analyser (1977) The analysis of user needs. *Canning Publications*, **17, 1**, January.

Edwards, LE (1984) *Software Development Standards and Conventions*, Auerbach.

Egan, LG (1993) ISO 9000-3: Key to quality software and global success. *I&CS*, January.

Fowler, PJ (1986) In-process inspections of workproducts at AT&T. *AT&T Technical Journal*, **65,** 2, special issue on quality, March–April.

Frenkel, KA Toward automating the software development cycle. *Communications of the ACM*, **28,** 6, June, 578–89.

Fuchs, E (1986) Quality: theory and practice. *AT&T Technical Journal*, **65,** 2, special issue on quality, March–April.

Gibson, CF and Davenport, TH (1985) Systems change: managing organizational and behavioral impact. *Information Strategy: The Executive's Journal*, Fall.

Godfrey, AB (1986) The history and evolution of quality in AT&T. *AT&T Technical Journal*, **65,** 2, special issue on quality, March–April.

Goksel, AK, Sekino, WT and Troutman, WW (1986) Tools and techniques for VLSI quality. *AT&T Technical Journal*, **65,** 2, special issue on quality, March–April.

Hamilton, MH (1986) Zero-defect software: the elusive goal. *IEEE Spectrum*, March.

Hatley, DJ (1985) A structured analysis method for real time systems. *Fall DECUS U.S. Symposium*, December.

Heller, M (1987) Of quality assurance, support and price. *Journal of Engineering Computing and Applications*, Fall.

IEEE Transactions on Software Engineering, **SE-3,** 1, January, 1977. Note: Entire issue devoted to structured analysis.

Inglis, J (1986) Standard software quality metrics. *AT&T Technical Journal*, **65,** 2, special issue on quality; March–April.

Jones, C (1996) Software change management. *IEEE Computing*, February.

Kackar, RN and Shoemaker, AC (1986) Robust design: a cost effective method for improving manufacturing processes. *AT&T Technical Journal*, **65,** 2, special issue on quality; March–April 1986.

Katz, RH and Lehman, TJ (1984) Database support for versions and alternatives of large design files. *IEEE Transactions on Software Engineering*; **SE-10,** 2, March.

Kinnaird, R (1987) Configuration management for software engineering. *EXE Magazine*, 1987.

LaPlante, A (1995) Scope grope. *Computerworld*, March.

Lowe, J and Daughtrey, T (1993) Software quality: international perspectives. *ASQC Quality Congress Transactions*.

Mazzucchelli, L (1985) Structured analysis can streamline software design. *Computerworld*, December 9.

McCarthy, R (1975) Applying the technique of configuration management to software. *Quality Progress.*

O'Neill, JM (1993) ISO 9000, an easy method to document requirements. *ASQC Quality Congress Transactions.*

Olson C, Webb, W and Wieland, R. (1985) Code generation from data flow diagrams. *Proceedings of the 3rd International Workshop on Software Specification*, August, pp. 172–6.

Paradis, JW (1993) Great documentation for ISO 9000 certification now! *ASQC Quality Congress Transactions.*

Parnas, DL (1996) Why are software jewels rare? *IEEE Computing*, February.

Parnas, DL (1972) On the criteria to be used in decomposing systems into modules. *Communications of the ACM.* December.

Perry, M (1993) Company-wide quality using ISO 9001. *ASQC Quality Congress Transactions.*

Pettijohn, CL (1986) Achieving quality in the development process. *AT&T Technical Journal*, **65,** 2, special issue on quality, March–April.

Phadke, MS (1986) Design optimization case studies. *AT&T Technical Journal*, **65,** 2, special issue on quality, March–April.

Quantitative Software Models (1979) *DACS.*

Ramamoorthy, CV *et al.* (1982) *Techniques in Software Quality Assurance.* Teubner, 1982.

Ramamoorthy, CV *et al.* (1984) Software engineering: problems and perspectives. *Computer*, October, 191–209.

Robertson, LB and Secor, GA (1986) Effective management of software development. *AT&T Technical Journal*, **65,** 2, special issue on quality, March–April.

Ross, D. and Schoman Jr, RE (1977) Structured analysis for requirements definition. *IEEE Transactions on Software Engineering*, **SE-3**, 1, January, 1977.

Ross, D [Guest Editor] (1977) Reflections on requirements. *IEEE Transactions on Software Engineering*, **SE-3,** 1.

Saltmarsh, T. (1983) *Qualitative Risk Assessment*, Auerbach.

Surette, GJ (1986) The AT&T quality system. *AT&T Technical Journal*, **65,** 2, special issue on quality; March–April.

Teichroew, D. and Hershey, E (1977) IV PSL/PSA: A computer-aided technique for structured documentation and analysis of information processing systems. *IEEE Transactions on Software Engineering*, **SE-3,** 1, January.

US Department of Defense (1980) Requirements for Ada programming support environments – Stoneman.

Waters, SJ Towards comprehensive specifications. *Computer Journal* **22,** 3.

Wulf, WA (1984) Trends in the design and implementation of programming languages. *Computer*, June, 14–23.

Yourdon, E Structured system life cycle. *Computerworld.*

Zimmerman, JS (1986) The right stuff. *Datamation*, January.

Books of Note for the Reader of this Guidebook

Software quality assurance and software engineering books

Abelson, H and Sussman, GJ with Sussman, J (1985) *Structure and Interpretation of Computer Programs*, McGraw-Hill.

Babich, WA (1986) *"Software Configuration Management" Coordination for Team Productivity*, Addison-Wesley.

Barra, R (1983) *Putting Quality Circles to Work – A Practical Strategy for Boosting Productivity and Profits*, McGraw-Hill.

Beizer, B (1984) *Software Systems Testing and Quality Assurance*, Van Nostrand Reinhold.

Beizer, B (1983) *Software Testing Techniques*, Van Nostrand Reinhold.

Bell Systems (1978) The UNIX time-sharing System, ISSN 0005-8580, *Bell System Technical Journal*, **57**, 6, July–August.

Ben-Menachem, M (1988) *US Department of Defense Std-2167/2168 Companion and an Aid and Training Guide for Use of the Military Standard for Mission Critical Software Development* and *DoD Standards 2167/2167A/2168 Auditor's Manual (in a five volume set) for Data Item Descriptions and Procedures*, MIV-Meda.

Ben-Menachem, M (1988) *Software Development Procedures Manuals: Software Technical Procedures Manual; Software Management Procedures Manual*, MIV-Meda.

Ben-Menachem, M (1987) *The PATRIARCH Series in Software Quality Assurance: The PATRIARCH SQA Handbook, The PATRIARCH Manager's SQA Guidebook; The PATRIARCH Developer's SQA Guidebook; The PATRIARCH Implementer's SQA Guidebook; The PATRIARCH Document Quality Assurance and Verification and Validation Handbook; The PATRIARCH SQA Planning & Auditing Manual*, MIV-Meda.

Ben-Menachem, M (1988) *Review and Inspection Manual for Philips Corporation*, MIV-Meda.

Ben-Menachem, M (1994) *A Software Configuration Management Guidebook*, McGraw-Hill.

Ben-Menachem, M (1988) *Software Development Procedures Manuals: Software Technical Procedures Manual; Software Management Procedures Manual*, MIV-Meda.

Ben-Menachem, M (1987) *English/Hebrew, Hebrew/English Quality Assurance Dictionary*, People and Computers.

Berlack, R (1991) *Software Configuration Management*, Lockheed-Sanders.

Bersoff, EH, Henderson, VD and Siegel, SG (1980) *"Software Configuration Management." An Investment in Product Integrity*, Prentice-Hall.

Birrell, ND and Ould, MA (1985) *A Practical Handbook for Software Development*, Cambridge University Press.

Boehm, BW (1981) *Software Engineering Economics*, Prentice-Hall.

Brooks Jr, FP (1978) *The Mythical Man-month*. Addison-Wesley.

Buckle, JK (1982) *Software Configuration Management*, Macmillan.

Cave, WC and Maymon, GW (1984) *Software Lifecycle Management, The Incremental Method*, The Macmillan DataBase/Data Communications Series.

Charette, RN (1986) *Software Engineering Environments: Concepts and Technology*, Intertext/McGraw-Hill.

Crosby, PB (1979) *Quality is Free*, McGraw-Hill.

Dahl, OJ, Dijkstra, EW and Hoare, CAR (1972) *Structured Programming*, Academic Press.

DeMarco, T (1978) *Structured Analysis and System Specification*, Yourdon Press.

DeMarco, T (1982) *Controlling Software Projects*, Yourdon Press.

DeMillo, RA., McCracken, WM, Martin, RJ and Passafiume, JF (1987) *Software Testing and Evaluation*, The Benjamin/Cummings Publishing Company.

Deutsch, MS (1982) *Software Verification and Validation Realistic Project Approaches*, Prentice-Hall Series in Software Engineering.

Dunn, R (1984) *Software Defect Removal*, McGraw-Hill.

Dunn, R *Quality Assurance for Computer Software*, McGraw-Hill.

Evans, MW (1984) Productive Software Test Management, Wiley-Interscience.

Evens, MW and Marciniak, JJ (1987) *Software Quality Assurance and Management*, Wiley-Interscience.

Ferraby, L (1991) *Change Control During Computer Systems Development*, Prentice-Hall.

Fitzgerald, J (1978) *Internal Controls for Computerized Systems*, Jerry Fitzgerald & Associates.

Gane, C and Sarson, T (1979) *Structured Systems Analysis: Tools and Techniques*, Prentice-Hall.

Glass, R *Software Maintenance Guide Book*, Prentice-Hall.

Hed, SR *Project Control Manual*, Sven R. Hed.

Hetzl *Complete Guide to Software Testing*, QED.

Humphrey, WS (1995) *A Discipline for Software Engineering*, Addison-Wesley.

IEEE *Software Quality Assurance; A Practical Approach*, IEEE Computer Society Press.

Ince, D (1994) *ISO 9000 and Software Quality Assurance*, McGraw-Hill.

Ince, D, Sharp, H and Woodman, M (1993) *Introduction to Software Project Management and Quality Assurance*, McGraw-Hill.

Jones, C (1991) *Applied Software Measurement*, McGraw-Hill.

Kernighan, BW and Plauger, PJ *The Elements of Programming Style*. [This is one of the best books on quality coding styles ever written.]

Martin, J and McClure, C (1983) *Software Maintenance The Problem and its Solutions*, Prentice-Hall.

McMenamin, SM and Palmer, JF (1984) *Essential System Analysis*, Yourdon Press.

Myers, GJ (1976) *Software Reliability: Principles and Practices*, Wiley.

Myers, GJ (1979) *The Art of Software Testing*, Wiley-Interscience.

Myers, GJ (1975) *Reliable Software Through Composite Design*, Petrocelli/Charter.

Orr, KT (1977) *Structured Systems Development*, Yourdon Press.

Page-Jones, M (1980) *The Practical Guide to Structured Systems Design*, Yourdon Press.

Perry, R *Effective Methods of EDP Quality Assurance*, QED.

Perry, R *A Structured Approach to System Testing*, QED.

Perry, R *Hatching the EDP Quality Assurance*, QED.

Peters, LJ (1981) *Software Design: Methods and Techniques*, Yourdon Press.

Quirk, WJ (1985) *Editor Verification and Validation of Real-time Software*, Springer.

Raheja, DG (1991) *Assurance Technologies, Principles and Practices*, McGraw-Hill Engineering and Technology Management Series.

Smith, DJ and Wood, KB *Engineering Quality Software*, Elsevier Applied Science.

Sommerville, I (1985) *Software Engineering*, Addison-Wesley.

Spencer, RH (1985) *Computer Usability Testing and Evaluation*, Prentice-Hall.

Staber, E (1987) *Approach to Testing and Maintaining Telephone Exchanges and Networks*, Standard Telephone und Radio AG.

Stevens, WP (1981) *Using Structured Design*, John Wiley.

Ward, PT. and Mellor, SJ (1985) *Structured Development for Real-Time Systems, Volume 2, Essential Modeling Techniques*, Yourdon Press.

Warnier, JD (1974) *Logical Construction of Programs*, Van Nostrand Reinhold.

Weinberg, GM (1982) *Rethinking Systems Analysis and Design*, Little, Brown.

Whitgift, D (1991) *Methods and Tools for Software Configuration Management*, Logica Cambridge Ltd.

Wirth, N *Systematic Programming*, Prentice-Hall.

Yourdon, E (1975) *Techniques of Program Structure and Design*, Yourdon Prentice-Hall.

Yourdon, E (1982) *Managing the System Life Cycle*, Yourdon Press.

Yourdon, E, and Constantine, LL (1979) *Structured Design: Fundamentals of a Discipline of Computer Program and Systems Design*, 2nd edition, Prentice-Hall.

International Standards

The world has a fantastic quantity of standards – some of them completely local or specific to a particular group of people or applications, some of them more or less international standards. Nobody knows the total quantity of standards. Among other things, there really is not a standard definition for what is a standard. Who creates all of these documents? How are they written (composed) and "closed" – affirmed as a standard? Of what value are they and to whom? Obviously the answers to all of those questions are very complex. We shall try to present a brief picture here. Nearly every country has a standards-making agency. Some of them do not really do much other than translate the documents into the local language and manage their distribution. Many of them do create standards. Also, there are many nongovernment organizations which create standards. Some commonly known standards making bodies are listed in the table opposite. This list is very far from a complete listing of the organizations. It appears to be the most important ones, for our purposes.

A good example of the information overload comes to us courtesy of the United States Department of Defense. They produce standards for their own use. Some of them, by the way, are quite good and very useful. One of the more interesting and useful publications that they have produced is the software quality engineering handbook developed in 1984, by Dr Raghu Singh. It was, we believe, the first real attempt to rectify differences and recognize similarities between management information systems and embedded systems. It set forth both quality goals and traits. Another example is DoD Std 2167A (which, fortunately, has been replaced, by something now called IEEE Std 1498). This enormously complex standard attempts to organize the relationship between the producer

Some of the more well-known standards bodies

Acronym*	Full name	Organization	Categories	Examples
AFIPS	American Federation of Information Processing Societies	Industry	Information technologies	
ANSI	American National Standards Institute	Government	General	
ASME	American Society of Mechanical Engineers	Industry		
ASQC	American Society for Quality Control	Professional	Quality	A1 – definitions, quality symbols, formulas, terminology, tables B1 – control chart method Q90 – quality management Z1 – sampling
ASTM	American Society for Testing and Materials	Industry	General	
BSI	British Standards Institute	Government	General	TickIt✓
CCITT	Consultative Committee for International Telegraph and Telephone (International Telegraph and Telephone Consultative Committee)	Government/ industry collaboration	Electronic Communications	X25; X400
CEN	European Committee for Standardization (Comité European de Normalization)	European Union	General	
CSA	Canadian Standards Association	Government	General	
DIN	Deutsches Institut für Nomrung e.V.	Government	General	
DoD	Department of Defense (US)	Military	Everything	DoD 2167A, 2168
EIA	Electronics Industries Association	Industry	Electronics	
ESA	European Space Agency	Government	Space technologies	
IEC	International Electro-technical Commission	Intergovernment	Electric, or Electronic	
IEE	Institute of Electrical Engineers	National Industrial	Electric, or Electronic	
IEEE	Institute of Electrical and Electronic Engineers	Professional	Electronics, or electricity	ANSI/IEEE Std 730
ISO	International Standards Organization	Intergovernment	General	
JIS	Japanese Industrial Standards	Government	General	
MOD	Ministry of Defence (UK)	Military	General	
NASA	National Aeronautics and Space Administration (US)	Government	Space technologies	
NATO	North Atlantic Treaty Organization	Military	General	
NEMA	National Electrical Manufacturers Association	Industrial	Electric, or Electronic	
SII	Standards Institute of Israel	Government	General	
UL	Underwriters Laboratory	Corporation	General, or safety	

*These acronyms do not appear in the glossary as they are only used in this table.

of a software system and the user of it via a series of documents. It can be useful, but usually, it is overkill. One of the more unfortunate aspects of it, was that it only discusses "assessment of ..." software items, not actually how one may achieve quality – not "doing it"! Also, there are no guidelines to the application of quantitative measures, nor are any supplied. However, without respect to the discussion of any specific document, the really impressive fact is the existence of some 60 000 active documents. By active we mean that there have been some 150 000 historical documents, but some of them have been made obsolete. There are some 400 new or revised documents, per month. The document catalog is about 2000 pages long, in three columns.

Alternate Software Quality Assurance Plans

As you probably imagine by now, there are a great number of standards which can, or could, be relevant to the managing the software process in general and to the QA of software, in particular. Only two sources really seem to us to be of any importance or interest – though we must admit that we do not recommend that you spend much time on them.. The European Space Agency (ESA) has published several documents of interest. ESA PSS-01-21 Issue 1; Software quality assurance for ESA spacecraft and associated equipment, ESA PSS-01-101 Issue 1; Software quality assurance plans and ESA BSSC (84) 1 Issue No. 1 ESA software engineering standards; (handbook, not standard).

In addition, there is a Bellcore document (for those interested in telecommunications): TR-TSY-000282 – Software Reliability and Quality Acceptance Criteria (SRQAC).

Notes

1   Ada is a registered trademark of the United States Government, Department of Defense (Ada Joint Program Office).
2   Parnas, DL (1996) Why are software jewels rare. *IEEE Computing*, February.

INDEX